THE CONNECTION BETWEEN THE LIVING AND THE DEAD

RUDOLF STEINER (1915)

THE CONNECTION BETWEEN THE LIVING AND THE DEAD

Eight Lectures Held in Various Cities
between February 16 and December 3, 1916

Translation by Aria Jackson
Introduction by Christopher Bamford

RUDOLF STEINER

SteinerBooks

CW 168

This book is supported by a gift in memory of
HARVEY AND LOUISE LISLE

SteinerBooks
Anthropsophic Press

610 Main Street
Great Barrington, Massachusetts 01230
www.steinerbooks.org

Original translation from the German by Aria Jackson.

This book is volume 168 in the Collected Works (CW) of Rudolf Steiner, published by SteinerBooks, 2017. It is a translation of the German *Die Verbindung zwischen Lebenden und Toten* published by Rudolf Steiner Verlag, Dornach, Switzerland, 1995, based on transcripts not reviewed by the speaker. Published by permission of the Rudolf Steiner Nachlaßverwaltung [Rudolf Steiner Estate], Dornach, Switzerland

Print: 978-1-62148-075-4
e-Book: 978-1-62148-077-8

Printed in the United States

CONTENTS

an early death, with the example of Theo Faiss. The life led back by the spirit self to the world of effects (kamaloka). Being led by the life spirit to implant forces for the new life on earth. On heredity, with the example of Goethe: the influence of identity on subsequent generations. The philosophy of "as if" and Fritz Mauthner. Views of current science on thinking, feeling, will. The "high point" of materialism was around 1840. On experiments about the correlation between brain configuration (occipital lobe) and criminality; additions by spiritual science. The increase of materialism in materialistic spiritism. The example of Meister Bertram's representation of the Fall as old clairvoyance(Lucifer as a serpent with a human head). The ideal of spiritual science. The separation of the anthroposophical movement from the theosophical movement and world events.

3. The Death Event and the Time after Death

LEIPZIG, FEBRUARY 22, 1916

The elements of the human being. The relation between the internal and external aspects of the physical body; turning during the Moon period. On the building and casting off of the physical body; the remains of intrinsic warmth in the Earth. The igniting of I-consciousness after death by looking at one's death and the "empty space" left behind in the world. Looking at the life panorama; its transition to the outside world. Human fortunes as actions of the gods. Elements of the human being after death: formation of the spirit self through the etheric aspect interwoven in the universe. Living backward. Casting off the astral body as transition to a completely spiritual life. The internal arising of the life spirit; connection to the body gradually "becoming weary" during life. The cosmic midnight: we construct our next incarnation from the wisdom collected as a result of our becoming tired as we aged; all the hierarchies influence this activity. The head as an impression of the wisdom of the gods. The soul finding itself after death: surrender of the internal aspect, active formation of the spiritual form. Looking at the living. The depiction of Lucifer as a serpent with human head: the old clairvoyance with the example of Meister Bertram's painting of the Fall. The significance of sacrificial death and the human being's consciousness of it.

4. How Can Today's Poverty of Soul be Overcome?

ZÜRICH, OCTOBER 10, 1916

Development of the spiritual soul as a task of the fifth Post-Atlantean cultural epoch. The intellect and the mind in the fourth cultural epoch. The difficulty of getting to know and understand one another today because of increasing individualization; loneliness and egotism as characteristics of the consciousness soul. Gradual consciousness of karmic relations through inner activity. The ideals of today's cultural epoch: (1) Human social understanding: necessity of practical psychology and biology and a real attention to the other's individuality. Danger of sympathies and antipathies in personal and national interrelations. (2) Freedom of thought. The necessity of religious freedom of thought and tolerance in place of the old group religions. Danger of faith in authority stemming from Jesuitism, with the example of the medical field. (3) The importance of acknowledging the reality of the spiritual world.

5. Karmic Effects

ZÜRICH, OCTOBER 24, 1916

The meaning of spiritual science for this period. On exposure to life enigmas. Questions of fate with the example of the early death of a family member; the experiences of the one remaining behind (pain, loss) and the dead person (inner living together with the thoughts of the one remaining behind). Invigoration of the I-consciousness by an previous violent death (accident). The typical effects of the subconscious. The necessity of spiritual research regarding the connection of human beings to the spiritual world. Spiritual-scientific ideas assimilated in life as a window into earth-life after death. Reading aloud as living nourishment for the dead. The reverse effect of assimilated spiritual-scientific realizations on the Earth after death. The crumbling of the Earth's surface and of spiritual life. The revival of thought, feeling, and impetus to will by seeing the spiritual connection. Today's lack of connection in thought with the example of a brochure by a theologian (A. W. Hunzinger): ethically-based pessimism; conflict between morals and tendencies; attempts at conflict resolution by rejecting: existence (Buddhist), materiality (Platonist), and individuality (Mystic). The thoughtlessness of the "solution" proposed in the book (freeing the human being from awareness through love).

6. The Great Delusion of Contemporary Culture

ST. GALLEN, OCTOBER 26, 1916

Coming to terms with spiritual science and the difficulties associated with this (isolation, anxiety). The necessity of spiritual realization. The spreading materialism of the nineteenth century; the opposing spiritism of occult circles as an attempt at proving the spiritual world. Discrediting of spiritual science with machinations. The difficulties important people have in recognizing the spiritual world, with examples of Jaurès and F. Mahling. Materialism in medicine and the possibilities of spiritual science in this field. The confusion today between the natural-scientific and theological concepts of mind, with the example of a theologian (A. W. Hunzinger). The necessity of thoughts that truth and recognition of the spiritual world are the basis for a new natural order of life.

7. The Connection between the Living and the Dead

BERN, NOVEMBER 9, 1916

The elemental world and its influences. The development of imaginations in the etheric body by one's living together with our fellow humans and the soul's interest in its surroundings. The relation of the etheric body to many elemental entities. The special relationship to one's own etheric counter-image; the unification of the etheric body with it after death and the creation of a sort of planetary system with other elemental entities. The etheric body of the dead person as "switch" in interactions between the living and the dead. The conditions of receiving imaginations from the dead: soul interest in the dead person; immersion in something personal, such as their handwriting; participation in pain of the family members. The spiritual world. Shared relationships of different people with the same astral beings. Inspiration from the dead by immersion in their habits. Perception of the ahrimanic-luciferic influences on human beings by the dead; impartial interest in fellow humans as a condition for their coming near. The earlier instinctive knowledge of the influence of the dead (father-son succession, pedagogy). Real influence of the dead on the inner aspect of the living begins thirty years after death. Influences of the dead as causes of inner soul conflicts. The effect of the dead on people's views by intuition; comparison to the effects of the archai. The necessity of joining with the impulses of the dead.

INTRODUCTION

Rudolf Steiner opens this volume with the statement that the work of anthroposophy is based on the recognition that the world we customarily inhabit is only "a small fragment of the actual world." That is why, he continues, anthroposophy seeks to cognize—to penetrate cognitively—those creative worlds that, because they lie beyond the senses, are closed to ordinary intellectual awareness. According to this imperative, the task of the anthroposophist is to find ways—entrances, gateways, or portals—into the larger, suprasensory worlds surrounding us.

One such portal, open to everyone, is our relationship to the dead—above all, and in the first place, our own dead.

As Steiner puts it: "Part of the ethos that emanates from our spiritual science is our belief that souls who have left the physical plane and have been received in another world remain as connected with us as they were when they still looked at us with physical eyes and could speak to us through the medium of the physical body." Since they remain connected with us, though we now live in different worlds, a loving, cognitive-communicative relationship is not only possible, but also spiritually and ethically necessary. Denying, or ignoring, this relationship amounts if not to a kind of betrayal of love and relationship, then at least a regrettable missed opportunity open to everyone.

On the other hand, by maintaining and continuing to cultivate relationships with those we have known and loved in this world but who have crossed the threshold into the spiritual world, we all have the possibility of entering the invisible world that surrounds us by entering through the gate of our relationship to those we have known who are there now. With their aid, we can both gain access to the worlds of spirit and begin the process of forming community with them—two deeds, Rudolf Steiner tells us, that are vital for human-earthly-cosmic evolution. In other words, the spiritual worlds and the beings manifesting them await only our approach. All we need do is approach them selflessly and with love by showing ourselves vulnerable and willing to be seen by them. In return, they will open to and communicate with us generously and gratefully. Such was Rudolf Steiner's own experience from the beginning. The reality and the path to cognitive experience of the ongoing life of the dead through our love for them—indeed, finally for all the dead, insofar as we are able to experience and affirm the unity and solidarity of all human beings—was of central importance to him from his earliest years and continued to be so throughout his life.

Thus, one of the first spiritual experiences Steiner recounts is his meeting when he was nine with the soul of a distant relative, who had committed suicide and sought him out for help. Just as his living in close proximity with nature would open his awareness to the presence of elemental and nature spirits at work in natural phenomena, so, too, this sad soul of his relative, lost and distraught at the very fringes of the spiritual world, helped him understand and subsequently work to transform the constrained, narrow view of human life held by most people under the influence of materialism. To do so became for him both a practice and a mission.

Gifted in this regard, he soon grew able both to follow souls after death and to communicate with them. Taught by this experience, he began to understand not only the cognitive-consciousness nature of the community formed by human beings on both sides of the threshold, but also how potentially productive conscious earthly participation in that community could be both for those on earth and those in the spiritual world.

At the same time, intuitions experienced in the course of earthly relationships—sometimes fleeting and apparently chance encounters—awoke him to the equally powerful reality of past lives, past encounters. Thus, his sense of this community of humanity was extended to include not only the present, but also for all time.

From such beginnings, over many years of study, meditation, and initiatory encounters, illuminated at a critical moment (around

1899-1900) by standing "spiritually before the Mystery of Golgotha in a deep and solemn celebration of knowledge," Rudolf Steiner developed his Christ-centered capacity for conscious cognition of the spiritual world, including the continuous lives of human souls (before conception, on earth, and after death) into the research method of spiritual science.

The range of this research was manifold. By the end, its application would cover nearly every aspect of life—human, earthly, cosmic, and divine-spiritual. Yet, for all that, and one reason why it is called "anthroposophy" ("the wisdom of the human being"), what lay at the very center of Steiner's worldview, at its heart, was always *human life* as it is lived on earth and in the spiritual world, or what we might call "the spiritual ecology" of humanity on both sides of the threshold.

From this point of view, the present volume, representing as it were the "middle period" of his research, provides a good introduction to this "field of the human," viewed under the aspect both of the life of the "so-called dead" and our relationships or connections across the threshold with them.

*

When, under the aegis of theosophy, Rudolf Steiner assumed the mantle of spiritual teacher at the turn of the twentieth century, his spiritual path was already in large measure determined. The pivotal experiences that had taught him the reality of our relation to the dead, of reincarnation, and of the centrality of the sacrificial work of Christ in earthly and cosmic evolution through the Mystery of Golgotha formed the generative center of his teaching. Through these, and through reading in their light the Western traditions of philosophy, literature, alchemy, Rosicrucianism, and esoteric Christianity, he would gradually transform theosophy into anthroposophy. The mission of reintroducing karma and reincarnation in a new form perhaps came first: it fitted more naturally into theosophy as it then existed. At the same time, more slowly, he began to introduce and move to center stage the deed of Christ.

The work with the dead, which began at the same time, necessarily took a more private form, developing as it did within the intimacy of the growing inner circles of his students, spiritual friends, within the Esoteric Section of the Theosophical Society. Here the emphasis was on building a spiritual, meditative community. Death, however, is always present, and members of the Esoteric Section and other spiritual friends soon began to cross the threshold. Advice, consolation, spiritual guidance was needed, and in response to this need the teaching first took form.

Thus, in 1905, when Rudolf Steiner wrote a letter of advice to one of his students, Paula Stryczek, who must have written to him seeking spiritual guidance in the face of the death of her friend, Anna Wagner, the wife of another student, Günther Wagner, he said:

> When those dear to us pass over into the world beyond, it is particularly important that we send them our thoughts and feelings—without allowing the thought to arise that we wish to have them back. The latter makes life more difficult for the departed in the sphere into which they must pass. We should send the love we give them—not the sorrow we experience—into the worlds where they now are. Do not misunderstand me. We do not need to become hardened or indifferent. But we ought to be able to contemplate the dead with the thought, "May my love go with you! You are surrounded by it." In my experience, a feeling such as this is like a winged garment that carries the loved one upward. On the other hand, the feelings of many of those who mourn, which we might express as "Ah, if only you were still with us," becomes an obstacle to the loved one ....
>
> More particularly, may I now give you the following advice. I will write down for you thoughts that I have not yet quite formulated in very good German; nevertheless, they are based on ancient esoteric tradition for such a case.
>
> Compose yourself inwardly three times a day, of which one of these times should be immediately before sleep at night, so that you take these thoughts over with you into the spiritual world. It would be best if you were to fall asleep with the thought:
>
> May my love be the sheaths
> That now surround you—
> Cooling all warmth,

Warming all coldness—
Interwoven with sacrifice!
Live, borne by love,
Light-endowed, upward!

It is important here that you have the right feeling for the words "warmth" and "coldness." Physical "warmth" and "coldness" is not what is meant, but something like "warmth of feeling" and "coldness of feeling"—though it is not at all easy for a person clothed in a physical body to have any idea of what these qualities mean to a disembodied soul. Such souls have to become aware that the astral body, which they still have around them, is effective, though it cannot make use of the physical organs. Much of what humanity strives for here on earth is given by our physical organs, which are no longer there. This lack of the physical organs is similar—but only similar—to a feeling of burning thirst transferred onto the soul. Those are the strong feelings of "burning thirst" experienced after a person has left the body. And it is just the same with what the will desires to do. The will is accustomed to making use of the physical organs, but no longer has them. This "privation" approximates a feeling of coldness in the soul. It is precisely in relation to such feelings that the living can help; for these feelings are not merely the result of a person's individual life, but are connected with the mysteries of incarnation. For this reason it is possible to help someone who has died.

Now, there is something else I would also ask of you. Let the above sentences be preceded by a few thoughts about our Mr. Wagner. They should contain something like the following: "[Mr. Wagner] You were surrounded by your faithful love until now; this love still surrounds you; it is unchanged; may it hold you fast in the power of the spirit, as it has previously illuminated you in the visible present."

... Of course, you may feel free to communicate what I have written to anyone you yourself feel it is right to do so. I would wish that the hearts of many people are turned toward this dear person. (*From the History & Contents of the First Section of the Esoteric School 1904-1914,* pp. 103-104.)

This basic teaching would remain unchanged. It would only become deeper and expand in every direction to become, as it were, a Rosetta Stone or interpretative framework for the interfusion of earthly and cosmic, spiritual life.

During most of this early period, although beginning the practice of saying words of remembrance for society members who had died, Steiner did not extend his teaching. However, as the separation of anthroposophy from theosophy approached (1912-13), his spiritual researches and lectures began to shift focus toward the manifold aspects of life between death and rebirth in all its forms. At first, the emphasis was more on reincarnation and the path of the soul after death through the planetary spheres to its next incarnation. Slowly at first, and then more insistently, until it came like avalanche, Steiner emphasized the living reality of the presence of the dead in earthly life—and conversely. He began by speaking of his own experiences: how those on the other side had helped him with his researches. Then, gradually, the emphasis shifted toward the vital, existential need for humanity to awaken to the mutuality and reciprocity of humanity on both sides of the threshold. As in any relationship, however, these two sides cannot really be separated, since the reality—the relationship—is in-between.

Therefore, as Rudolf Steiner's research deepened and he began to comprehend the full complexity and ubiquity of the commerce between the living and the dead—paradigmatic of that between the earthly and spiritual worlds generally—he increasingly brought the two spheres into ever-closer proximity. Nevertheless, as his exposition developed, his emphasis changed.

At first, impelled by the First World War with its huge numbers of dead, Steiner focused more on what we might call the "personal" aspect: the one-to-one relationship between the living and the dead. The lectures in this volume, which were given in 1916, come toward the middle of this latter period. Then, as his research deepened and expanded, and the war receded, Steiner turned more and more to the universal aspect of the dead's concern and mission on earth and among the living, researching and illuminating their activities in all spheres of life—political, cultural, social, even ecological. Always implicit in his teaching was the reality that the dead, who are for us the fringe of the spiritual worlds, fully inhabit these worlds which are a whole, so that they as it were constitute a potential opening into the entire spiritual world, to the work of the angelic hierarchies.

*

Steiner begins by stressing the need to overcome our tendency to theorize. Obviously, we cannot rise to or awaken into the world of the dead with ordinary, materialist thinking. Ordinary materialist, "dead" thinking must be transformed; it must become flexible, and pliant. It must become living thinking. To help us do so, and to begin to live into the living experience of the potential connection, or community of support, between the living and the dead, Steiner turns to describe the life of those who have died.

When a person dies, first the physical body is left behind—is cast off—and falls away from the rest of one's being—the etheric body, the astral body, and the I—to become one with the earth. For a materialist, this means, ultimately, that its "atoms" merge with the earth's material base. For spiritual science, however, this view is a fantasy. There are no "atoms" in this sense. The gift of the body to the earth is a gift of warmth. And for the dead, this is also a great gift: casting off the body, deeding it to the earth, is a great experience for them too. Without this experience, which we all participate in when we die, we would never develop I-consciousness after death! In other words, just as we achieve I-consciousness within the body when we enter the body through conception and birth, so, too, we achieve I-consciousness in the spiritual world when we leave the body. We experience "the triumph of spiritual existence over bodily existence." (Perhaps something of this kind was alluded to in the early medieval practice of *speculum mortis*, the mirror of death: that in the mirror of their own death every person would discover the secret of their own individuality.)

Human beings thus enter the world after death with both I-consciousness and their etheric and astral bodies. The etheric body stays with them for a short time, during which they can still think as they did while still on Earth. But, rather than *thinking* their thoughts, they *see* them as a great tableau within the panorama—the life-review—which they behold as their whole life passes before them. The etheric body then separates. Yet it continues to remain visible to them, though outside them, united with the universe, throughout their further life. They look upon it with their I and astral body.

In other words, when we on earth rise into the spiritual world to accompany, contact, or follow our dead, we must learn to distinguish in which of two ways we are doing so. For we may be "contacting" either their etheric being, consigned to the etheric world, or their astral body and I-consciousness. Discovering this, Steiner says, can be a shattering experience. Equally disturbing perhaps can be the discovery that the etheric being left behind by the dead is actually all around us in the earthly world we live in. In other words, *we are separated from the spiritual world only by our state of consciousness*. A world surrounds us in which the etheric bodies of the dead live.

Thus the dead live on in their I and astral body With these—up to the point when the astral body, too, "dissolves," separates, or is left behind, and the I continues on its way—they are close to us. During this period, just as they perceive their own etheric body, the dead can likewise see our thoughts and they can easily distinguish through their own experience between those "thoughts" that they receive as impressions of the spiritual world and those we have in our soul, which, in and for them, are love. Indeed, our love-filled thoughts are to them what art is for us on earth: they are something additional that is at once superfluous and uplifting, delighting, warming. In fact, for the dead our thoughts are more powerful than art is for us, for they cognize them with feeling and will, not thinking—as we, too, must learn to cognize with feeling and will.

Such descriptions, however, are only partial. To begin to grasp spiritual phenomena in earthly language requires observing them repeatedly from different points of view. Thus, in these lectures, Steiner continually amplifies his previous accounts in remarkable ways.

For instance, he reveals that what he has been calling I-consciousness after death is not to be understood as the I is in earthly life. On earth, this I "appears" as the highest element of human nature, but after death, in the world between death and rebirth, it is the lowest element, "enveloped as in a mist by the astral aspect." At the same time, just as when we incarnate we envelope ourselves in earthly elements, so in excarnating after death we envelope ourselves in those higher spiritual elements into which our present nature will metamorphose in the future course of evolution (as described in *Theosophy*): first with the "spirit self," which allows us to relive our last earthly life in reverse; then with the "life spirit," which enables rhythmic movement in the spiritual space; and finally with the "spirit human." Thus, whereas on earth, the I stands "above" the physical, etheric, and astral bodies, after death the I, enveloped in the astral, stands "below" the spirit self, life spirit, and spirit human, which takes over to lead the I when the astral body departs. Then again, amplifying the way in which for the dead the experience of dying or "deceasing," the moment of death, remains accessible to them (unlike our experience of birth), Steiner explains that the "feeling-like, image like impression" of "where" we died is nothing, not even space. Nothing is there, for the dead, where the physical body was. Rather, a new world arises: spirit floods, forges in on all sides, giving rise to a feeling of deep fulfillment, as one expands into the whole world. From emptiness, the void, one fills the all—and there is joy in that.

As for the etheric body, and the way it separates and expands after death, while also permeating the etheric on earth, Steiner now tells us that this is especially so in cases of those who have died at a young age, in which the etheric body still has an excess of forces that are then available as a support and aid for those on earth. How sad it would be if what they had to give remained unknown—or known only by a small group. One can only imagine how powerfully such words must have impressed those listening in 1916 amid the carnage of eight thousand young deaths a day—how vitally important it must have seemed to overcome the materialist view.

In these lectures, then, Steiner returns repeatedly to the same terrain, but always amplifying and adding to what he had said before, in the hope that those who attended the previous lectures will continually deepen their perspective. In the third lecture, for instance, he emphasizes that our understanding must begin in the physical-sensory world with human beings as they present themselves to us. First, the physical body, known through sensory observation and scientific analysis. Next, the the living form or organizational body—the etheric—which cannot be sensed with the senses, but can be grasped by imaginative, suprasensory perception and is, in that sense, still "outer," while the astral body, on the other hand, can be experienced only "inwardly." The same is true of the I. This said, it is also true that the physical body, the oldest member of the human being, must also be understood inwardly. Consideration of this leads us to realize that in the course of evolution we have been turned inside-out: the internal has become the external, the external the internal. In other words: "there is much that is extrasensory about it [the physical body]—its whole method of construction is extrasensory and turns its outer aspect to us only when we see it as a whole." But when we die only that part of our body that comes from the Earth returns to it. What originates from Saturn, Sun, and Moon stages of human/Earth evolution and exists in the form of extrasensory forces is taken up into the cosmos. Only the warmth element remains behind on Earth, while the extrasensory forces welcome us into the spiritual world: "When we are living between death and rebirth, we are everywhere in the world with the extrasensory forces that form the basis of our physical body here." We are everywhere, except in that space where we were as physical beings, which is void and marks our belonging to to the world. Apart from this, the world we enter after death is alive with the forces living and weaving through it. These we experience as spiritual sound, light, and warmth.

As Steiner circles around the relationship between life between birth and death and life after death, and the two-way connection between them, he offers different ways in which spiritual science approaches these questions. One fascinating perspective follows another to build up a vast and complex picture. In the fifth lecture, "Karmic Effects," for instance, he begins by placing deaths under the general category of fate or destiny. Such deaths, indeed nearly all deaths, are twofold, for death almost always occurs in a relationship. Few die completely unknown by anyone. That is, a person dies into the spiritual world, while those related to him or her remain "left behind" on Earth. Both suffer the loss of one another, but in a different way. Of course, it makes a difference how long they have known each other. If the loss was unexpected, it is as if "the foundations of life have been cut off." The one left behind in the physical world experiences the loss in the physical world; the other experiences it spiritually, in the spiritual world, where the sense of "inner togetherness" is intensified. What happens then in their relationship? How does it develop? They met in physical life. Beneath the threshold of consciousness, a bond was formed. Had both lived, it is not clear that "life"—or karma—would have permitted this bond to develop in the fullest manner. We do not know. But now, from the other side, the one who has died can help bring about the necessary deepening of the relationship, because he or she is now able to penetrate and flow through the thoughts and feelings of the other. Thus the bond can grow and prosper. Thus, as Steiner concludes, "correct fulfillment of karma often involves pain being borne on one side, and a more intensive togetherness with the thoughts of the one who remains behind here on the other." Naturally, this is true not only of intimate relationships, but of group relationships too. Furthermore, when at last the one left behind on earth also dies, then the karmic bond can be renewed and transformed in the spiritual world. Karma must always be seen as whole—ongoing.

What happens, Steiner then asks, when a person's life ends through some misfortune—perhaps in a motor accident or in a violent death? In this case, the sublime vision of death, which gives us I-consciousness in the spiritual world, is different than when a person dies of natural causes. It is different in the same way that ordinary-time, daily experience, differs from those rare, transformative moments when time seems as it were collapsed and in an instant or a few minutes or hours we have experiences that will take a lifetime to unpack. Thus, the experience of I-consciousness of one who passes violently into the spiritual world is intensified. Karmically—as Steiner stresses, there are no "accidents"—the necessity lying behind such events is related to previous (and future) incarnations. In other words:

> We will always find that in the past this person has experienced through the lives between death and rebirth and through various

> circumstances in repeated earth-lives up until the unfortunate event that the I-consciousness developed for the purely spiritual world needed strengthening, invigorating. And this invigoration occurred by the person's physical life having been ended, not from within, but from without.

Thus the needle of karma weaves its way through the threads of our lives.

Insights of this kind used to be much more common. Spiritual science now seeks to reintroduce them in a new way that gives meaning and direction to our lives. Reimagining the connection between the living and the dead, the earthly and the spiritual worlds, is central to this mission. It can begin with something as simple as reading to the dead, which puts into practice the reality that, as the dead are in our thoughts, they see our thoughts. By such means "death" loses its sting. But this does not mean we should lose sight of the unique preciousness of the Earth and its mission—which depends, as it were, on "open communication" with the spiritual world. As the communication diminishes, the Earth suffers and is gradually depleted, for the Earth depends on human beings maintaining the connection. As people's thoughts become lifeless and dead, so too the Earth begins to crumble: its surface changes, becoming increasingly lifeless also. Though the gods seem to have withdrawn, this is only the sign that humanity must learn to stand on its own feet and bring to life what they once brought to life.

Sadly, today, such thoughts still find as little traction—and as much opposition—as when Steiner spoke. Well aware of this, Steiner sought consistently and repeatedly to warn his listeners not to become discouraged. He recognized that anthroposophy was very small movement. Only a few people took spiritual science seriously and into their hearts. He understood the loneliness and isolation from the larger culture than many anthroposophists felt, as well as the poisonous doubts and hesitations that this situation could plant in their souls. Nevertheless, anthroposophy's fundamental teaching of the spiritual nature of the world, of the dependence of the phenomenal, sensory-physical world on the spiritual worlds, was an evolutionary necessity. Hard though perhaps it was to believe—given "the great delusion of modern civilization," as the sixth lecture calls it—spiritual science was not a choice: it was the only and truth path to the overcoming of materialism. As he puts it:

> We are in the middle of the struggle for existence that is waged outside of our circle with means that are sharply different from ours. And those who reflect even just a little on all that anthroposophy is trying to be for life will be able to observe how entirely different the goals of thinking, feeling and willing under the influence of anthroposophical ideas are from the goals that the great majority of people set for themselves today. Because thoughts and feelings are actual facts, we should understand that our little handful of people, that is every single one of us, is thus part of a comparatively small life-group that is—one can say in most cases—completely opposite to the thoughts, sensations, and feelings of the rest of humanity.

We may ask: what underlies this materialism or "unconscious spiritual cowardice in regard to precisely the most important thing humanity needs today"? Steiner distinguishes two forms of materialism: first, scientific or theoretical materialism, which peaked in the second half of the nineteenth century; and second, and much more pernicious, what he calls the "practical materialism"to which it led. This is the reduction of spiritual life to materialist spirituality that came to dominate ethical, social, and religious life and feeling, and which meant that even the best-intentioned people failed to comprehend the primacy of spirit, that is, spiritual beings and spiritual forces, and instead humanized and rationalized them. This is as true of theologians as it is of the best and leading social, political, and scientific figures. In this context, anthroposophy, based on the foundation of spiritual science, stands quite apart as "a completely new movement, based on something that is new to the world." This demands of anthroposophists great courage and determination:

> We live in an atmosphere, so to speak, that demands a potent development of strength, a powerful perseverance. Those are the

> deeper reasons why one can often become disheartened and feel lonely; perhaps why a few, here and there, although declaring support for spiritual science, cannot cope very well with life. But when we have clear insight as to how great is the thing that we are part of in the whole human nexus, and how it seems like a small thing today only because we are still at its beginning, we can find this strength; then we can really find it. Every great thing in the evolution of humanity must begin small.

From this point of view, the first goal is to live together with and relate spiritually to the spiritual worlds in the same way that we do sensorily-physically with the physical world. These worlds are spread out around us, beginning with the elemental world or the world of imagination. Though we live within it, we cannot bring this world into our awareness with our ordinary consciousness. It floods through virtually our entire organism unnoticed, above all from and through our relationships with others. From these relationships, streams of images flow through us, giving rise to feelings of sympathy and antipathy, as well as less defined feelings and inclinations, and in all that develops into the deeper connections of love and friendship. At the same time, these images also form our whole soul disposition: how we relate in an implicit "imaginative togetherness" with the other beings and the world and develop particular interests in our surroundings. In this way, we participate in the elemental world and through this process build up a kind of counterpart to our own etheric body—a cosmic etheric counter-image—through which we relate to the entire cosmic-elemental world. And when we die, and our etheric body is cast off, it is absorbed or taken up into the spiritual world by this cosmic counter-image. This is a great gift, our gift to the spiritual world:

> Our etheric body creates a sort of sun, so to speak, with its cosmic counter-image, and the other elemental entities surround this sun like a sort of planetary system. And when this interplay takes place, the forces are created that add what our etheric body can bring to the elemental world in the correct way through a gradual becoming.

Thus all that we have acquired etherically, the fruits of our life in feelings and thoughts is thus given to the cosmos. We have not lived in vain: all we have felt, thought, and willed has meaning for the cosmos. And this becomes also the image-medium through which connections, relations can be maintained and continued between those on Earth and those in the spiritual world. This is because, at the same time, a connection continues between the true identity of of the one who has died and his or her etheric counter-image. We can communicate with them: through images they can speak to us as imaginations.

Besides the elemental or etheric-imaginative world, of course, we are also surrounded by the soul or astral world and its spiritual or "heavenly" beings. When we are asleep and the astral body has risen out of the physical and etheric bodies, the connection with these beings is direct and unmediated, but they are always present, acting in our lives through insight and inspiration. They give us our life's sense of direction: the will-gesture of our lives. Therefore to begin to make conscious our relation with one who has died astrally or from this soul perspective, we must inwardly imitate or make our own something of the "life direction" of the one who has died as this is expressed in habits and even physical behaviors:

> The spiritually trained must be able to transform themselves in a certain way, at least for a short time, so that they take on something of the habits, of the behavior of the being—let us say the human being—with whom they wish to communicate. They must be able to settle in so that they can say to themselves, I have taken on their habits to such an extent that I could do what they could do, feel what they could feel, sense what they could sense, will what they could will; it has to do with "could"! The possibility must be there. We must be able to be more intimately together with the dead.

It is important to realize, however, that the connection with the dead goes both ways. Though they are not interested in our egotistic thoughts and feelings, the dead do nevertheless see into our souls, take part in our soul lives. Indeed, a certain part of the world order and the progress of humanity is based upon the dead having an inspiring influence on earthly human life. This used to be common knowledge—that the "ancestors" participated in the life of generations coming after them. Habits thus passed almost physically from generation to generation. Now it is different. It must become a matter of awakened consciousness. It can no longer be instinctive. In fact, it is imperative that it become conscious. As Steiner says, "We had better not believe that the dead do not have an active interest in human beings." They send their influences into the human world. Above all, they see where our egotism—our personal likes and dislikes—comes from, whether Lucifer or Ahriman, and in order to connect with them, we must achieve non-judgmental relationships with others, free of likes and dislikes. Everything depends upon our soul disposition, our mood, our state of being. We must learn to become lighter, less solid, less selfish—in a word, more selfless, freer.

The question of freedom, of course, suggests the presence of Christ. Rudolf Steiner speaks of Christ's centrality to the spiritual tasks of our time in several ways throughout the lectures, always stressing how important the individual's development of the relationship to Christ is to our present moment of evolution. At the end of the last lecture, however, speaking of our relationship to the dead, he does so in a particularly moving manner:

> Consider what it means that human beings must carry within themselves the feeling—namely, at a certain time between death and rebirth—that they carry the hierarchies within themselves as their inner experience! That is true! It could lead people to the most terrible arrogance, which could live in the soul as a dark feeling when they are reborn. In ancient times a barrier to this arrogance was made by the fact that people more or less knew, when they passed through death's gate and entered the spiritual world, that it was not they themselves who were seeing, but rather the highest beings of the highest hierarchies who were conveying sight to them. But people lost this connection in the spiritual world, just as they lost the old atavistic clairvoyance in the physical world here. It is because of this that what Paul spoke of in the words, "Not I, but Christ in me"—and what true spiritual

perception is contained in the phrase "We are born of God; we die in Christ"—must occur…

If we experience the gate of death with the correct feelings of "In Christo morimur," then we find, looking in from the surrounding space, among those beings whom we see—who are part of the higher hierarchies and are also elemental beings, and also beings that are embodied here as human souls or are even disembodied human souls—and among all of these we also find our own I-being. And we see the relation of this, our I-being, to the other beings, which I have just described, from the outside. To be able to have these sensations after we have passed through death's gate is incredibly important because we are only able to correctly come to terms with the embodiment of the flesh if we can have these sensations for our own I. We can only have them if we know that they are due to correctly passing through the gate of death with the feeling of, "We have died in Christ."

This being connected with Christ gives us the opportunity to see our relationship in the spiritual world with Christ's spiritual eye; to see ourselves as an I-being among other spirit-beings…

In a word, this is a transformative and vital collection of lectures that deserves close study, repeated reading, and meditation.

THE CONNECTION BETWEEN THE LIVING AND THE DEAD

Rudolf Steiner

During the war years, the following words were spoken by Rudolf Steiner before every lecture that he gave to members of the Anthroposophical Society in the countries affected by the war:

My dear friends, we call to mind the guarding spirits of those who are out on the battlefields where war is now raging:

Spirits watching over your souls,
May thy wings bring
Our petitioning love
To the human beings on earth entrusted to thy care,
That, united with thy power,
Our plea may radiate help
To the souls
Whom we seek lovingly to reach.

And as we turn to the guarding spirits of those who have, because of these tragic events, already passed through the gate of death:

Spirits watching over your souls,
May thy wings bring
Our petitioning love
To the human beings in the heavenly spheres entrusted to thy care,
That, united with thy power,
Our plea may radiate help
To the souls
Whom we seek lovingly to reach.

And may the Spirit whom we have for some years sought to approach through our spiritual science, the Spirit who passed through the Mystery of Golgotha for the salvation of the Earth and for the freedom and advancement of humanity, may He be with thee and thine arduous duties!

Lecture 1

Life between Death and Rebirth

Hamburg, February 16, 1916

Our striving is to cognitively penetrate, as far as possible, the worlds that are closed to the familiar sense-oriented, intellectual awareness connected to the physical plane. Indeed, over our years together, we have come to understanding that human beings, when in the physical body, inhabit a world that is only a small fragment of the entire actual world. But, because we meet so seldom, even at these meetings everything cannot be explained—that is, not everything from the ground up. Other gatherings and writings will reveal that what is spoken of at these meetings (which we are able to hold only rarely) is well founded. Our focus at such meetings should be to become conscious of the important and essential aspects of the actual larger world that encompasses the physical world.

Since we last met here, various events have taken place within the circle that cultivates our spiritual science. A large number of dear friends have crossed the threshold of death since the beginning of this difficult time of war. These friends who have passed through the gate of death have directly participated in these major events. This means that we ourselves, within our circle, have also been affected by the great spiritual world in that these souls who were among us entered the spiritual world when they laid aside their bodies. Part of the way of thinking that emerges from spiritual science is that these souls who have left the physical plane and have been received in another world remain connected to us, as they were connected to us when they still looked at us with physical eyes and could speak to us by means of their physical body.

It is precisely when we draw near to the so-called dead in the world where they exist that we become aware of all that is soul-shaking there, and that must at some time be released within our soul. Then we attempt to look over the threshold that divides us from the spiritual world and to enter a world that can be regarded only from the disembodied soul state. You can understand that over the years since we last saw each other various experiences have passed through my own soul, and out of such experiences words will be spoken and will be considered together here today.

Indeed, over the last year I have often discussed with our friends the fact that for those who can see into the conditions of existence real trust can mature only when they realize that those who were loyal, sympathetic souls here on earth, remain so after they have passed through death's gate. For our work, we certainly do not lose those souls who have gained an understanding of our cause through their connection with us here before passing through the gate of death. There are such loyal colleagues among these souls that although opposition and lack of understanding toward our cause here in the physical world are at times so great and become ever greater, as we have seen, we must still believe in our cause taking its place in the evolution of humanity. We can reach this conviction through the connection with the disembodied souls who have acquired an understanding of the whole meaning of our cause for the evolution of humanity.

Indeed, only when we approach with an open mind the world in which the so-called dead exist—we can say it in this way, although the dead are clearly present in the entire spiritual world—only when we are capable of approaching this world as a visitor, as a companion to the dead in the spiritual world, will we then learn to know more and more what has already been emphasized here. We will learn that the concepts, thoughts and ideas that we have formed about this world because we are in physical bodies must be changed in many ways, must be made pliant, so that they can also encompass the mysteries of spiritual existence. Contemporary humanity is used to looking at the environment in a purely material way, and therefore forms ideas from this purely material view. Thus it is difficult, above all, for us to penetrate the spiritual world, even with our imagination. Many believe that an understanding of the spiritual world cannot be gained if one cannot see into it. They believe this only because they have made their thoughts inflexible and desolate as a result of becoming too accustomed to thinking only of the physical world.

After having started by saying all of this, I would like to speak to you today about some points that have to do with the life of the so-called dead. If we want to understand life between death and rebirth, we must start by considering the way in which a person is composed of the four aspects that we already know well: the physical body, etheric body, astral body, and the I. If we first examine the outermost fact of death that is visible from the physical plane, we can say that one lays aside the physical body. We need not go into the different ways in which the physical body returns to the earthly elements; whether through cremation or decomposition, these are different essentially only in terms of the time each takes. But if, when we consider the fact that in death one's physical body falls away from one's entire being and becomes one with the earth, we examine this fact only in terms of its significance for the physical plane, we have actually considered death only in a very incomplete way. Spiritual movements that see only to a certain degree into spiritual realms often consider this in a very imperfect way. They allow themselves to be misled by all sorts of moral beliefs, which are actually in many ways unsuited to understanding correctly how the spiritual works into the physical world.

All physical events also have spiritual meanings. There is no physical event that does not also have a spiritual meaning. Thus, the physical event of the physical body's falling away is (more or less) that its parts, its molecules, its atoms break apart and are consigned to the earth. Now, a great bias in today's materialistic worldview, which has long fundamentally ruled humanity, is that the human body as we bear it from birth to death (or, let us say from conception to death), decays into the smallest parts, into atoms. These atoms are then absorbed into the earth or the earthly realm, where they remain atoms, and then, as atoms, become other beings. One can easily arrive at this bias through today's materialistic point of view. But even this way of seeing the world is actually fundamentally nonsense in light of spiritual science, because there really are no atoms in the sense meant by chemists. The smallest parts of our body, regardless of the way in which we as a body are united with the earth, become, in the end, warmth. In one way or another, over a shorter or longer period of time, our whole physical organism basically becomes, in the end, warmth.

This is why we speak of warmth in spiritual science as the fourth state of matter, while physics does not accept it as a fourth state of matter, but rather only as a characteristic of the body. This warmth is, in fact, what is actually consigned to the earth. It is shared with the earth. Thus, from our physical body, we give warmth to our earth. What humans leave behind of themselves is really intimately connected with the warmth found in the earth. Human beings do not become air, or water, or something else. Those are only transitional states that they go through. The part of them that becomes air and water, in the end, becomes warmth. Yes, even if it takes centuries, the last remains of matter become warmth. And even if the skeletal system becomes warmth perhaps only after millennia, nevertheless, it does become warmth in the end. If you see in a museum the ancient skeletons of people who walked the earth in ages long past, the time will come when these too will remain only as warmth within the earth-body. The fact that the physical body remains with the earth at all has a great, a significant, meaning for those who have passed through the gate of death. The departing soul enters the spiritual world and bequeaths its physical body to the earth. This is an endeavor, an experience, for the so-called dead. The soul undergoes this experience: my body has left me. We must try to imagine what an experience like this would be. What is this experience? Now, you can form a concept of this from experiences on the physical plane. Such an experience might be, let's say, when you have some new experience that you haven't had before, and you learn from it. In this case, you have added something to your soul that it did not possess before—a new concept, a new understanding. But now think of this expanded to a much greater scale. It is an immensely powerful experience for human beings that they lay aside the body and bequeath it to the planet they are leaving. This gives them the possibility when they are between death and birth of being able to see, to think, to understand. This is a great, powerful experience that is comparable to no other earthly experience. The value of an experience for us here is that we have something in our soul that remains as a result, a consequence, of the experience. Thus we may raise the question: What remains as a result, as a consequence, of the experience of the departure of the physical body from our total being?

Were we not to have the experience of consciously participating in the laying aside of our physical body as we cross the threshold of death, we would never develop an I-consciousness after death! I-consciousness after death is stimulated by our experience of the departure of the physical body. It has great meaning for the dead: I see my physical body going away from me. I perceive the feeling growing within myself from this event that I am an I. We could also state this paradox in another way. If we could not experience our death from the other side, we would not be able to have I-consciousness after death. Just as the human soul comes into being at birth, or even at conception, and adapts gradually to using a physical body and thus achieves I-consciousness within the body, so does the human being achieve I-consciousness after death from the other side of existence by experiencing the falling away of the physical body from our total being.

Just think what this actually means. When we look at death from the physical side of existence, it appears to us to be the end of our existence. There appears to be nothing beyond it. But seen from the other side, death as such is the most splendid thing the human soul could ever face, because it means that human beings can experience the triumph of spiritual existence over bodily existence. We do not remember the experience of our birth here into physical life. But, although we cannot witness our birth into physical life, if we become fully conscious after death we will always have the event of our death immediately before us. The event of our death is not frightening in any way, but is rather the greatest, most splendid, most beautiful experience that our soul can have. Death then shows us continuously the great fact that our consciousness, our self-awareness in the spiritual world, originates from death; that death is the stimulator of this self-awareness in the spiritual world.

Now we must look at the second component of our human existence: the etheric body. We know from the basic presentations we have all participated in together in the course of our branch meetings that this etheric body remains with us for a comparatively short time after death, and that then it is laid aside. We know, too, that a certain significance lies in the fact that this etheric body, such as we had, remains united with us for some days after death.

As long as we still have this etheric body with us after death, we can still think thoughts as one can think them on earth. Thus we can view as a great tableau all of the thoughts that we have carried within us. It has often been described to you that after death we view the thoughts we experienced during life in a life-tableau. In the days in which we still have our etheric body with us, we see our whole life as in a panorama before us, and we see all of it before us simultaneously—that is, we see everything at once. What we call memory here in the physical world arises in the etheric body, but is bound to the physical body. But we have discarded the physical body. We see our thoughts. We do not bring them up from the depths that are connected with the physical body, but we see them as in a panorama and look over the life that we have experienced.

Then we lay aside the etheric body. But this etheric body, which is now laid aside, remains visible to us throughout our entire further life after death. It is outside of us but remains visible. It unites with the whole universe, but we can see what happens to it; it remains visible to us. And this belongs to the mysteries of death: that as long as we bear the etheric body with us we see in a panorama what we had within us as thoughts while we lived, and that we unite this with the world outside of ourselves; we see it interwoven in the world. After death this etheric body belongs to the world, not to our own I. The experience is really that what had woven through and lived within us as our own etheric body during earthly life now becomes a part of the outer etheric world.

The time then comes when, as you know, only the I and the astral body remain of what we carried with us on the physical plane, as well, of course, as the view of what we were. We experience ourselves in a much different way than here in the physical body—we have an elevated awareness established in us by death. We must never, however, give ourselves over to the idea that the life between death and rebirth is unconscious on the part of the soul. The consciousness bound to the life after death is a stronger and more acute consciousness than the one here in the physical body, but the consciousness is formed in quite a different manner. Here on earth, we can approach the dead in the way we are trying to imagine them by gathering everything that spiritual science offers, in order to reshape the ideas that have been adapted to the purely physical objects and events here on the physical plane. In this way we can understand that after death we live in the I and in the astral body. We have put aside the etheric body; it is now connected to objective existence.

My dear friends, for those who enter into the spiritual world it is a truly soul-shaking experience to visit, to accompany, the departed, with whom one may come into contact, and to follow not only the individual life of the person between death and rebirth, but also to experience what the deceased sees. The part of the individual is seen in the form of the etheric body that has been interwoven with the world—a world that is now an outer world, an objective world to the person—and one observes what the departed has actually given to the etheric world. And thus we may, in a certain respect, experience in two ways those who have departed. We can experience what they have given to the etheric world and we can experience what resides in their consciousness after death.

The first contact with what the departed has left to the etheric world is quite soul-shaking. This is what was woven into the etheric body during earthly life but is now spread out for the departed as an objective, outer world. It would be shattering if we were not able to establish a connection with those beings living on between death and rebirth, who carry the consciousness and self-awareness of the dead, but rather only with what they left behind. Even then, such an experience deeply affects the soul that actually has contact with the spiritual world.

Above all, what is soul-shaking is the real, living experience that such spirituality (the etheric spirituality such as that just referred to; that is, the etheric spirituality left behind by the dead) is actually continually around us. Just as we live in the air that surrounds us everywhere, what the dead have left behind as their etheric world surrounds us. This spirituality that I am now speaking of exists in the world in which our physical bodies also exist. Just as air surrounds us, so does what the dead leave behind. We are separated from the spiritual world only by our state of consciousness; we are not separated by spatial relationships, but by our state of consciousness.

Take, for example, a person who strives to practice soul exercises. I want to explicitly emphasize that such soul exercises must be done in absolute inner quite. Those who become restless during these soul exercises do themselves harm. When soul exercises are done in the way I have spoken and written about them, and in the way we have discussed them before, so that they are truly soul exercises, and not affected by the physical body, they will never harm the human being in any way. We will never achieve true spiritual knowledge if we do not remind ourselves of these things now and then.

So, now imagine practicing the following exercise. You see colors with your eyes: red, blue, and so on. And now you shift to trying to experience the red, blue, green, and so on, as something living, in a certain respect. In doing this exercise, we gradually realize that as human beings in the physical world—especially in our present materialistic time—we are present in it in a very crude way; we do not respond to the finer, more subtle impressions we may experience. We experience these finer things when we pay attention to the soul impression that colors make on us (or that other sensory impressions make as well). Of course, we all know roughly that if we let a blue surface affect us, it affects us differently than a red surface. For those who can feel it without becoming nervous in the process—I emphasize this explicitly—a red surface is something that "attacks"; something that reaches out of its surface to affect us. Something always comes out toward us from red. Blue brings about the opposite feeling in us. It remains peacefully in its place. Nothing comes out at us from blue. On the contrary, we have the feeling when we can feel more finely into the colors that we can penetrate the color blue with our soul forces, that we can enter into it. Green is effectively in a state of rhythmic equilibrium. That is why it is so beneficial as the earth's vegetative cover. Green affects us so that, in part, we penetrate it, and in turn, it comes back to us. When we see a field of green plants, we have the feeling that we are entering into something, and then it comes back out toward us; into—and then back out. The refreshing feeling that we have from seeing a wide, green field comes from this rhythmic, balanced movement.

You can be sure of the fact that such a thing has been noticed before by human beings—that one can live with colors, so to speak. If you read the chapter in Goethe's *Theory of Color*‡ on the moral effects of color (although it is understood by few today), you will find there the corresponding feelings that one can have with all colors. In this way, one can live with colors, as well as with other sense impressions, but we will talk about colors here in order to give an example. One can live with colors in such a way that with blue something arises from our soul like a strength that is equal to the longing that issues from our soul, and this is readily absorbed by the blue. With red, it is as if something is created that meets us but it does not want to accept us, that wants to conquer us in a certain subtle way. When we feel colors in this way, we can have a sort of moral-soul experience. Of course, not everyone can master such exercises in one incarnation, but I describe these exercises so that you can see how the different worlds are interrelated. If you were to practice such exercises, you would live much more purely in the world of colors. If you practiced such exercises for other sense impressions, you would live in the world of those other sensations more purely. And soon, something else would also enter in.

Suppose that one were to experience the blue firmament as being alive in this way. Then the blue would not be just overhead (and this is a very subjective blue at that, because in reality there is no vault there), but it would be like a benevolent inner hemispheric expanse that absorbs one's soul life everywhere, a hemispheric expanse that (behind its two-dimensional quality), can come to terms with soul experience. Such is the way it is for those who witness the world in the deeper sense. Jakob Böhme,‡ for instance, did not say, "When humans see the blue firmament...." Instead, he said, "When humans see the depths."‡ Therein lies the whole act of witnessing blue: seeing the depths.

But an accompanying phenomenon occurs when we become so at one with the life of colors that our soul aspect glimmers at once in their presence. The opportunity to make use of a very short period of time is kindled, a moment that cannot otherwise be used at all. When you come into contact with an external object in ordinary physical life, you see it in this way; you see a particular color. This is, in fact, where your impression begins. Then you can reflect, form an idea, about the color. When you see the color, your witnessing of the object begins. But that is not the beginning of what takes place. Today, even the experimental psychologist knows that a certain amount of time passes between the effect on the eye and the appearance of the idea of blue. That is, the blue color affects the eye first. We do not perceive it immediately; rather, a certain amount of time passes, and only then do we become aware of it.

You can read in commonly found books how experiments about this are carried out in laboratories today. Experimenters construct certain apparatuses and attempt to cause an impression for the "guinea pigs," the subjects sitting there. The subjects must now indicate by means of another apparatus when they notice an impression, so that the experimenter can determine the short period of time, the instant that passes between the "attack" on our sense organs, so to speak, and the moment we become aware. A certain period of time elapses. During this time period, we do not yet experience the blue color (if we are talking about a blue impression), but during this period of time we do already experience the moral impression of the color. It already affects us. So, the way in which the soul pours forth into the blue, into which it is readily absorbed, is already within us. The soul aspect of a color in fact takes effect before we experience the color, although it remains in the unconscious. Humans do not perceive it. We do not notice what precedes the perception of color. We only begin to develop our consciousness when color appears.

Just think of when one is forced to pay close attention in a certain way to this moral impression of the color, to this soul experience of the color—then something special takes place. You must pay attention to this when you place color on a surface; that is, when you paint, when you use colors that must arise from within your thoughts. When you are involved in true painting, then you work from the soul impression of the colors. In this case, you do not proceed as an artist who is simply reproducing a model; rather, you know that to evoke a specific soul impression you must use red, so you use red. You put blue in another place because you want to evoke a different soul impression. This is how all the painting is carried out in our building in Dornach. There, what surrounds us as color has come completely from the soul aspects, which appear through the colors. In this case, it was necessary to create the building as a soul being in the highest way. Just as we encounter the construction of the world, so the building has grown as a construction out of a soul being. You would perceive what is manifested in the Dornach building if you could use that short period of time that passes between the instant in which the building affects the sense organs and the instant in which the impression becomes conscious. Those who took part in the construction had to create all the colors and forms in the building precisely from this short period of time.

I have led you in a somewhat scientific way into something that may seem difficult to you. But such difficulties must be overcome. As things are today, it may well be that someone can be as if blessed in some way (we are always blessed in a certain way in that we are present in the world) and is able to retain this moment. If we can become more aware as we are looking at something, we will at times have the impression that, in fact, an interaction has already taken place between ourselves and what we see. We will see something and think, it seems to me that I have already seen it before.

You may be very familiar with the experience of encountering a being or object and having the feeling that it is there not just in the moment when we become conscious of it, but that it had already approached us, it already had come close. We might say that one can at times notice something subtly approaching. But for everyday life, what takes place in this short instant lies completely beyond our consciousness, beyond the threshold. In the moment when we can become aware of what lies just outside of our consciousness—in this moment—we make an important spiritual discovery. I want to illustrate this with a specific instance once again. A number of you may have already heard this; I have mentioned it here before. Last year a young boy died near our building; he was crushed by a furniture truck.‡ The etheric body of this child is united with the Dornach building; it forms the aura of the Dornach building and lives in its aura. When we set out to create something artistic here, forces come from this etheric body, which then naturally appear larger. One feels these forces within, as one feels the building at a soul level.

Why is this? It is because the etheric bodies of the dead are preserved in the world that the dead see—the world of which I have just spoken that always surrounds us—and which we do not perceive simply because it remains unnoticed before the impression comes to us. What the departed see of our world, what they look at, is contained in the etheric world surrounding us. And indeed we too would always see it if we could cross this threshold even a little and, in a way, see just beyond the threshold before we look into the physical world.

But our not seeing does not prevent the dead from being affective continually in this world through what they have left behind. A world surrounds us in which the etheric bodies of the dead live. They are connected to it in some way. But we do not perceive in our world the powerful interwoven state of what remains etherically present from the dead, although what remains in the ether has an effect on our physical body and sets the instrument of the physical body in motion. However, we must adopt the feeling that our world must be expanded in order to take in what is present in the entire etheric world through the etheric bodies of the dead.

First of all, the dead are not present in this world, but only their etheric bodies, which were left behind. The dead live on further in the astral body and the I after they have put aside the etheric body, but the dead themselves are not so easy to find. You can comprehend from this how we must re-form our ideas if you consider that everything pertaining to thought is separated from us along with the etheric body, which passes over into the outer etheric world. Thoughts that we have accumulated here in our physical body do not remain within us after death. Thought becomes the outer world. We do not behold our thoughts after death the way we did during life when we could recall them from memory out of our subconscious. After death we look upon our thoughts as if we were seeing an etheric painting; we see our thoughts outside in the world. Thoughts are something external for us when we have passed across the threshold of death, whereas what reveals itself to us on earth through feeling and willing remains after death connected with our individuality. It lives on in the astral body and the I. In beholding the moment of death, the I awakens into self-awareness. The astral body awakens in such a way that the thoughts before us in the etheric painting penetrate into our astral body. Thus we experience them in our astral body. Here in the physical body, we experience thoughts by bringing them out from within. After death we experience thoughts by looking on them as on stars, worlds, or mountains, and they make an impression on us. We receive this impression and experience it in our astral body and in our I. That is, it is exactly opposite from the way it is in physical life. While we are here, we refer to thoughts as something internal, but we must refer to them as something external after death. Then we live merged with the world, poured out into the world. It is important that we see this, that we do not surrender to the idea that the world after death is only something like a fine, thin repetition of the physical world here, as is often assumed in spiritist circles. It is something quite different. It is something quite different because our thoughts are beings outside of our own being.

Precisely when we bring such ideas before our soul, we realize that we not only need a bit of impartiality in order to declare ourselves in agreement with spiritual science, but also that we must be able to make our concepts fluid, to change our concepts somewhat; that we cannot claim we can imagine what is in the spiritual world with the concepts we have here in the physical world. Thus it is necessary for those who are in the position, let us say, to visit the so-called dead to learn how to communicate with them. When we encounter an individual here in this world, we come into relationship with that person's inner self through words, facial expressions, and gestures. The departed, when we come into relationship with them, show us in the objective world what they want to express. They show us in imaginations what they experience, what they have to say to us. When one asks the dead something, they say, "Look there, there you will find what I am now experiencing."

But all this is a quick process; the dead have the ability to perceive thoughts suprasensibly because they are outside of things. We cannot see thoughts because we experience them inwardly; our thoughts are within us. Only when we acquire the ability to behold thoughts suprasensibly, as the dead do, can we experience along with them. Through this, the so-called dead have the highly unique ability to experience our thoughts.

There is one circumstance in particular where this occurs, which I would like to touch on here. When someone whom we have loved has left us, we carry on the thoughts of the person in our soul. We think of the things we experienced together, what we felt together, and so on. I have said that the dead see thoughts. They can very quickly distinguish between the thoughts that they themselves have as impressions of the spiritual world (which signify imaginations of what is in the spiritual world) and the thoughts that incarnated people have in their souls. The departed can make that differentiation. They make the distinction through their inner experience. It is actually quite a big difference. If the dead are to experience thoughts about something that is only in the spiritual world, they must actively experience these thoughts; it is exactly the same with initiates. They must follow each part of the thought they experience themselves. It is indeed difficult to make the process clear. Suppose a painting were before you, but you could see this painting only if you sketched and traced each detail yourself. The dead can do this. They trace every thought they see, recreate the thought, so to speak, and experience this re-creation. The re-creation of what is present in thought-formation in the spiritual world fundamentally represents a significant part of the life between death and rebirth. We re-create it thus, and then we know that we are dealing with thought-formations that belong only to the spiritual world.

The experience is different when one looks from within the spiritual world at thoughts that live in human beings in the physical world. There it is not as if one re-creates them; rather the thoughts really confront one in such a way that one can behave passively in relation to them. Just as a plant need not be sketched first, but actually immediately forms an impression in us, so are the thoughts of the living. They really come about in a way similar to the way impressions of the physical world do here. And that is what uplifts, delights, warms the dead about the thoughts of the living whom they loved. It is a very special realm for the dead, looking into the thoughts of those who love them and stayed behind. It is a special world for them. If one could experience the world here only as what comes into being physically in the mineral, plant, animal, and human kingdoms, then there would be no art. Art is created in addition to, beyond, what we actually need physically. Those who understand at all the evolution of humanity as being spiritual know that art cannot be absent from the world, in spite of the fact that even if there were no art, nature would be just as complete as it is now. If necessary, the dead would have to live in the way that incarnated human beings would live in a world of nature, bleak, dead, and bare without art. The dead would have to live in this way if they were forgotten immediately after their death by their loved ones. What is seen in the thoughts left behind in the souls of those who love the dead is certainly added to the world that the dead need directly, but it also elevates, improves, the existence of the dead. We can compare this, in a sense, to art in the physical world; but these thoughts are uplifting, an improvement, in a far superior way for the dead than the improvement in the physical world for us through art.

Thus it is deeply significant for the whole world when we unite our thoughts with those of the dead, specifically in the way we have often spoken of here—when we bring to the dead the kinds of thoughts that are formulated in the conceptual language common to the living and the dead, in the language we speak here in spiritual science. The dead can understand the content of spiritual science just as well as the living can; it never becomes foreign to them.

I believe we gradually form a vivid picture of the spiritual world precisely by gathering such concepts. We can find our way into what lies beyond the threshold through these concepts, and basically all that is available to us on this side of the threshold.

In relation to these phenomena, we must consider that humanity today is short-sighted when it comes to looking at the world, although this is somewhat justified because it belongs to the world plane. But actually, humanity is more short-sighted than it should be. When modern people who are quite materialistically-minded form their ideas about the world, they think that these ideas, these notions, are universally human. Indeed, you know how difficult it is to teach a materialistically-minded person that it is possible to think differently. Materialists are firmly rooted in the physical world when they say that those who do not think as they do are fools. There is no greater inner intolerance than that of materialistically-minded people. Such people basically always think that in earlier times people believed that all kinds of spiritual beings were present, that they did hardly anything in life without conjecturing or even seeing spirits everywhere. But the materialist claims that all that was meaningless fantasy, and that finally humanity has come far enough to have abandoned this childishness. And yet it is possible for people to notice at every turn how nonsensical such an idea actually is.

I want to explain this to you with an example that seems far afield and comes from a much different side than what we have discussed today. Let us think of the image—which we have often examined from different perspectives—of the first stage of the Earth, of the Paradise-existence of human beings, as it is described in the Bible. Let us think of an image of the first humans, Adam and Eve, in Paradise: Eve taking a bite of the apple, giving the apple to Adam; the serpent in the tree, seducing Eve. Indeed, this motif has been painted from time to time, and even in the present, with a woman portrayed as realistically, as naturalistically as possible, and also a realistic man, because it is modern. Whether impressionistic or expressionistic, either way a woman as realistic as possible and an even more realistic man; and a naturalistic landscape and a naturalistic serpent, bearing its naturalistic voracious teeth, and so on, are represented. But it was not always painted this way, because such an image would not show the actual facts that can be seen within it. Of course, we know that the symbol of the ultimate seducer, of Lucifer, can be seen in the serpent. However, Lucifer is a being that, as we know, stayed behind at the Old Moon stage; a being that can have the serpent as its symbol only as it appears on Earth—the serpent itself is not Lucifer. Rather, the serpent must somehow be seen in a spiritual way. That is, this Lucifer must also be seen with soul powers. With our inner effort, Lucifer must be seen from the inside outward. So how could one see him, my dear friends? We all basically carry the impressions of Lucifer in us, just as we do the impressions of Ahriman. Without any demonstration or detailed explanations, which you can search for yourselves on the basis of what we already have in our literature, I want to show you how one could imagine Lucifer.

Human beings carry impulses of the Lucifer aspect in themselves. We carry them in such a way that they sit in our head; they penetrate from our head into the astral body (the stage at which Lucifer remained behind). Thus, whereas the spirits of form have shaped the head, the Luciferic impulses penetrate into the head and also into what is shaped by the astral aspect—the spinal cord. So if we drew the head and its extension, the spine, separate from the human body, we would have a serpent, a snakelike creation with a human head. Of course, the whole thing must be thought of astrally, with the head somewhat reproducing the human head and the spine, which is attached to it, snaking down. Think of this objectively projected outward—it is a serpent with a human head. That is, seeing Lucifer externally in an image one could actually say: a serpent with a human head. Not a serpent with a serpent head; that is not Lucifer but an earthly serpent, which the spirits of form have already shaped into an earthly form. So we would have to say a serpent with a human head. This means that the artist who wanted to paint Lucifer in a tree would have to depict a serpent with a human head, winding around the tree. Thus the artist would paint from the perception of spiritual science. We would thus have to imagine Adam and Eve near the tree, and curled in the tree, similar to the body of a serpent, the now astral spinal cord with something resembling the human head. When the woman first sees it, of course, it resembles the female face.

Go to the museum here, to the art gallery, and look at the painting by Meister Bertram,[‡] and see how he painted, in the middle of the Middle Ages, this serpent on the tree as I have just described it. It is striking! It is superbly striking because it is proof that a painter in the Middle Ages painted from the real, actual imaginations of the spiritual world. This is fully valid proof that we do not have to go back so many centuries in order to obtain evidence, even now, that people already knew something in those days that people today in this materialistic age have forgotten.

Of course, this subject that I have just explained is never touched on in conventional art history. Nevertheless, everyone in this materialistic time could be convinced not just in attitude but also in their way of thinking that we ceased looking at the spiritual only a few centuries ago. Whoever goes to the art gallery and looks at this painting of Paradise by Meister Bertram has fully valid proof, brought to the outer physical plane, that it really has not been so long ago that people could see into the spiritual world with atavistic clairvoyance and knew its secrets in a much different way than we know them in the present. Just think how blindly people move through the world today; if only they wanted to, they could see for themselves externally on the physical plane that evolution is present in humanity.

This is what is important: in the course of the last three to four centuries, the old, unconscious, more atavistic clairvoyance has retreated. Of course, Meister Bertram could not have developed spiritual science. He simply looked—looked into the etheric realm to see Lucifer, and then he painted it. This was unconscious, instinctive clairvoyance.

In order for our outer sight to come about, this old beholding of the spiritual world had to recede. But we must regain it. And the time must gradually come when what has been lost is regained, but in the area of consciousness. Therefore, this must be prepared through spiritual science. Humanity will approach the spiritual world only by studying spiritual science. But this spiritual science must truly give insight into the spiritual world.

Today we can scientifically prove how much the natural sciences can achieve. When purely scientific thinkers speak about consciousness, they are actually speaking of the soul implement, the bodily instrument of the soul life. Today, one can test what the descriptions originating from the most important scientific minds of the present say about the soul aspect. In their words, the soul organization is called psychophysiology. There you will find that these people always examine, in a highly peculiar manner, the sensory life and the imaginational life. The soul instrument belongs to these, and they describe what is happening in the brain and in the nervous system when a person senses or imagines. In their view, a parallel process turns up everywhere in the physical body. If these researchers would go on to examine feeling and willing, they would find no bodily parallel processes.

The fact that something like this does not actually emerge—is not noticed—is simply because the natural sciences and their rearguard, the monists, simply boast about the fact that for every thought and sensory process a certain physical process is present, and that thinking and perception are bound to the brain. (Perhaps one cannot really say "rearguard" because a rearguard is valuable, but the monistic rearguard of the natural sciences is highly superfluous.) They do not speak of feeling or willing. At the most they speak of "shades" of feeling; that is, a certain nuanced visualization. But they do not come to feeling and will. The honest scientists say that science does not extend to feeling and will. You can read what I am now talking about in any scientific literature. It is proven everywhere. For instance, you can most easily find what I am now saying proven in the work of Dr. Theodor Ziehen, a very well-known psychiatrist and psychophysiologist of our time.[‡] He shows the individual processes that correspond to thinking and perception. He gets to shades of feeling, but not to actual feeling and will.[‡] He thus denies feeling and will. He says that they simply do not exist. One could not scientifically prove more clearly that scientific thinking extends only over the temporal, extends only over what we cast off with death. What goes beyond, what lives precisely in feeling and will, as I have mentioned, belongs so minimally to the body that scientists cannot even find it; and they even dismiss, deny it! Such people boast that there is no feeling or will because these cannot be found with normal science. Science itself proves to us today that feeling and will are not connected to the body, as such, in the way that thoughts and perceptions are!

This distinction has to do with the fact that our thoughts will separate themselves from us and appear dispersed outside of us after death. Feeling and will remain with us. And from feeling and will spring the strength to create the thought tableau. Those who wish to, can show strictly through science that feeling and will have nothing to do with what nature is; rather, they go forth after death as the astral body and the I. Feeling and will remain with the human individuality; they awaken into a new consciousness in the way I have described. Because the entire act of spreading out is etheric, it is reflected in the astral body and then in the I, when the astral body, too, is laid aside.

Everything is basically in order because modern science does not refute spiritual science, but rather confirms it! If people could only muster some understanding, they would see precisely how natural science, through real understanding, proves the legitimacy of spiritual science, including its specific assertions.

Spiritual science is, as you see, something that must begin entering into the evolution of humanity in our time, must begin to take hold of humanity, or else humanity will come to grasp only the temporal and will know nothing of the eternal that lives in us. The time will come when human beings will realize this, and then will become more engaged in the evolution of the life of the will, in the evolution of the feeling life. Because only through feeling and will do we unite ourselves with the world, which is not void of thoughts.

Of course people will argue we just feel the spiritual world, we do not will it! But, indeed, we are united, precisely through feeling and will, with the objective world of thought—with thoughts that really live, not with thoughts that we merely think. And just as humanity could see into the spiritual world in antiquity, so must humanity regain this view into the spiritual world in the future. We will be able to achieve this, however, only if we first decide to engage with the thoughts in the spiritual world, which in our time are dismissed.

For us to engage with the thoughts of the spiritual world, there is much that must be corrected in the concepts and ideas that are swirling around in the present. It is hard to believe how basically unthinkingly people in our time think (permit me to use this paradox). They give definitions, which they are adamantly convinced are correct and cannot be disputed at all. But more than ever, spiritual scientists have the task of testing those ideas of which people are adamantly convinced because they seem completely logical and people are convinced of them. If, for instance, someone in today's materialistic age is asked, "What is a true concept?" That person would give a reply like, "A true concept is an inner picture of an object that is actually present outside in the world." That is, everyone today would define a concept as a truth consisting in the correlation of an outer manifestation with an image that one makes in one's thoughts. Now, if we investigate the concept, we can very easily prove that the true concept has absolutely nothing to do with what is usually called a concept. We can easily prove that the object travels very different paths than does the image that a person makes as a concept. If a concept is true only when it correlates to an object, then it would of course be true only as long as the manifested object confirmed it. Thus we could compare a concept to, for example, a painting made as a portrait of a person. The portrait is good if it resembles the person. But it has nothing to do with the person's inner being. The correlation of the picture with a self does not come near to the inner truth of the picture. Imagine that you paint a portrait of a person, and then the person dies right afterwards. The picture corresponded at first to that which is; and afterwards, to that which is not. The being has absolutely no relation to whether the picture is true or not, no relationship with the outer manifestation. For those who look at the subject in a really logical way, the relationship is completely contrived. The essential thing is to experience things inwardly. Humanity must learn to experience inwardly again.

But above all, humanity must achieve a sense for real truth again; and we can be led to this, in particular, through our time, which is so difficult and full of suffering. Little by little. through materialism, we have basically deviated from the truth completely. We have lost ourselves through materialism, precisely in relation to the sense for truth. Compare something you can verify today; compare the journalistic description (many people today read nothing other than newspapers) of some event that you witnessed yourself with your own senses. If you read about it in the newspaper, you will find that it is depicted in a way that the journalist thinks will make an impression on readers. But the feeling that everything should correspond to the truth—this is diminishing more and more. But that is only a part of it. And as long as a feeling for truth does not permeate humanity, the impulse that leads out of the sensory world to the spiritual world will not be able to arise in our souls because in the absence of these concepts that correspond to truth, the concepts secretly become false. For example, how often have we experienced the following? Someone writes about spiritual science, let us say, about what I have published on spiritual science. He writes, and of course cannot help saying, based on his materialistic concepts, that it has all been invented from fantasy, and that inventing from fantasy is not allowed. And then he decides to investigate how someone could come to be such a fantasizer.

Such an article was really published not long ago![‡] It investigates how a person could be so fanciful. It explains where that person comes from (in this case, it was myself), where he lived earlier, and how he could have such fantasies based on a certain miscegenation. The author dreams up the most unbelievable things with his materialism. And that is what I am saying. One simply takes the lie into one's own hands; one twists the truth inwardly.

Of course, this cannot be directly proven. But what dishonesty lies therein, when one is able to accuse someone of fantasy, and then to dream up things about him! If you look more closely at life today, you will see how tremendously prevalent is this lack of a feeling of responsibility; this lack of concern that everything we say be consistent with reality. Without acquiring this sense in the most intensive way, we cannot find the entrance to the spiritual world. We simply will not be able to comprehend why something must be true that spiritual science elicits from the spiritual world as truth. But we are much too closed-minded to really contemplate the present day in this way, and we are too attached to our interests to really look at all areas to see how untruth pierces through and fragments every one of life's circumstances.

To contemplate true perception, true visualization, is one of the first preparations for spiritual science. And such reflecting must become a conscious preparation time for what the future of humanity must really be, because the future salvation of humanity can come about only by reuniting our souls with the spiritual. Spiritual science is not something that we seek like another sensation; rather, spiritual science must be something that we know must arise in the present time because humanity needs it. And if we look at the course of the evolution of humanity in an unobstructed and lucid way, we must to a certain extent feel an obligation to it.

What boundless enrichment we experience through what spiritual science can give us. The world is expanded little by little because to the physical truth of the evolution of humanity is added spiritual truth. In this materialistic age, we are cut off more and more from the world in which human beings exist between death and rebirth. Through spiritual science we must again live together with the whole human being, even when the human being doesn't have a physical body. Our materialistic world offers us nothing of this.

Precisely in our difficult times, it can really be a blow to the soul to see something like the book, for example, that has just been published by Ernst Haeckel.‡ He calls this book *Ewigkeitsgedanken* [*Thoughts on Eternity*]. Now, Ernst Haeckel is one of the most outstanding minds of our time. These "thoughts on eternity" tie directly in with the Great War of the present. What is its essence? The main content of this newest book from Haeckel is his question: What can this war show us? Needlessly, thousands upon thousands of people are dying violently in it. Can we not see in this war the proof, says Haeckel, that all thoughts on eternity and infinity are absurd? Should not this war convince us that human life perishes through external coincidence, by bullets and so on; should this war not show us, according to Ernst Haeckel, that there is nothing beyond ordinary physical life?

Of course, there are also other people today who come to thoughts of a very different kind about eternity through these difficult events, to thoughts on eternity that at least evoke the feeling that those who pass through the gate of death in such times continue to carry on their tasks for humanity in other worlds; that what they have sacrificed is, in fact, the starting point for what they must achieve without a physical body.

With current science, one can prove this and that. Just as we can make excellent machines that help human culture progress in a peaceful way and also the most terrible machines of destruction, the very same science can create this and that, and prove this and that.

In order to really penetrate the world in which the eternal lives, spiritual science is essential. Spiritual science shows us, among other things (I have already spoken of this before, at least to a number of you here), that those who leave the physical body early, before the usual age for the physical plane has run its course, who give their etheric bodies to the etheric world, live on in their individuality. Spiritual science also shows that such an etheric body, which could have continued to support the physical body for decades when it was consigned to the etheric world, still has life forces, and it is present in the etheric world, as I have shown you through examples.

What the departed gain with their sacrificial deaths lives on in their individualities. It lives on precisely in such a time as ours, when we can grasp the true meaning of what is happening with the soul-eye of spiritual science. Spiritual science makes us aware of the spiritual counter-image of what is now taking place on European soil as the violent and traumatic events play out on the physical plane. The spiritual correlate, the parallel spiritual process, must flow into the future, into the physical events of the evolution of humanity because all that is physical is guided from the spiritual world. But this will become fruitful only if human souls incarnated on Earth are conscious of receiving something beneficial from what lives on in the spiritual world that the dead have brought about through their sacrificial deaths. This effective and useful gift lives on in the spiritual world and helps us to work into the future on earth when we unite with the dead through our consciousness of the reality of the spiritual world.

That is what spiritual science must give to human beings, including for this situation. Then they will be able to make the spiritual aspect of this most violent world event fruitful in the correct sense for the future—and to conceive and sense and perceive in the right way:

From the combatants' courage,
From the blood of battle,
From the suffering of those abandoned,
From the people's sacrificial death,
Spiritual fruit will grow—
May souls guide their senses, conscious of spirit,
Into the realm of the spirits.

Lecture 2

The Elements of Our Being between Death and Rebirth

Kassel, February 18, 1916

The times in which we live suggest powerfully to us how necessary it is for human beings to investigate the meaning of life on earth. But we will never understand the meaning of life on earth if we look only to what is happening in the sense world because the deeper meaning of all that happens there comes to expression only when the spiritual aspect also comes to expression in the sensory. This is a difficult time of testing. And particularly those who are firmly and devotedly determined to hold to our cause must understand that its meaning will be revealed within our soul only when we raise ourselves up to what is expressed spiritually, even in the very difficult events taking place on the physical plane.

In light of the fact that we look upon battlefields where in innumerable instances the gate of death opens, and in light of the thought that a great many of our friends have already left the physical plane, perhaps we will do well, particularly today, to turn our attention to what can be said about the world into which human beings enter when they step through the gate of death. Today we will examine the life between death and rebirth from this viewpoint. Of course, there are many viewpoints from which our approach may originate.

In spiritual science, we try first of all to understand people as they are before us. We know that they stand before us in both their physical and spiritual aspects. We know that these spiritual aspects remain suprasensible; the spiritual can reveal, announce, itself only through the physical. And when we observe human beings here on the physical plane in order to understand them in the sense of spiritual science, four main parts or elements of the human being are initially unveiled to us. We call them the physical body, the etheric body, the astral body, and the I. You know this from my description in *Theosophy.* Beginning with the etheric body, the elements of human nature are suprasensory to physical observation. But we do experience our own I and astral body; we experience them inwardly. We experience them in that we are able to know ourselves as I, even though this I remains hidden, suprasensory. And so, you can understand why we consider human beings according to all of these four parts, even when we focus only on what the physical world reveals.

Now, let us consider the fact that we can also look at those who are living between death and rebirth in a similar way; that it is also possible to speak of the elements or members of one who is in the life between death and rebirth. Indeed, you know that we leave our physical body to the material elements, the substances of the earth; and we leave our etheric body to the universal etheric world. After a time, what is particularly present in our astral body, but of which we know nothing on earth, also dissolves, as it were, and our I then continues through the world that we experience between death and rebirth.

We should think of human beings who exist between death and rebirth as differentiated, structured beings, just as human beings are here in the physical world. We can also speak of the different parts or members of our human nature between death and rebirth, but in this case we will have to speak in the following way.

When we observe human beings here on the physical plane, the I appears to us as what comes across to us as the "highest" aspect, if we may use the expression. Here, human beings have a physical body in common with all minerals, an etheric body with all plants, an astral body with all animals. But the I belongs to human beings only. In the spiritual world, the I, which on earth is the highest aspect of human nature, is the lowest aspect in the world between death and rebirth. As we begin with the physical body here, so must we begin with the I in the spiritual world. The I is the lowest part of the human being between death and rebirth and is enveloped as in a mist by the astral aspect while the individuality moves through the soul world. And just as we envelop ourselves here with various members when we enter the physical world from the spiritual world through the gate of birth, so do we also, after death, envelop ourselves in the spiritual world, as it were, with spiritual members. We actually already know the names of these spiritual parts. It is just that we look at them a bit differently on earth. To begin with, we envelop ourselves in "spirit self" when we have passed through the gate of death. The spirit self is in fact a part of human nature that humans will develop in themselves in the future during the Jupiter stage of evolution. What I am now calling the spirit self for the world between death and rebirth is not exactly the same as what will develop when human beings evolve onward from Earth stage to Jupiter stage. What will develop during the Jupiter stage will be a sort of outer reflection, a counter-image appearing to the senses, of the spiritual being that human beings take on when they pass through the time between death and rebirth. So we can also characterize this aspect in which human beings envelop themselves there when they pass through the time between death and rebirth as the spirit self.

With further progression in the spiritual world, human beings envelop themselves in the part we can call "life spirit," which is a spiritual counterpart to something that will develop in our physical progression only during the Venus stage of evolution. And the true "spirit human" will develop within human beings as the spiritual counterpart of what human beings will have as a physical reflection in the highest sphere of their physical evolution toward which we can look today—the Vulcan stage. Thus we can say that just as human beings envelop themselves in the astral, etheric, and physical bodies on earth, so do they envelop themselves in the spirit self, life spirit, and spirit human as they grow into the spiritual world.

Now I would like to describe a bit more precisely out of initiation knowledge, as one might put it, how these things come about. Indeed, you already know much of this. When human beings pass through the gate of death, the physical body is given over to the elements of the earth. This release of the physical body is extraordinarily important for the life between death and rebirth, and although it certainly seems trivial to say that death is actually birth in the spiritual world, even so, it is accurate. We must simply become accustomed to making our concepts somewhat flexible, so that with our concepts we do not immediately cling to what the earth presents to us.

We are used to forming our concepts only according to what the earth presents to us. We must be able to transform these concepts. Life in the spiritual world is completely different from life on earth. The spiritual experience that human beings have in the spiritual world by stepping through the gate of death is this: the physical body falls away. That is a meaningful, an immensely meaningful experience! And the first thing that should be said about this experience is that it relates quite differently (with respect to the beginning of the spiritual life after death) than a person's birth relates to physical life between birth and death.

We cannot observe our birth with earthly physical powers of perception. Human beings do not experience their birth here on earth with their physical powers of perception because we do not then have memory. Memory itself begins only later. This is proper for earthly life, and must be so, but it is the opposite for the life between death and rebirth. Because the moment, the instant of death (I cannot say of dying, but the moment of death) remains as something the person can look at again and again during the whole progression of the life between death and rebirth. Though we do not remember the event of our physical birth, in contrast we have the moment of death before us clearly throughout our entire life between death and rebirth, but from the other side, from the perspective of spiritual life—from the other shore, so to speak.

Death can be fearful for human beings on earth, and this reaction has a certain rightfulness. It represents the decline of the physical nature of the human being. Exactly the opposite occurs when human beings between death and rebirth look back on their death. Then death continuously shows the triumph of the spirit over the physical; death then represents the most beautiful, most splendid, most exalted thing that we can essentially ever experience. And being capable of observing our death throughout our entire spiritual life between death and rebirth gives us consciousness after death. We know that we have laid aside our physical body. Just as we gain our self-awareness here in the physical world by having a physical body, the fact that we experience our death and that we always have it before us gives us our self-awareness after death.

When we are outside the physical body with the astral body and I during the time between falling asleep and waking up, we have no consciousness of the physical world. When we awake, we must physically sink into ourselves, and then our I-consciousness can blossom again. After death, each time we look at our death, when the whole event—this exalted, beautiful event as seen from the other side—stands before our soul, then consciousness awakens again and again after death. Consciousness completely depends on the continuous observation of this moment.

Something else is connected to this, as well. It is somewhat difficult to speak about these things because, as I said, there are no corresponding experiences here in the physical world, but we must try to characterize these things as they really are. If, during our life after death, we look back at our death, above all we have the feeling and the ideational impression that where we died, from then on, there is nothing, not even space. As I said, it is difficult to describe, but it is so: nothing is there. And expressed in an outer way: the whole thing from its foundations appears splendid, exalted, because everywhere other than that place a new world arises for us. The flooding spiritual world surges in from all sides, but nothing is there of the place where we died.

To describe these things theoretically in this way might seem grim, but there is nothing grim after death about this perception. A deep fulfillment wells up in the soul from this perception after death. One learns to expand into the whole world and to look back upon something in the world that is as if empty. And from this arises the feeling: that is my place in the world; the place that is made of all the far expanses, and that is mine. And one has the perception that precisely from this emptiness one gains a sense of the meaning of the whole world; that every single human existence—one has it of course first as an explanation for oneself—must be there. "This place would always be empty if I were not there"—so each soul tells itself. The perception is that each one is given a place as a person in the universe. This perception, which is incredibly warming internally, arises from this observation: the whole world is there and the whole world has sent forth, as out of a symphony, the single note that is the person. And this note must be there, or there would be no world. This feeling is what arises from looking back on our experience of death. It remains because it primarily gives the I-consciousness, self-awareness between death and rebirth.

Then, there is a comparatively short but sufficient time for a togetherness with the etheric body. For a number of days, everything one has experienced in life, even the smallest events remain; it is all there together in a great life tableau. During this time, one has the very intense feeling that the earth on which one has stood keeps moving on, but one's own self remains behind; one begins to stand still. One no longer goes along with the spatial movement of the earth. And because of this the life tableau spreads out.

When we speak of this remembrance of life, we are not speaking of memory in the actual sense of when we have memories by looking back in time. That is not the case here; rather, it is simultaneous; it is a tableau, a living tableau. And, as I mentioned before, it includes even the smallest events. Then one separates oneself from this etheric experience. The detaching of the etheric body takes place, as we say. One now has as outer form what one had experienced inwardly with the etheric body. What was experienced inwardly is now outside of us and grows bigger and bigger, and weaves itself (that is actually the correct expression) into the spiritual world one has just entered. But in the spiritual world, the void emptiness of which I have spoken remains, and the etheric body weaves itself all around it externally, and becomes bigger and bigger.

Now we must hold on to the fact that it would be an erroneous idea—I must admit that I have been convinced that in every case it would be a mistake—to think that we could not see what we weave with the universal spiritual world as an etheric body during the life between death and rebirth. We see it eternally, see it continuously; it is part of our outside world. What was in the etheric body until now, what was part of our inner world, is now part of the world outside of us. We look at it. And it is important that we are able to look at it, because through it so much of the outer spiritual world becomes understandable to us as a relationship between what we have woven into it and the entire outer spiritual world.

You may remember the lectures I once gave in Vienna‡ concerning the time between death and rebirth, when I said human beings are first of all interwoven in a world full of wisdom. Whereas here on earth we search, straining for wisdom, there we are completely surrounded by the light of wisdom. The wisdom with which we are surrounded overwhelms us there. And it would continue to overwhelm us if we could not weave into the world the wisdom we have taken into our etheric body during life on earth. What we bring dampens down the immense overabundance of light in the universal world ether, and we begin to understand what in the universal world ether weaves through the world and imbues it with soul and spirit.

With this is described what falls away from us, so to speak, when we are taken into the spiritual world, because essentially then only the I and the astral body remain from the earthly parts of human nature. The physical body has fallen away. In its place, what I have called the void or emptiness remains. The etheric body is accepted into the universal world ether. We continue on our way. What we have now given to the world ether as our etheric body, we replace by enveloping ourselves in what we have called the spirit self. It is now more or less an outer member of our being. The undifferentiated etheric presses around us; it envelops us with a sort of spirit self.

It would be good to spend a bit of time now on our concept of the human being. We need not talk about the void that remains because it has great meaning only for those who have died, who have experienced it in the way that I have described. But it is somewhat different for the etheric body. The etheric body weaves objectively into the universal world ether. This human etheric body is now inside it.

You will understand that to a certain extent the etheric body of a person who dies at a young age is somewhat different in the world outside than the etheric body of a person who has reached old age. Of course, every etheric body has its task, and to wish to die young or to die old should not result from what I will now say—that would be a distorted misconception, the greatest misconception, of the matter. But nevertheless what I have to say now is accurate.

The etheric body of a person who dies at a young age could possibly have worked within the physical body and sustained the physical body for decades more. Energy in the spiritual world is not lost any more than it is in the physical world. That is, if the person dies at twenty or thirty years old, a force is present in the etheric body from which the person is released after death that could have sustained the person's physical body for decades more. This etheric force is no longer within a physical human body; it is outside in the world. Perhaps this can best be understood with an example.

I have already spoken to some of our friends about this subject. There was a young child‡ who perished under tragic circumstances at the age of seven near our building in Dornach. He had gotten some food that evening from our cafeteria, which is near the building. A strange chain of events resulted in the child's going out of the cafeteria and through some bullrushes that were near a road on which a fully loaded furniture truck was passing at that moment. The truck overturned and crushed the little boy. It was a very tragic event. Right after the evening of lectures, after 10:00 pm, word came to us that the child was missing. So we searched for the boy. At first we could only see what happened to the furniture truck. The extenuating circumstances were also very strange. The boy had wanted to leave fifteen minutes earlier, but was detained by someone who wanted to walk with him. And he had wanted to go through a different door, in which case he would have passed the furniture truck on the right side, whereas he was crushed on the left. Someone told him that he should go out through that particular door; he was directed, literally, to go out that door. And besides that, no furniture truck had driven on that road for years, and perhaps no truck will drive on it for years to come. It was a truck that was bringing furniture to one of our members just that one time. The furniture truck was so heavily laden, and fell haplessly in such a way, that it could not be immediately lifted. The people who were driving the furniture truck had nothing with them to lift it, and simply left. They wanted to wait until the next day to lift the truck. But, of course, we had to lift it that night, and we found the dead child underneath it.

Thus in the time after his death, this little boy had been in the surroundings of the building for a while. Now it is really true that in the time after his death, his etheric body was interwoven into the building's aura. It is surely not immodest to say that whoever, like myself, is involved in the artistic aspect of the building notices how the stimulation one needs to integrate various things artistically into the building comes from this child's unused etheric force.

Of course it might be more congenial to human egotism to ascribe it all up to one's own ingenuity. But it is absolutely the case that what comes to us inwardly originates from outer spiritual influences. And we can concretely verify each of these spiritual influences. Here we are concerned with the boy's etheric body, which was seven years old and thus could have sustained the physical body six or seven decades longer. It now exists in the etheric aura of the Dornach building with the whole immensely wise constructive force necessary to artistically form the physical human body.

And I even dare to say with complete certainty to artists that the art necessary to form the physical body from the etheric body is much greater than any art we practice on earth. Human beings are indeed the greatest artistic creation. And all the impulses that form the physical human body are contained within the etheric body. Artists, as well, produce impulses from their etheric body when they create artistically.

This is just one example; others can be given in which the supporting capacity of unspent etheric bodies can be seen. Even during this year, dear young friends of ours have passed through the gate of death. And so we see how, in precisely this time, countless people are passing through the gate of death at an early age, leaving their etheric bodies, which all could have worked on the physical bodies for decades more. These etheric bodies, which in addition have been invigorated and strengthened by going through sacrificial death, are present and will be present. In future times, there will be people living on this European soil who will be able to live in a spiritual, an etheric, atmosphere where these unused etheric bodies exist. And when there are people on earth who understand what lives spiritually, not just as abstract memory but as true etheric forces—we will be able to have this understanding only through spiritual science—then they will no doubt feel the inspiring forces of what is present from these etheric bodies.

And that is part of the feelings that now weigh heavily on our hearts; we say heavily because when we look at the enormity of what could happen if a good many people became aware of what is sown through the deaths that are now taking place around us in the great events of our time, we see that the number of people who can understand these things is still so small. And it could easily be that through people's lack of understanding regarding spiritual science, as a result of the materialism filling all humanity, people in the future could live on without any hint of an idea of what can come about as a result of these deaths.

We must let such a statement live in our own hearts in no other way—in as much as it is incumbent upon us—than that we fill ourselves with such a consciousness and do what we can to create an understanding of it. We should not just fill ourselves with the fearful worry of how much materialism exists. We must recognize how much materialism exists on earth, but we should not close ourselves off, for instance, to the materialistic worldview that is spreading more and more; rather, we should do all the more to carry out our tasks.

So much for what there is to say about the etheric-physical aspect. In the spiritual world after death, we human beings then advance another step. We first envelop ourselves in a sort of spirit self, which is formed in a slightly different way than all that is formed when we are here on earth. One could say that the spirit self is something that presses toward us from all sides, and we feel as if we are at its center. Then we settle further into the other members of our human nature by experiencing at the same time a sort of spiritual course moving backward, as I have described now and again. We experience a sort of antithesis to earthly life, but now in a much different way than through the pure tableau I described. We realize how, subsequently, time proceeds after the etheric body is put aside, and we live on with the astral body and the I enveloped in the spirit self.

This spirit self is a sort of driving force. It leads us back, so that we experience our last earthly life in reverse, from death to birth; we really move backward. For example, here on earth if we say something to a person and harm that person, we experience that event in our physical body from our own point of view. We cannot experience it from the standpoint of the other person. We would not be able to live in the physical body at all if we wanted to live otherwise than having our own experiences. Let us take a case in which in order to get revenge, someone hurts a person very badly by saying something. Here one does not experience what the other person feels or senses. With our going backward after death, which I just described, we experience in the spiritual world what the other felt, always as the effect of what we have done. That is, there we live within the world of effects. We experience, in reverse order, what others have gone through with us during our physical life, completely separate from ourselves, until we come to the point where we have reached birth. Then we envelop ourselves with what one could now call the spiritual counterpart to what will develop during the Venus stage of evolution; we envelop ourselves with life spirit.

And this life spirit determines later life, which I have also described before. You will, for instance, find it described from the most varied viewpoints also in the Vienna lecture series on life between death and rebirth.‡ Today I want to describe it here from another viewpoint.

In the spiritual world, we are now surrounded by life spirit, and it expresses itself in a certain way, which is essential that we understand. The spirit self first leads us back—the spirit self mainly has to do with our essence, with our individuality—and then it leads us further on. After it has brought us back to re-experiencing birth, it leads us on to the paths we are to follow in the spiritual world.

Our further envelopment by life spirit is different. Here in the physical body we are permeated by the etheric body, which also contains life ether and all that enlivens us. We are more or less permeated by the etheric body, and we live through this etheric body. You know that the etheric body extends slightly beyond the physical body, but otherwise has a very similar shape. Without an etheric body one cannot live on the physical plane.

When we have put aside our astral body, we realize that we are enveloped in life spirit. We were enveloped by life spirit the whole time that spirit self was leading us back. But only now do we notice it. We notice it only after we have gone through the whole process called the kamaloka period. And we now become aware of something interesting: life between death and rebirth is possible only by being enveloped in this life spirit. Here in the physical body we must live within our skin. But we cannot live within ourselves in the spiritual world between death and rebirth. If we wanted to live only within ourselves in the spiritual world, more or less only in one single place in the spiritual world, then we would have to die perpetually; that is, we would not be able to live. Rather, we must live with the entire universe. We must know the whole universe to be a great living being with which we must live.

Now this can happen in two ways. We could flow out into the whole universe. But if we flowed out, the consciousness we would have, which I have described, this self-awareness, would also flow into nebulousness. Rather, we must move around within the great, living world organism. Here in the physical body, an element of ourself, say a hand, is in a specific place. In the spiritual world we must always be led around; we must always be carried from one place to another. The life spirit does that. That is how we leave one place and arrive at another. However, this happens rhythmically so that we always return to the same place. But we must be led around in the spiritual world. A spiritually dynamic life develops for us. Here, as physical individuals, we are for the most part stuck in one single place. Something of the spiritual is always carried into the physical; and thus we are able to move around on the physical plane. This is essentially an ahrimanic effect because the spiritual is carried into the physical by Ahriman. But after death it is right that we are led into the spiritual through the whole associated world organism, and in this way, we settle into the whole environment surrounding earthly life, whereas here on earth we settle into one place. And while we are led around within this spirit environment after death, from spirit place to spirit place (you can find more details on this in my Vienna lecture series),[‡] at the same time, the forces are implanted in us that we need to prepare for our new earthly life; to be drawn toward earthly life again. The first half of the life between death and rebirth proceeds in such a way that we make our way away from our former earthly life; in the second half, we find ourselves preparing for a new earthly life.

You see, materialism today essentially creates the opposite out of all things. It misleads people to the worst misconceptions, making them seem not only credible, but almost obvious. When a genius appears, such as Goethe, people take him materialistically. A very thick book was written and published about Goethe‡ in which all of his ancestors who could be found through research were analyzed in a materialistic way, both physically and mentally (though the materialist looks only at the body). The authors showed how Goethe inherited this from one ancestor, that from the other. Goethe himself said ironically, "I have my stature from my father,‡ my happy nature from my mother." Here in Kassel, during a lecture series,‡ I once showed how people take so materialistically what is "bequeathed" through the stream of physical hereditary, including genius in particular. And I have frequently said that this is absurd, laughably foolish; and yet, again, so credible. It makes immediate sense to the materialists that certain characteristics are enhanced through many generations, and then appear to be bequeathed to the genius. The materialists think that they are speaking of real experiences. But it expresses nothing more than, for instance, that someone who has fallen into the water and has been pulled out is wet. The soul naturally passes through all its ancestors in a certain way, and thus everything that it drew from those ancestors is attached to it. Just as someone who has fallen into water is wet, so, too, do we have the characteristics of our ancestors as we go through the generations. It would be different if the opposite occurred—if one could prove that genius is bequeathed to one's descendants; but it is not. People should prove *that*! But they leave that out. They research Goethe's ancestors, but then they neatly leave out his son and his grandchildren! Just look to see if the characteristics of being a genius are bequeathed to descendants! Although there may be cases where the matter is concealed, bequeathing the characteristics of genius to descendants is out of the question. Only if it would manifest, would one experience it. But there is no such bequeathing of the characteristic of being a genius.

However, something else is the case. When we try to follow a human individuality further back (the individuality enters a physical body at a certain point in time—it comes from the spiritual world, after all), it is this same individuality that brings father and mother together; that plays a part in the father and mother coming together for its creation. Indeed, it plays a part even further back. It affects, more or less, the entire series of generations in such an order that at last the two people, through whom this one individuality can find its embodiment, find each other. This individuality plays a part in all that takes place through centuries, from ancestors to descendants. As unusual as it sounds, it is true. Goethe had a father and mother, grandfather and grandmother, and so on. If we go back through the centuries, we will see that Goethe's individuality had an effect from the spiritual world in such a way that people always found each other; so that finally the senior Kaspar Goethe and his wife Aja were produced. The individuality of Goethe affected the series of generations over centuries from the spiritual world.

This is exactly the opposite of what is assumed. What we human beings carry in our souls is not bequeathed to us physically by our ancestors; rather, we assemble our ancestors from the spiritual world, from the Cosmic Midnight of the world, which lies at the midpoint between death and rebirth, so that we can find our way into earthly life. This is the mystery that results. This is immensely significant. And through it, we see clearly that really an inner link exists between what happens in the spiritual world and what happens in the physical world. And at the same time we see how uniquely is our spiritual-soul life between death and rebirth interwoven with what happens here. This is simply not noticed here.

Recent philosophy speaks of spirit in a very strange way. There was a professor in Halle,[‡] now seen as a very important light in the field of philosophy, who published a book, *The Philosophy of "As If,"* in which he tries to prove that such concepts as spirit and soul do not represent reality, but that they are useful in humanity's worldview. He says that one should not look at human beings in such a way as to think that they have souls. They move their hands and speak, so we can say that we behold them *as if* they had souls. Otherwise, let the soul be soul. We deny it—we do not worry about it—but we behold it as if human beings had souls; as if the soul wanted to have an effect on all of this.

This is a comfortable philosophy, but also terribly void of thought. Indeed, whoever tries to put this philosophy to use in tangible practical life sees that this "as if philosophy" is not much good, even as a method. A person such as Fritz Mauthner, who wrote a philosophy of language[‡] and traced everything back to language, must be examined from the point of view of this "as if philosophy"; as if such a person could also have spirit. But if we make this attempt, we find that this method is not much good. We do not say that we can be observed as if we had a spirit; it is not applicable. It is not applicable when no spirit is present. Of course you know how I mean that. But I only mention this Fritz Mauthner because he is someone who completely denies the whole significance of history and who said, most evidently from the standpoint of present materialism, that history can never be a science. He said that when a raindrop falls on the earth one can discover the raindrop's laws scientifically because many raindrops fall according to the same laws.[‡] One can compare the individual cases with each other and then find the laws. Contemporary philosophers believe that observing many instances in which the same thing always occurs leads to individual laws. But things happen only once in history—the Thirty Years' War happened only once, and so on. Thus, to Fritz Mauthner, our entire history is only a series of accidents. People today must come to such conclusions if they truly deny spirit because history would be only a series of coincidences if precisely what we just described—which has an effect from the spiritual world, and which people between death and rebirth contribute to—did not affect history in a real way. We weave, as it were, between death and rebirth what happens here on earth; we weave only according to those impulses that come to us from the spiritual world.

An objection cannot be seriously raised against spiritual science from any scientific perspective, because when we compare to spiritual science what today's science can truly accomplish, today's science is the best support for spiritual science. We must simply approach the subject in the correct way.

If you take up any book today in which a materialistically-minded person voices views, perhaps half psychologically and half physiologically, you will find the following. These people attempt to imagine how humans visualize things by showing the intellectual "apparatus," the physical organs—the life of the nerves, the life of the brain. They test this intellectual apparatus and can really show that when some idea takes hold in us, a process takes place in the brain. Thus they claim they can prove to you that without a process in the brain, a thought or idea could not be conceived at all; then what do you need an autonomous soul for? Only an intellectual apparatus is there! But they also come to something else, these materialistically-minded people. Look through the usual textbooks and you will find that in them these people show the intellectual apparatus and connect all thinking and visualization with the mechanical processes in the brain and nervous system, but they must deny feeling and will. Feeling and will cannot be explained by bodily processes. Thus they are simply discarded. And today when you open these books you will find everywhere that although people have acquired will and feeling through their biases, these are in fact treated as nonentities; as if they do not exist at all.

Thus natural scientists stop short of feeling and will. As we now know, after death, thoughts separate themselves from us along with the etheric body. This explains how the separated part, which leaves us along with the etheric body, also works on our exterior here on earth and forms the intellectual apparatus. When the intellectual apparatus is formed, then thinking occurs with the help of the intellectual apparatus formed by thinking itself. Feeling and will remain with us in the astral body and the I. We carry them into the spiritual world. Science does not force materialism on us; quite the opposite. True science today justifies spiritual science all around. Today's materialism is completely dependent on people's having no inclination toward spiritual life, on their having no interest in, or any appreciation for, spiritual life. Understanding does not have to be missing, either. Because truly, when we engage with what the spiritual scientist is able to give from the spiritual world, even for such a period as the life between death and rebirth, it can indeed be understood. We need only a finer, subtler understanding than the coarse understanding modern human beings employ in many cases for the outside world. But we also live in a time when materialism has just reached its high point. Spiritual scientists can, in fact, give the exact year in which materialism reached a high point—about 1840–41. Since that time, it has already begun to recede somewhat, but there are of course major aftereffects. But this materialism—what does it mean for our concepts about physical human life? It is exactly the most astute minds of our time who are misleading people under the influence of materialism to lamentably gross misconceptions.

There is a truly very astute man who is a criminal anthropologist by profession. He has analyzed many criminal brains.[‡] He proposed a well-known, important theory on criminal brains: the theory that in most criminal brains, in the greatest number of cases, the posterior lobe, which covers the cerebellum, is underdeveloped, as is also the case with monkeys. Monkeys are distinguished precisely by the fact that they also have a small occipital lobe. That was, of course, grist for the mill because one could say that when people are criminal it is a regression to monkey nature; they are born with an occipital lobe that is too small!

But think what an enormous consequence that must have for moral life for people who say that humans have only a physical body. Then such people must say, "What is all this responsibility you talk of? What do you mean you want to morally improve people through this or that educational method? It is all nonsense. Those born with an occipital lobe that is too small, which of course cannot grow over the cerebellum during this life, become criminals—of necessity, they become criminals." And then, if this materialistic thinking were realistic, it would also be true: We are not executing people because they have killed someone, but because their occipital lobes are too small! Materialists would have to admit this; they could not live in the world if they did not admit such a thing. People could not be materialistic in this sense at all if they did not admit that they would hang people because their occipital lobes are too small. Anything else would only cover up the truth.

But is it the truth? We must speak of the etheric body of the deceased, as we have done today, in the sense that it is also still present; of this etheric body, which actually expands after death and weaves itself into the general world ether. Now, if we have a young person whose occipital lobe is too small, we cannot just make it grow, because no physical science has accomplished that. But we can set up education in an appropriate manner when we see that there is also an etheric body present and that part of the etheric body corresponds to the occipital lobe. We can develop the etheric body of the occipital lobe precisely through appropriate education. The etheric occipital lobe is just as effective in life, maybe even in a certain sense more effective, as the physical occipital lobe, because it must overcome a certain force. And the comfort then streams forth from our knowledge that the physical form of an occipital lobe is not the only thing that matters. Rather, if we notice those who have this or that disposition to do wrong, we can develop the etheric lobe of such people, whose occipital lobe is too small, by evoking specific feelings in them. Then we will be able to save them.

You see, that is the truth. That is the moral aspect of spiritual science! It, too, is present. If people were honest, they would see desolation and dreariness arising from the materialistic worldview, specifically in moral-ethical relationships. One can see, arising from what spiritual science can give us, the consoling possibility of actively engaging in what people become. If we can observe at the right moment certain tendencies in a child that could lead to criminal behavior, then we will be able especially to develop through a certain type of education the aspect of the etheric that affects the occipital lobe particularly strongly. Thus we could weave this strength into people, which then lives on with them between death and rebirth. This would develop the occipital lobe especially well, even into the physical nature in the next incarnation. We help them not only for this incarnation, we also create the disposition for an especially well-developed brain, which they can then carry through the life between death and rebirth, to be incorporated in their next bodily incarnation.

Thus spiritual science engages us practically in life. But it will have to do something that goes beyond what people do today. People today think, much too much, that they have done enough with spiritual science if they listen to it for a while, and if they believe that it has a beneficial, uplifting effect on the soul. That is not enough! Spiritual science must have practical application in all aspects of life. The fruits of spiritual science must come forth in all aspects of life. Pedagogy is especially bleak today because people believe only in what humans are physically; pedagogy especially must be stimulated by spiritual science.

Today there are still many people who say, "Well, you can tell us a lot about spiritual science, but why should we believe what you tell us? We cannot see it ourselves." At best, someone who finds the way, to a certain extent, into the spiritual worlds could see it as it is depicted in *How to Know Higher Worlds*.‡ But it is a totally egotistic point of view when people want above all to see something practical, and believe that by looking at spirit in the same external way as they look at the physical—because they are too comfortable to search for spirit in a spiritual way—that this will somehow carry spirit into the physical world. And if materialism today is connected with egotism—it is after all a worldview!—then materialistic spiritism is even more egotistic, because at least materialism goes about simply accepting only the physical world and then satisfying this physical world. Materialistic spiritism, however, tries to have first a sensory view of the spiritual world; and second, perpetual satisfaction—and of a physical kind at that. But in its lack of clarity, this spiritism imagines the physical to be spiritual. In short, it wishes to remain in the physical world, and yet also have a spiritual aspect! Deplorably, the increase in materialism, which is flourishing especially in America, has become possible through the popular spiritism that emerged there, because of its tendency to materialize the spiritual, to present the spiritual aspect and spiritual events materially.

But to return to the earlier thread—there are many ways to identify things on the physical plane as impressions of the spiritual world. And one of the ways (of course not all of them can be mentioned here) is by seeking the spiritual where it is working, for instance, in children—where it should develop. Pedagogy must be stimulated there. Pedagogy will become living only if people reach the point of cultivating a sense, a feeling, for the spiritual, so that the teacher not only gives every kind of pedagogical instruction but also, above all, is intent on observing the potential of the individuality to see what wants to develop from it. This must be achieved, really achieved! And we would do well to be aware, so that we can keep faith with this effort, that people in our time are actually incredibly shortsighted. They believe that we have come remarkably far in our time; that we have finally gotten rid of all the naïveté of earlier centuries. But it is not true that we have gotten rid of biases. We had to get rid of the old atavistic clairvoyance, which was done away with in its last remnants not so very long ago, in order to see the physical plane clearly and to attain freedom. I spoke the day before yesterday to our dear friends in Hamburg about a particular example of this clairvoyance.[‡] If you were to look around, you might be able to find such an example here, too. I would like to tell you about the Hamburg example; maybe you can look for a similar one yourselves in Kassel.

When the Fall from Paradise (the powerful image in the Bible that stands for the seduction of humankind by Lucifer) is painted by an artist today, Adam and Eve and the serpent are depicted realistically; the serpent has a typical serpent's head. We know from spiritual science that this serpent is Lucifer. A physical serpent on earth can at most be a sort of symbol for Lucifer, but this physical serpent is not Lucifer; the long serpent that artists depict encircling a tree, with a typical common serpent head on top, is no Lucifer. Lucifer is a being who remained back at the Moon stage of existence; a being who we, of course, cannot see with our senses. Seeing with the sense of sight did not occur during the Moon stage; the earth has produced this sensory aspect. We see an earthly serpent with our senses. Of course, we cannot see Lucifer with our senses; we must look at him inwardly.

When we look inwardly, it is an inner sensing. And we sense that the upper part has something similar to a human head with bulging eyes. "Your eyes shall be opened, you shall see."[‡] The serpent is inside the head and fills out the nervous system right down into the spinal cord; that is, a human head that continues into the body of the serpent. This, however, is all to be thought of only etherically. Thus, it would have to be perceived inwardly. A painter who wants to paint Lucifer according to the Bible would have to paint the etheric nature of the spinal cord, and above that something that is still etheric, not yet physical—the human head. This is our lesson today, in an image.

You can see Bible images by Meister Bertram, including the Fall as I have just described it, in Hamburg.[‡] He painted no ordinary serpent; rather, a serpent with the usual form, but with a human head. In the fourteenth or fifteenth century, in the middle of the Middle Ages, artists could paint that way; that is, they still perceived the reality of the etheric realm. There you have tangible evidence of how things were at that time. Artists did not portray an ordinary serpent in those days because atavistic clairvoyance was still present. This capacity has disappeared completely over the last few centuries; and now it must be regained. It can be regained only by preparing ourselves to understand the spiritual world again through spiritual science.

And so, those who stand with spiritual science with their whole heart and whole soul see that the most important task of our time is to learn to understand what is in the spiritual world in order to prepare themselves to be able to look into the spiritual world, into what plays a part in the world around us. How differently we will go through the world—and not just the visible world (after all, light is not otherwise visible; colors are visible)—when we know that air is not all that surrounds us; rather, that the air is permeated by weaving forces, and the etheric bodies of the dead also weave within the light. Spiritual science will be there for all people; it will bring something to all people. Natural science and spiritual science will then be well connected.

I believe it is exceptionally important in our time that we feel a strong commitment to allowing such truths as we have been able to experience today about the life between death and rebirth to enter into our meditation quite often. Another good content for meditation is to let the beginning of the life between death and rebirth—the emptiness that assigns us our place in the world—to let this assignment of the etheric world, this interweaving of our own etheric body into the etheric world, come before our soul quite often while meditating. Thus, what is within us will be stimulated to grow more and more into the immediate experience of the spiritual world. And humanity today really needs that. When you look at the events of our time, you can feel how important it is for humanity today to become part of the spiritual world. The present time of testing will be experienced in the right way only if a number of people can perceive faithfully and with devotion what is alive in spiritual science, and how spiritual science must prepare humanity's future.

The signs of the times are truly grave, and this gravity reveals itself precisely when we think about what is close to us. Just think, we are talking about what should imbue our path with a serious principle:

To seek what is alike among all human souls and throughout all nations and races.‡ We rightly see this as a high ideal of humanity, but we must not conceal from ourselves what an immense contrast there is between life in present-day Europe and this ideal. Can we say that what European humanity expresses today is even remotely close to this ideal, to what it expresses? It is so far away from this ideal! And may—I say specifically *may*—may we then see this ideal as one we might put into practice immediately today? Are we not obligated as Germans to be clear (so that we do not fool ourselves), that given European relations today, we cannot even think of realizing such an ideal in the slightest? We would complete very poorly the mission ordained us specifically as Germans if we simply got carried away today by general, ambiguous ideals. Our times require us to unfold something specific within our Central European being. And we may see this connected with the karma that has accrued especially for us.

If you look at world events today, you will see that we have been guided rather well in the sense of these great world events. Karma brought about the fact that our movement was first part of the general Theosophical movement. Long before this war showed what it could teach the German people today, our German movement completely separated, broke away from the Theosophical movement. We have emphasized how important it is that our spiritual movement, which carries us and which will also have to carry the spiritual world, grows specifically from the qualities of the German people. We could say that we, as the Anthroposophical movement, have already for years felt the hatred of, especially, the British toward our specific field of spiritual science. It has simply increased now, because they cannot remain silent there; what has recently been written about us on the part of the so-called English theosophists exceeds anything forgivable.‡ Thus, if we look over the course of our movement, we can well say that we also find our karma somehow through our own movement; that it is in complete harmony with what the great movement in the outside world shows us today. Because our karma led us early enough to an independent emphasis on German spiritual life, we may certainly in all modesty make karma out to be favorable to us; and we may regard the fact that anthroposophy found its center in German spiritual life as a sort of luminous morning star for our karmic stream. And since the signs of what is now taking place outside in the world appeared to us much earlier, we can derive the belief from this one single fact that there is something in our movement that has a power for the great general movement of humanity.

Let us learn, my dear friends, to trust that the spiritual force latent in our movement is among the best our souls could possibly join with. Let us learn to experience the whole gravity—the whole meaning of thought and feeling and the will impulse—and the whole meaning of the fact that there must be individual souls who understand in relation to the great challenges of our time how spiritual impulses must cooperate with what will play out in our future history here on earth. Let us learn to understand, not just in the abstract, but also in the concrete sense, what meaning and significance the countless dead now flooding the earth have. Let us learn to understand that we must remain faithful to our movement, so that there will be people who can correctly look into the sphere in which the etheric bodies of those who have sacrificed themselves for our time will continue to play a part on the great fields of history and cooperate with those who will walk the earth later in times of peace. Let us learn to understand what it means to find the correct meaning, so that spirituality permeates even what is taking place today on the physical plane, so that followers of spiritual science will give meaning to what arises spiritually from the courage and sacrifice of our time. Let us learn to understand the correct meaning of the words with which we now close these reflections:

From the combatants' courage,
From the blood of battle,
From the suffering of those abandoned,
From the people's sacrificial death,
Spiritual fruit will grow—
May souls guide their senses, conscious of spirit,
Into the realm of the spirits.

Lecture 3

The Event of Death and the Time after Death

Leipzig, February 22, 1916

We live in a time when we are reminded daily, hourly, of death—of people passing through the gate of death, of this momentous human life event. Death becomes a life event for people in the true sense of the word only through spiritual science, which shows us how the eternal forces that go through births and deaths are working internally within us. These forces create a particular form for us during the time between birth and death that enables us to take on a different form of existence after passing through the gate of death. Thus death, which from the materialistic viewpoint can be only an abstract end-of-life, becomes through spiritual science a real event, even if a difficult one, for our whole life.

Dear friends among us have passed through the gate of death primarily as a result of current historic events, but also from other causes beyond those. So perhaps it seems especially fitting in our reflections today to give some thought precisely at this time to the death event and the facts of human life that follow after death.

Certainly, examinations of the life between death and rebirth have come up again and again in our spiritual-scientific reflections, and we have already gathered much evidence of this matter specifically. You well know from spiritual science's course to this point that everything can be presented from only one particular point of view at a time; and that basically we can come to know things more specifically only by having them illuminated from different points of view. Thus I will add a few things today to what we already know of the suggested subject that may be useful to us for our total worldview.

We observe people in a spiritual-scientific way (and this is good), standing before us in the physical world as expressions of their total being. We must first of all begin with what human beings present in the physical world. That is why I have called attention again and again to how we can gain something like a guiding overview, as it were, of the total person‡ if we first take the physical body as our basis, which we come to know from the exterior through sensory observation, through scientific analysis of sensory observation here in the physical world. We then take as our basis the formative body, which we characterize as the etheric body. This already has a suprasensory character and cannot be observed with our ordinary sense organs (not even with the intellect connected with the brain), and is thus already inaccessible to ordinary science. We can say, however, that this etheric body is a construct that was known by Immanuel Hermann Fichte, the son of the great Johann Gottlieb Fichte, as well as Troxler and others.‡ This etheric body is something in humans that can really be grasped only by imaginative perception because it is suprasensory; it can, however, be seen outwardly with suprasensory perception, just as the sensory physical body can be seen outwardly with sensory perception.

Now we go further in our observation to the astral body. The astral body is not something that can be seen with the outer senses as the physical body can, nor with the inner senses as the etheric body can; rather, the astral body is something that can only be experienced inwardly. We must be inside it ourselves in order to experience it, just as with the fourth aspect that we must first of all grasp here in the physical world, the I. We build the whole human being out of these four members of human nature. We also know from our observations up to now that what we actually call the human physical body is something very complex; this human physical body was developed over a long period through the Saturn, Sun, and Moon stages of evolution‡ and has already played a part in earthly evolution from the very beginning of Earth-existence until our time. Our bodies have built up a complex history. The physical world really shows only its exterior to us, also to ordinary science. One could say that through ordinary physical seeing and physical science we know only as much about the physical body as a person knows about a building by going around it outside and never going inside, never finding out what is inside the building or who lives there. Now, of course, those who take their stance from outer science in the materialistic sense will say they know the inner nature of the physical body very well! They will say that they know this inner aspect because they have looked at the brain within the septum, because they have looked at the stomach and the heart during dissections—and so, they know it!

But the inner aspect that can be seen externally in this way, the spatial-inner aspect, is not what is meant here when we speak of the "inner." This spatial-inner aspect is also only an external thing; this spatial-inner aspect in the human body is actually much more external than the true spatial-inner aspect. It certainly sounds strange when I say this. But you know from previous descriptions from spiritual science that our sense organs, which we carry on the exterior of our body, on the spatial exterior, were developed already during the Saturn period. They are made of forces much more spiritual than are, for example, our stomach or other organs that are internal in a spatial sense. Internal organs are made of the least spiritual forces. As strange as this sounds, this fact must nevertheless be pointed out. People speak about themselves incorrectly; this is natural because of living here on the physical plane—but, indeed, what they express is incorrect. We actually should call the skin on our face the internal, and the stomach the external aspect. We would come much closer to reality that way! We would come closer to reality if we said that we eat from inside to outside (we send food from inside to outside by sending it to the stomach), than if we said, as we do now, from outside to inside because the closer to the surface our organs lie, the more the spiritual forces touch them, and the less the spiritual forces touch them, the further into our spatial-inner aspect they lie.

You can see this easily if you recall what has been brought up in the descriptions from spiritual science up to now: you will know that during the Moon stage of evolution, and again during the Earth stage, something split off, and then went out into space from the Saturn, Sun, and Moon stages of evolutions. Something strange happened during this splitting off. We were turned, really turned like a glove is turned inside out, the internal to the outside, and the external to the inside. The human face, which is turned outward today, was really turned inward during the Saturn and Sun periods (in its very first beginning, of course), and also during a part of the Moon period. Organs that are internal today were formed from outside during our Moon-existence. Since that time, we have really been turned inside out like a skirt. (A while back, turning a skirt inside out was commonly done so that clothes could be worn for a longer time. Of course, this is not customary today.) When we speak of the physical body, we must also be aware that there is much that is suprasensory about it. Its whole method of construction is suprasensory; it is built from the suprasensory and turns its outer aspect to us only when we see it as a whole.

Now we come to the etheric body, which is no longer visible at all to physical-sensory observation. The etheric body is very important when human beings have gone through the gate of death. Initially, in the first days after we enter the spiritual world, this etheric body is of especially great importance. We must learn to think differently in relation to the physical body, really learn to think differently, if we want to contemplate correctly what is waiting for us after we pass through the gate of death. Indeed, you know—because it can be observed even from the physical world—that we cast off our physical body when we pass through the gate of death. The physical body is given over to the earthly element through decomposition or burning—the two processes differ only in length of time. Now it could seem for the person who has passed through the gate of death as if the physical body, as such, were simply disposed of. But that is not the case; we can give over to the earth only the part of the physical body that comes from the earth itself. We cannot give over the part of the physical body that originated from Old Moon-existence, from Old Sun-existence, from Old Saturn-existence. What originated from Old Saturn-existence, from Sun-existence, from Moon-existence, and indeed, even from a large part of Earth-existence, are suprasensory forces. And these suprasensory forces in our physical body (which show us only their exterior in sensory seeing, as I have just described)—what happens to these suprasensory forces when we have passed through the gate of death? Only what was given to our physical body—to this most wondrous structure that exists first of all as structure in the world—only what is given to it by the earth is given back to the earth. What happens to the rest, then, when we pass through the gate of death? The rest pulls away from what sinks into the earth through decomposition or combustion and is taken up into the whole cosmos. When you think of all that you can sense in the environment surrounding the earth, with all the planets and fixed stars, and when you think of this process as spiritually as possible, then in this spiritual thinking you will have the place in us where our spiritual essence is. But only a part of this spiritual aspect, that which lives in warmth, is separated and remains with the earth. Warmth, our inner warmth, our own warmth is separated, remains with the earth. But all the rest of the physical body that is spiritual is carried out into the whole of space, into the entire cosmos.

When we now leave the physical body, where do we go? What are we submerged in? Upon our death we are submerged quickly, lightning-fast, into what formed the physical body from all of the suprasensory forces. You should imagine that all of the creative forces that have worked on your physical body since the Saturn period expand out into the infinite and prepare the place where you live between death and rebirth. All of that had been simply concentrated in the space enclosed by our skin between birth and death.

We are now outside of the physical body, and we have an experience that is important, above all, for the entire life between death and rebirth that follows. I have already mentioned this often. This experience is of an opposite nature to the corresponding experience in life on the physical plane. Here in life on the physical plane, we cannot look back to the hour of our birth with ordinary sensory perception. None of us can remember or look back on our own birth in this way; none of us has an actual experience of our own birth. We know only that we were born; first, because perhaps someone told us, and second, because we know that all the people who have come to the earth after us were also born.

It is exactly the opposite with the corresponding experience after death. Whereas the vision of our own birth does not stand before our soul in physical life, the moment of death, if we look at it spiritually, stands before our soul during the whole life between death and rebirth.

However, we must be clear that this moment of death is seen from the other side of the threshold. If death has something frightening about it, it is only because it is seen here as an extinguishing, so to speak, an end. From the other side, from the spiritual perspective, when we look back to the moment of death, death appears evermore as the triumph of the spirit, the wresting free of the spirit from the physical body. It appears as the greatest, most splendid, most meaningful event. And our I-consciousness after death awakens from this event. For the entire period between death and rebirth, we have an I-consciousness that is not just similar to, but actually a much higher sense than the one we have here in physical life. We would not have this I-consciousness if we could not look back and see (but from the other side, from the spiritual perspective), this moment in which we struggled out of the physical aspect with our spiritual aspect. We know that we are an I only because we know we have died; we have released our spiritual aspect from our physical aspect. When we do not look back at the moment of death from beyond death's gate, it is for our I-consciousness after death like the experience of sleep for our physical I-consciousness here on earth. Just as we know nothing of the physical I-consciousness during sleep, we know nothing of ourselves after death if we do not see this moment of dying. Seeing it is one of the most splendid, one of the most sublime moments.

You see, even in this case, we must learn to think very differently here about the actual spiritual world than about the sensory-physical world. If we comfortably stay only with concepts we have here in the physical-sensory world, we cannot accurately grasp the spiritual at all, because the most important thing after death is that the moment of death is seen from the other side. Through looking at the moment of death, our I-consciousness is awakened on the other side. Here in the physical world we have one side of I-consciousness; after death we have the other side of I-consciousness. I described earlier where the suprasensory aspect of the physical body is after death; where we must search for it. We must search for this physical aspect, as much as we can sense it, as a relation of forces, an organism of forces, a cosmos of forces in the whole world. This physical aspect prepares for us the place through which we must pass between death and rebirth.

Thus, enclosed here by our skin in the physical body, in this small body compared to the whole world, is really a microcosm, really an entire world. It is really just rolled up, if I may speak lightly; and then it unrolls and fills the world, with the exception of a small space that always remains empty. When we are living between death and rebirth, we are everywhere in the physical world with the suprasensory forces that formed the basis of our physical body, everywhere except the one particular place that remains empty. That is the space we take into ourselves here in the physical world within our skin, and that from the spiritual world we always look upon as empty.) There, we see ourselves from the outside, and look into a hollowness. What we look into is empty. Because it remains empty we have a basic feeling concerning it. This is not a detached looking, like when we stare at something here on the physical plane; rather, this looking is connected to a powerful inner life experience. When we look at this void, a feeling arises that then accompanies us throughout our whole life between death and rebirth, and which shapes much of what we call this otherworldly life. It is the feeling that there is something in the world that we must fill again and again. And then we attain the feeling that we have a reason for being in the world, a purpose that only we can fulfill. We sense our place in the world. We sense that we are a building block of the world, without which the world could not exist. That is the vision of this void. When we look at this void, we are overcome by the fact of our belonging to the world.

All of this is connected with what the physical body then becomes. From these elementary descriptions, we will be able to demonstrate only schematically, as it were, what really requires images for the reality in the spiritual world. But we must have these images first, in order to gradually bring ourselves to concepts that penetrate further into the reality of the spiritual world.

We know that we then experience after death a sort of memory that lasts for approximately three days. (We use the word "memory," even though, strictly speaking, it is not memory in the common sense.) For a few days we experience something like a tableau, a panorama, which is woven from all that we have experienced in the previous life. But we do not have anything like an ordinary recollection within the physical body. A recollection in the physical body is such that we call it up chronologically from memory. Such memory is a force that is bound to the physical body; a thought in which we call up memories chronologically. The memory after death is such that everything that played out in life is around us in our imagination at the same time, as in a panorama. One can say that for days we live within this experience. Events that we have just experienced in the last period of time before our death are there, simultaneously, in powerful images, and, also simultaneously, what we experienced in childhood is there: a life panorama, a life image, that shows us in a web woven of ether what happened during that time. Everything we see lives in the ether.

Above all, we experience what is around us as alive. Everything is living and weaving. Then we experience it as spiritual sound, as spiritual light, and as spiritual warmth. This life tableau disappears after several days, as we know. But how does it end? And what is this life tableau?

Indeed, when we investigate what this life tableau really is, we must realize that everything we experience in life is woven into it. But experienced how? By our thinking during life! Thus, everything that we experience conceptually, or with thought, is in the tableau. To give a specific example, let us say that you lived with someone during your life; that you spoke with that person. Through speaking, his thoughts were communicated to your thoughts. You received love from him; you let his whole soul affect you; you experienced all of this internally. When you live with other people, you witness their experiences. They live and we live, and we experience something of them. What we experience of a person is interwoven into this etheric life tableau. It is the same as what we remember. Imagine a moment when you experienced something with another person ten, twenty years ago. Imagine, remember. After death, you will not remember as we usually remember in life, where everything fades; rather you will remember in such a way that the memory will be as alive in you as the experience itself. In the tableau, your friend will stand before you as at the time of the experience. In physical life our experiences are often quite dreamlike. Strong experiences on the physical plane ease off and lose their strength. When we have gone through the gate of death and have an experience in the life tableau, it is not weakened; it is there with all the freshness and strength that was originally present during life. Thus the experience weaves into our life tableau; thus we experience it ourselves for days.

Just as after death we have the impression in relation to the physical world that our physical body has fallen away from us; so too, do we have the impression after some days that our etheric body has fallen away from us. But this etheric body of ours actually has not fall away in the same way that our physical body did; rather, it is woven into the whole universe, the whole world. It is within the universe and makes impressions in it during the days we experience the life tableau.

And what we have as a life tableau thus passes into the external world that lives around us; it is taken up into the world.

During these days, we will again have an important, vivid experience. This is because our experiences after death are not only experiences like the memories of earth-life; rather, they are building stones for absolutely new experiences. How we come to our own I is itself a new experience in that we look back on our death. We cannot experience such a thing here with our earthly senses. This reveals itself only to initiated knowledge. But also what we experience during those days when we have this life tableau around us, this etheric weaving that breaks away from us and weaves into the universe; what we experience then is also something exaltingly sublime, something very powerful for the human soul.

Here in physical life, indeed, we confront the world; we confront the mineral, plant, animal, and human kingdom. We experience what our senses can experience, whatever sense experiences the brain-bound intellect can have, what the mind connected to the vascular system can experience; we experience all of that here. And in fact, seen from a higher point of view, we humans here between birth and death are exceedingly large "drips" (forgive the expression); giant drips. We are exceedingly ignorant in the face of the wisdom of the larger world if we think that what we experience here, in the way described, is all there is; and that in carrying in our memory what we have experienced, we think we have acquired it. We merely believe it to be so. But while we experience, while we create concepts and emotional perceptions during an experience, in our process of experiencing, the whole world of hierarchies work in this sequence. It lives and weaves within it. When you meet other people and look them in the eyes, the spirits of the hierarchies live in their gaze and in what their gaze transmits back to you; the work of the hierarchies lives in it. What we experience presents only the outer side to us; the gods work within the act of experiencing. And whereas we believe that we live only for ourselves, the gods are working something out through our experiencing, until they have something that they can then weave into the world. We have conceived thoughts; we have had emotional experiences; the gods take them and share them with their world. And after we have died, we know that we have lived so that the gods can weave together what comes from our etheric body and give it over to the whole universe.

The gods have allowed us to live so that they can spin something for themselves, with which they can enrich their world a bit. That is an earth-shaking idea! If you take only one step in the world, this step is the external expression of a god-event and is a piece of the web that the gods will use in their world plan. When you go through the gate of death, they will take this step from you and incorporate it into the universe. Our strokes of destiny are also the deeds of gods, and what our lot is for us as human beings is only the outer side. This is what is meaningful, important, essential.

And now, what we have gained internally in life by being able to think, by having emotional perceptions, to whom does this actually belong? After our death, it belongs to the world! As we look back on our death with what we now have remaining—with the astral body and the I—we see what has been woven into the universe and the world. During physical life we carry within us as our etheric body what is later woven into the universe. After death, it spins off and is interwoven into the physical world. We look at it, observe it. As we experience it inwardly here in physical life, so do we look at it after death in the world outside of us. Just as we look at stars and mountains and rivers outside of us here, so too do we see after death—besides what becomes of the physical body as fast as lightning—what the world has taken into itself of our own experiences. And those of our own experiences that were incorporated into the whole world constitution are now reflected in what we have left, in the astral body and I, exactly as the outside world is reflected in our physical organs through our physical human body here. And as this is reflected in us, we receive something that we cannot have here during this Earth-existence, but we will have later during the Jupiter stage in the form of an external, physical impression. It is something that we receive now in a spiritual way because our etheric being is at this time outside of us and makes an impression on us. Instead of experiencing the etheric as we did earlier as our inner aspect, now it makes an impression on us from outside. The impression it makes is certainly first and foremost a spiritual one; it is pictorial, but as something pictorial it is already a model for what we will have outwardly for the first time in the Jupiter stage: the spirit self. That is, through our etheric aspect's being interwoven into the universe, the spirit self is born for us; but this is a spiritual model for the future and not an "outer" member of our being, such as we will have later on Jupiter. So, after we have discarded the etheric body, we have our astral body, I, and spirit self. Thus, of our earthly existence now remain our astral body and our I.

The astral body remains with us for a long time after death, as you know, just the same as when it was first of all subject to us as the earthly astral body. It remains with us because this astral body is pervaded by what is only earthly-human, which the astral body cannot bring out of itself immediately. We go through a period during which we can finally cast off, little by little, what earthly life has made of our astral bodies. Here on earth, we actually basically experience, at most, only half of our experiences, insofar as they touch the astral body. We really experience only half of what somehow takes place through us. Let us take an example; it is the same with good thoughts and good actions as it is with bad actions and bad thoughts, but let us take as an example this bad action. Imagine that you say something mean to a person, who then feels hurt about it. You have only what concerns you from this mean thing you said; you have the feeling within yourself concerning the reason you made this remark, that is, the impression on your own soul when you said it. But the other person on whom you inflicted this mean remark has a very different impression. That person has the other half of the impression, so to speak; the feeling of being hurt. This other half of the impression really lives on in the person. The one side is what you have experienced yourself here during physical life; the other side is what the other person has experienced.

We must live through all of these experiences again after death by going through our own life backward. We live in reverse through the effects of our thoughts and actions. That is, during the life between death and rebirth, we experience our earthly life in reverse. When the etheric body separates from us and forms the life tableau in which our whole life is displayed simultaneously around us, we look upon it from outside. But this going backward through our life is truly a *living through* what we have done. When we have gone backward to the point of our last birth, we are then ready to discard the part of our astral body that was permeated with the earthly aspect. Then the astral body separates from us, and with this laying aside of the astral body, a new state of being begins. The astral body always keeps us connected with the earth through our experiences. When we must go through our astral body in this way, not dreaming but reliving earthly experiences in reverse, we are still in earth-life; we are still within it. When we have "laid aside" (not the best words, but there is no other way to say it because our language does not have a word for it) the astral body, we become completely free of the earthly aspect and we begin to live in the actual spiritual world.

And then a new experience begins. This laying aside of the astral body is really only one side of the experience; the other side is something quite different. When we have laid aside the astral body after going through our earthly experiences, then we feel as if internally permeated with—we cannot say matter, but as if with—spirit; then we really feel present in the spiritual world for the first time. The spiritual world dawns in us internally. Before, we were aware of it externally, when we saw the universe and our own etheric body interwoven in the universe. Now we realize it internally; now we experience it internally. And our own I dawns in us internally as a pre-image for what human beings will have in physical expression first during the Venus stage of evolution. It is a pre-image or model of the life spirit; we now are made of spirit self, life spirit, and I. Just as we might feel dreamlike here in physical life from birth to the moment that we really become conscious as a child, the moment to which we can later remember back, so too do we live an existence that, though it is completely self-aware, is more conscious and higher than earthly life. But we do not experience a completely spiritual life until we have separated from our astral aspect and have retained from it only what fulfills us inwardly. From this time on, we are spirit among spirits.

But now another experience—an important, an essential experience—begins. Here when we work in physical life, we perform various actions, and with them we have experiences; indeed, we have just spoken of this. But we have experiences not only in the physical world, we also have something else during the experiences, which is simultaneous with the experiences. And I want to use a particular word, even if it is only a very general expression for these simultaneous experiences. One could say we become weary while we experience, worn out. That is indeed always the case—we become weary. And even if this weariness is balanced out through sleep (much less through sleep than through the peace during sleep), it is still really only a partial balancing out because, as we know, of course, our forces dwindle little by little: we age. We also become tired in a general sense. And as we get older, we cannot compensate for everything through sleep. Thus, here on earth we become worn out, tired. Indeed, after what has been said, we can now raise the question: Why do the gods allow us to get tired?

Why do we become tired? Becoming tired here, getting worn out, gives us something; it actually means a lot for our total life; it means ever so much. We must simply grasp the concept of becoming tired in a more comprehensive sense than we usually think of it. We must set it quite intensively before our souls, this concept of becoming tired.

You will best understand the concept of becoming tired if you imagine the matter in this way. If I were to ask one of you right now if you experience something of the inside of your body, probably only those plagued with a headache would answer that they are experiencing something now, in this instant, about the inside of their body. Only they feel the inside of their head; the rest of us live without feeling it.

We feel our organs only when they are not quite right; then, by feeling, we know something about our organs. In life we are constructed in such a way that we know about our physical body only when it is not quite right. We really have only a general feeling for our physical body. It becomes stronger when something is not right. But we have only a feeling; we know very little internally. Those who have had intense headaches know about the inside of their head—internally; not as an anatomist does, who knows only the container. But when we become more and more tired in life, this feeling of our inside, our spatial-internal, appears more and more in our body.

Just think: the more we become weary in life, the more the infirmities of life appear; the infirmities of age, for example. Our lives consist of gradually sensing this physical aspect of ourselves, learning to feel it. As it hardens us, enters into us, we learn to feel it. Because it happens so gradually, it is a subtle feeling for us. We would know how intense it is, if we, for example (forgive the simple expression, but it will express to you what I mean) could feel in one moment as sound as a bell, like a child bursting with health, and then immediately after, for comparison, as one feels when the limbs have become frail at eighty or eighty-five years old. Then we would immediately feel the contrast. But because it happens so slowly, we do not notice how we are spun into the experience of the physical, into becoming tired. Becoming tired is a real process, but actually it is not present at all at first because the child is bursting with life. Then, as life progresses, the life force is constantly drained by this becoming tired; then the tendency to become tired predominates. We become tired; while we become tired in this way (even if it is, let us say, only a slight feeling from within us), something internal actually develops within us.

Our life here in the physical world offers us only the external part of deep, significant, exalted secrets. Feeling, which is thus accompanied quietly in life by this process of becoming tired and of sensing the inside of our bodies, is the exterior of something that is woven within us—wonderfully woven from pure wisdom, a whole web of pure wisdom. By becoming tired in life and learning to sense internally, a fine knowledge of the wondrous structure of our internal organs is woven into us. We learn to become tired in our hearts, but becoming tired means that knowledge is woven into us, is constructed like a heart from the universe. We become tired in our stomachs. We make them tired primarily in that we ruin them through food; but even so, all wisdom, an image of wisdom from the cosmos, of the way the stomach is constructed, is woven into us as our stomachs become tired. The way our internal organism is constructed—sublime, wonderful. This formidable work of art forms an image that comes alive only when we have laid aside the external part of the astral body that was tied to the earth. And it is this image that fills us as life spirit and now lives in us. The wisdom about ourselves, about our wondrous internal structure, now lives in us.

And so the time begins when we learn to compare, as it were, what now fills us from out of wisdom in the form of life spirit to what was woven into the universe earlier as etheric presence. Now we work on this comparison, on how one can fit with the other, and we create as an image a human being as it should be in the next incarnation. We begin in this way, by gradually facing the Cosmic Midnight, as you will find indicated in the Mystery Drama *The Souls' Awakening*.‡ Thus after the Cosmic Midnight we carry out a task, which takes place by participating in the creation of the world, in bringing in what we enjoy here. During the life between death and birth, we work; we weave alongside the gods. We help weave part of the gods' images. We can be co-workers for the goals of the gods in that the gods put us in the world. We may prepare the next incarnation for ourselves. As we do so, not only processes that are egotistic in relation to us take place, but also all other possible processes. And this can arise from the following.

Here on earth, winter changes to summer, the sun rises and sets, everything that is earthly work takes place. In the spiritual world is a process that is much higher than that: what, at the very last, leads to our earthly incarnation, what leads to human existence. It is powerful, heavenly work that has not only a meaning for us, but a meaning for the entire world. When we are able to gradually experience this wonderful process through spiritual sight, we encounter something astounding. (It will indeed seem strange to you when I say it, but the higher secrets will always seem strange at first to our physical-sensory way of seeing.) What comes before our souls will shake us—the more, the better. These things, as they are, should not come to our souls at all in such a way that we absorb them in a rational, dryly cognitive way, and thus remain indifferent. Precisely through these things, we should gain a soul impression of the grandeur and greatness of the divine-spiritual world. One could say that were we to put spiritual science forward in a dry way that does not move the whole person and bring immediately an impression of the greatness and grandeur of what pulses and lives through the world as the divine-spiritual aspect, then all of us would be born headless; for, even after what I have just described and in spite of everything that we are capable of, the way things are in the world today we could not bring about the construction of our own head. The human head is such a sublime image or copy of the universe in its structure that human beings themselves cannot construct it; even with our life's wisdom woven into us, we could not prepare it for the next incarnation. All of the hierarchies of the gods must play a part in it. What is present in your head, in this sphere, broken only by the occiput—this somewhat transformed sphere—is a real microcosm, a real impression of the great world globe. Everything that lives outside in the universe lives within it; everything that is active in the various hierarchies works there. While we construct our next incarnation from the wisdom collected as a result of our becoming tired as we aged, all the hierarchies influence this activity in order to incorporate into us what then becomes the head as an impression of all the wisdom of the gods.

While all of this is taking place, our physical hereditary line is making itself ready through generations on earth. Exactly as we give over to the earth after death only what has come from the earth, so do we receive only the earthly part of ourselves from our parents and forebears. The earthly part of us is really only the external aspect, really only the external expression of this earthly aspect. Everything that we ourselves can first weave in the way described and everything woven by the entire hierarchies of the gods is woven into our heredity before we develop a relationship through conception to the physical body in which we envelop ourselves when we enter the physical plane.

As I have said, the more that we can take up of this sublime awareness in our feeling life, the better it is for us. Just imagine: we use our head, but we generally have no idea (at least to the extent that we are living with only a materialistic consciousness) that whole hierarchies of gods work to form our head, to form the spiritual basis for the head, so that we can exist at all. When we grasp this in the sense of spiritual-scientific awareness, it permeates us of its own accord with sensations and feelings of gratitude to the whole universe.

From this, what we approach through spiritual science should also produce an ever-increasing heightening of our feeling life. More and more, in spiritual science, our feelings should keep up with our knowledge. It is not good for us to remain behind in our feelings. As we get to know spiritual science more deeply, we should be able to develop more reverence for the secrets of the world, which lead at last to the secrets of humanity. True progress in spiritual science lies in the purifying spiritual warmth of our sensations and our feelings.

I must mention something else, because it seems to be an extension of this whole observation we have been making. We settle into the physical world first as a child, when we have a vague consciousness. At first we recognize our mother, and then get to know other people gradually. We think that as we settle into the physical world, we are always meeting new people. And that is the case for our physical consciousness. When we have passed through the gate of death, we have a true, real relationship to all those souls whom we had come near to in life on earth. They appear again before our spiritual gaze. We can say that we "find" those souls who came near to us in life, and who passed through death's gate before we did. The word "find" is descriptive for physical relations, but we can also characterize this experience of souls coming near to other souls as "finding." We must, though, imagine this finding of souls who have passed through the gate of death before us as coming near to them in the opposite way we approach people on the physical plane. Here we come near to people by first encountering them in an external-physical way. Then we gradually get to know their inner aspect; our experience of their inner aspect develops only from our "settling into" them. Thus, what we experience inwardly of a person develops only from our own inner aspect.

After we ourselves have passed through the gate of death and encounter the souls who passed through the gate of death before us, then we first of all know that the soul in question is there. We sense the soul; we know it is there. But we must now give over our whole inner aspect to what is there as a first impression, a most abstract impression. Here in life on earth, we must allow people to affect us; after death, we must devote or give over our inner aspect, and we must construct the image, the imagination, ourselves. The imaginative element, what we can see, we must construct for ourselves little by little. You can have an idea of this experience after death if you imagine that you do not see the other soul; rather, you only perceive the other soul when you create for yourself an image by comprehending the other soul's inner nature little by little. You construct an image for yourself. Thus, after death, you must actively construct inwardly the image of the souls that you encounter. You know in some way that you are now encountering a soul, but it does not yet have spiritual form! Which soul is it? That is the soul—this now surfaces in your own soul—to which I have had the feeling of a son to his mother.

Now you begin to feel: I can experience myself with this soul. Now you construct the spiritual form. You must be active within it, and then it will become an image. And by having to construct the spiritual form together in this way, you are already with the other departed person, even before you have constructed the spiritual form. It is this way with everyone that you were with in earthly life; that is, you now experience them in a world in which you must find them by first awakening the ability to see them. You have to be active in this process.

For those still here in the physical body, those who remain living after we have died, we have already encountered them here on earth as images. We look down on them from the spiritual world and do not need to construct an image; they look back at us as an image. They can then interweave something into this image that is like a warming spiritual sustenance for us through their thoughts about us, through their memory of us, and (as we know as spiritual scientists) by reading aloud to us.

All of this widens our view into the true world, into the really true world. When we let it come before our souls thus, we have an idea of how little human beings actually know of the spiritual world. It was not always this way. Only the most materialistic people of our time speak of how "wonderfully far" we have come today.[‡] In fact, we know that human beings had clairvoyance in the past, and that they lost this original clairvoyance—atavistic clairvoyance—for the sake of gaining certain characteristics that are connected with the experience of living entirely immersed in the material world. Truly materialistic people, completely materialistic scholars, would say, of course, that it is fantasy to talk of an original clairvoyance, of people in the past knowing something special. But if people truly saw the world, even a bit, with their physical eyes, they would find the materialist claim already disproved. It was not all that long ago that people knew more than they do now.

You know (we have often spoken of it, and I would like to mention it again here in closing) that Lucifer and Ahriman[‡] are part of the spiritual existence in which we live. We also know that Lucifer is symbolized in the Bible as a serpent, a serpent in a tree.[‡] The physical serpent as we experience it today, and as an artist in painting Paradise would surely paint it today—this physical serpent is not the true Lucifer; rather, it is the outer reflection, the physical reflection. The true Lucifer is a being that stayed behind during the Moon stage of evolution. He cannot be seen on earth among physical objects. Thus if an artist wishes to paint Lucifer, this would have to be done through a sort of clairvoyant inner sight, so that Lucifer could be comprehended as an etheric form. And Lucifer would then appear as he himself works on us: how he plays no part in our head or our organism, insofar as he is purely out of the earth, but in the continuation of the head down through the spinal cord. Lucifer must be painted this way if one is to paint him according to his etheric form, with a human head and a snake-like continuation in the human spinal cord.

And thus an artist who knows something of spiritual science would have to paint for us Adam and Eve, the tree, and up above in the tree, the serpent—that is, the serpent only as an expression—with a human head on top. If an artist painted something like this today, we would accept that it was painted from spiritual science, of course.

In the art gallery in Hamburg there is a painting from the Middle Ages by Meister Bertram‡ that depicts this scene in Paradise in this way. In this painting, the serpent is in the tree, as I just described it, painted correctly. You can see the picture there. People today, however, do not go about in the world with their eyes open, but blindfolded. It has also been painted this way by other artists. Perhaps there is something similar in Leipzig. What follows from this? People in the Middle Ages knew about this; knew it to the degree that they even painted it. This means it was not so long ago that people were first forced entirely onto the physical plane. And what informs us today from the material world as the course of the spiritual history of humanity is essentially nothing more than an outright lie. One is led to believe that human beings have always been the way they have become in the last few centuries, whereas it was really not so long ago that they saw into the spiritual world with clairvoyance. But they had to abandon this ability to see the spiritual world, because they were not free. In order to obtain full freedom and I-consciousness, it was necessary to give up this sight. And now, we must find our way again into the spiritual world.

Hence, spiritual science prepares something important, something essential: this living into the spiritual world again. And we should bring before our souls again and again the necessity that there are a handful of people who live today in the material world and are led by their karma to take on the most important tasks of humanity for the future. We perceive that these people have, through their soul-life, to perform most important things. Without being arrogant, we must show, in all humility and modesty, how great the difference is between a soul that is trying to find its way gradually into the spiritual world and all of the others today who have no idea, and who have no desire to have any idea, of the spiritual. It must not become simply a deplorable, painful feeling for us; rather, it must be a feeling that motivates us to continue working; that motivates us to be true to our work in the stream of spiritual science to which we have been led by our karma, our fate.

At our last gathering here,[‡] I also mentioned that when people pass through the gate of death before having completely lived out their life, what was given to them as etheric body force is not yet completely used up. If a person passes through the gate of death at a young age, the etheric body could have affected the physical body for decades to come. This force is not lost; rather it is still there. I have also already mentioned that because death daily and hourly approaches humanity in such great numbers at present, many etheric bodies that could have supported physical bodies for a longer time in the physical plane are consigned to the spiritual-etheric world, and continue to hover. And these forces, which could have taken care of the physical body for decades more, become spiritual forces that participate in the spiritual evolution of humanity. Thus a time will come in which the forces within these etheric bodies can be used for the spiritual advancement of humanity. This will come about only if, after today's terrible events have gone from this earth and peace has arrived once again, the souls here on earth,[‡] who still move on this earth in physical bodies, are able to understand that all those who entered the spiritual world in the past have their etheric bodies there and can radiate their forces into evolution. This must be understood by the souls here on earth. And these souls will be able to participate in this spiritual advancement, which is possible for the future, precisely because of so many sacrificial deaths.

Think what it would mean if spiritual science were to disappear now, and no one understood all that is being prepared in the spiritual world through their sacrificial death! The entire sum of these forces would fall to spiritual beings that would use them for a purpose other than what they should be used for according to the resolve of the rightful, further-developing gods.

This possibility, however, admonishes us, even from the events of our time, to be fully present with our consciousness to everything that the spiritual world is, because these current events, too, have a spiritual side. What is present outwardly in blood and death and casualties is the external expression of inner spiritual events, which must, however, be understood in the correct sense.

This is what I want to remind you of again and again, with the closing words of our reflections today:

From the combatants' courage,
From the blood of battle,
From the suffering of those abandoned,
From the people's sacrificial death,
Spiritual fruit will grow—
May souls guide their senses, conscious of spirit,
Into the realm of the spirits.

Lecture 4

How Can Today's Poverty of Soul be Overcome?

Zürich, October 10, 1916

What we seek as spiritual-scientific truths should not be just a dead knowledge for us, but a living one. It should be knowledge that can really find its way into our life, into all aspects of our life, and at the most important points in our life. Spiritual science today is often taken in quite abstractly. And people—especially those who have little understanding of spiritual science—may even come to a sort of detached knowledge that initially proves to be unfruitful for life, and they then have the following impression: "What does it matter that we know human beings are made of so-and-so many parts or members, and that humanity has evolved through different cultural epochs and will continue to evolve, and so on?" For those who believe, according to today's demands, that people should be completely present in practical life, spiritual science often seems quite unproductive. And it is often conveyed as being unproductive, even by those who already have some heart and feeling for it.

Nevertheless, spiritual science itself, as it is, is something infinitely full of life; it can come alive even in the most exoteric practices in life; and it also must come alive for the sake of the future. Today I would like to make this clear with a particular example by choosing something from our spiritual science that we all presumably know, that is well known to us, and to show how it will gradually become even more enlivened by our looking at it as being full of life.

Most of you will have heard before that our time was preceded by the so-called fourth post-Atlantean cultural period, in which the Greeks and Romans were the most important peoples. The impulses of this fourth post-Atlantean cultural period influenced the following centuries into the fourteenth and fifteenth centuries. We have been in the fifth post-Atlantean cultural period since the fifteenth century. We have been born into this period in our current incarnation, and human beings will live in this fifth cultural period for many centuries to come. We know, furthermore, and have often let it flow through our souls (at least, most of us have) that humanity particularly advanced outer culture and outer work during the fourth post-Atlantean—the Greco-Roman—cultural period, which developed the so-called intellectual- or mind-soul at that time. Our task now is to develop the consciousness soul.

What does it mean that the consciousness soul must be developed? Understood correctly, what was just introduced in abstract form will constitute the fate of humanity for our entire fifth post-Atlantean cultural period. The different peoples of this fifth cultural period must work together to give expression to the consciousness soul. This shows in all life's conditions and circumstances. If we look at life rightly, the truth is confirmed for us everywhere that our time represents the actualization of the consciousness soul. Human life was entirely different in the Greco-Roman period. Then, at the level at which humanity stood in the fourth post-Atlantean period, humanity was given the power of reason and the power of the feeling-soul [*Gemüt*]. Reason is something that includes many things. We no longer look at it so exactly today. The Greeks and Romans were dependent on their reason in a different way from people of today's fifth cultural period. As part of their natural state of evolution the Greeks and Romans received reason to the extent they needed it. Just as today natural dispositions develop as human beings mature, in a certain way natural reason developed then in them. This was very different from the way it is today. People then did not have to develop natural reason in the same way as is necessary today—and which will become more and more necessary in our fifth period—it developed then as a natural ability. People either had reason, if they developed in natural conditions, or they did not. If they did not, it was something pathological. It was also exceptional; it was not usual.

It was the same with the feeling-soul, which developed in the way appropriate to the fourth post-Atlantean period. When people encountered each other, they knew how to adapt themselves to the other person. History does not tell us much of such things, but it was so. In this respect, there is a particularly great difference between the people of the earlier centuries up through the fifteenth century and the people of our time. The people of those earlier centuries did not pass by each other indifferently, as is often the case today. Today, when people meet they often need a long time to really get to know each other. We each have to learn about the other person to begin to trust each other, until we gain each other's trust. What is achieved today only after long acquaintance (and even then, is often not achieved), was achieved instantly when people met each other in the Greco-Roman cultural period. Individualities coming together developed relationships very quickly; they did not need to exchange thoughts and feelings for a long time. A person's mind worked in a much more spiritual way into another person's mind. Relationships were made very quickly insofar as they served the well-being of the two people involved or insofar as this was necessary in some way for a number of people who formed a group.

Today we can correctly identify the colors of plants with our senses, but in the seventh post-Atlantean cultural period, people will no longer be able to do so without effort. Instead, certain circumstances will be necessary to even become acquainted with nature. Just as we can recognize plants immediately from the first impression today, and not just through closer contact, so it was then in relation to other people. We must remember that this kind of mind-connection between people was completely appropriate for that fourth post-Atlantean period. However, it sufficed only for the simpler living conditions of that time. Today, a much different web of feeling-connections extends over the world than was the case then. Just imagine that most of people's relationships in the fourth cultural era, by far, were based on personal encounters, and that whatever people had to work out together was worked out through personal encounters. Printing, which belongs to the fifth post-Atlantean cultural era, has enabled impersonal contact with others, and this will be increasingly so in our time. Modern transportation brings people together in such a way that relationships are formed quickly, and might actually not be beneficial at all. Thus, through these modern means of interaction, people encounter each other much more impersonally in the world.

As a result, the constitution of human beings now is such that it does not receive as fully developed either the mind with its ability to work instantly or the intellect with its penetrating effect, as was the case with the intellectual- or mind-soul. Rather, humanity is being developed by the consciousness soul, making us much more separate and individual, leading more to egotism and to awareness of our isolation within our own body. Because of our consciousness soul, we are now more separate as individuals, hermits who wander through the world, than we were with the intellectual- or mind-soul. The fact that people have closed themselves off has already become the most important characteristic of our time, and will become so more and more. The consciousness soul leads us to closing ourself off from the rest of humanity, to being more isolated. Thus it is quite difficult to get to know others, and especially to become close with them; to become familiar with others and to develop trust requires a lengthy process of first getting to know the other person.

So what, then, is all of this supposed to achieve? We will best be able to understand this if we contemplate thoroughly a certain spiritual-scientific truth, which tells us that the way we come together today is not coincidental—truly not coincidental. Our life path brings us together with certain people, and does not bring us together with others. Today, because we have entered a period in human evolution that in a certain way has brought the earlier karmic developments people have experienced to a high point, whom we meet is completely based on the effects of each person's karma. Just imagine how much less karma people had accumulated at the beginning of earthly evolution! Every time we incarnate, new karma is formed. Human beings at first encountered one another on earth without having been together before; at that time they needed to develop new relationships. But by being incarnated again and again in the world, we have entered into so many relationships that, as a rule, we now actually encounter only people with whom we have had some experience in earlier incarnations. We are brought together with people through what we have experienced in earlier incarnations. It seems "coincidental" when people meet one another; in truth, it is all based on meetings from earlier incarnations when the forces were generated so that these people are now brought together again in a certain way.

Now, the self-contained consciousness soul that must develop in our time can develop only when we give less attention to what plays out person to person in the present and allow the things that rise within us mysteriously as a result of previous incarnations to take effect. In Greco-Roman times, it was still the case that when two people met, each person immediately made an impression on the other, and the impression had a very strong effect. Now, so that the more isolated consciousness soul in people can develop, it should be more like this: one person meets another, and what emerges as a result of previous incarnations should gradually become more effective. This takes longer than immediate acquaintance at first sight; it implies that people, little by little, let what they have experienced with the other come up instinctively, feelingly. That is exactly what is called for today: that we get to know each other gradually, so that the sharp edges of our current outer personalities are smoothed down. For in this way of becoming acquainted, in this smoothing down of our individuality, lies the rise of still-unconscious, instinctive reminiscences, the consequences of our previous incarnations. And only when people thus enter into a relationship with others from out of their own inner being can the consciousness soul develop; whereas the intellectual- or mind-soul develops through the insightful getting-to-know-one-another of an outer encounter.

In this way individuals are correctly integrated with each other. What I have just characterized for you is only just beginning in the fifth post-Atlantean era. As this era progresses people will find it more and more difficult to relate to each other correctly, because bringing ourselves into relationships correctly requires inner development, inner activity. These difficulties have already begun, and they will spread ever further and become more and more intensive. How difficult it has already become today for people who have been brought together through karma to understand each other immediately. Perhaps because of other karmic circumstances they do not find the strength to develop an instinctive feeling for all the karmic connections that come from previous incarnations! People are brought together; they love each other. This is the result of certain effects from previous incarnations. But other forces work in opposition when such a reminiscence comes up, and people go their separate ways again. Those who meet in life in this way are not the only ones who must test whether what rises within them is really sufficient to establish a lasting relationship. It is also becoming more and more difficult for sons and daughters to understand fathers and mothers, for parents to understand their children, for siblings to understand each other. Mutual understanding is becoming more and more difficult because it is becoming increasingly necessary for people to really let arise out of their inner being what exists there karmically.

You see what a negative perspective this opens for the fifth post-Atlantean era—the difficulty in people's mutual understanding of each other. However, this difficulty necessitates that we squarely face this requirement of evolution, that we not wish to live on dreamily in the dark, because this requirement of evolution is absolutely necessary. Were it not imposed on humanity that getting to know one another is so difficult in this era, the consciousness soul would not be able to develop, and people would have to live together according to their natural dispositions. Then the individuality of the consciousness soul would not be able to develop. Thus, human beings must go through this test. This must be faced squarely because, of course, if only this negative side of the requirements of evolution in our fifth post-Atlantean era came about, then war and conflicts would occur even in the most superficial relationships. Thus we are seeing in this time a certain number of needs arising instinctively, which must be overcome ever more consciously. And to overcome them more and more consciously is one of the tasks of spiritual science for humanity.

I need only mention *one* term and it will immediately dawn on each of us that a remedy is being sought for the difficulty of mutual understanding that is necessarily arising. I need only mention the term. More and more a sense for *social understanding* must be awakened in this fifth post-Atlantean era, and awakened consciously, because we live in the age of the consciousness soul. That one term summarizes needs that were by no means present to the same degree during the fourth post-Atlantean era. Whoever is able really to study the structures of Greek and Roman cultures knows that individualism was not such a predisposition within humanity then as it is now in European, or even in the European-dependent American peoples. You will grasp this particularly if you compare human beings to animals. (In order to compare, we will use a radical example.) Why does an animal species live together within certain boundaries? Because it is predisposed to do so, as a result of its group soul, its species soul. Animal species are born with a group soul. That is a matter of course, but they cannot grow out of it; they remain in it. Human beings must grow beyond the group soul. Every single person must develop individually; and especially in the present day, the consciousness soul is one of the essential parts of this individual development.

There is certainly still a trace of the group-soul aspect in Greek and Roman cultures. We see that people were also still within a social order that had a definite form, even though its structure, its form, came about largely through moral forces. But these forms are being dissolved more and more in the fifth post-Atlantean era. The trace of the group-soul aspect, which still remained in the fourth era, no longer has meaning for this fifth era. In its place, however, social understanding must arise consciously; that is, all that comes from a deeper understanding of the truly individual human essence must arise.

Only spiritual science can develop this true understanding. When spiritual science develops more and more from the abstract to what is concrete and full of life, within the circles that follow spiritual science a very special sort of knowledge of and interest in humanity will be awakened. There will be those who have certain capacities to teach their fellow human beings about how people have different temperaments and dispositions; how the person who has a particular temperament should be understood; how another person who has a certain a disposition, a certain temperament, must be understood differently. Thus people with this particular social talent will teach other people who are ready to learn: "There is this type of person, there is another type of person, and we must look at the one person thus and the other person so." Practical psychology, practical knowledge of the soul, but also a practical knowledge of life will be developed, and through this a true social understanding of the evolution of humanity will result.

What has appeared until now as social understanding? Abstract ideals have appeared, the most varied, abstract ideals about world and national happiness—this or that form of socialism.[‡] If we really tried to introduce into the world such social ideas as are appearing here and there, we would soon see that we cannot accomplish it. Social understanding is not in any way about founding societies or sects with certain agendas, but about spreading knowledge of the human being, practical knowledge of human nature. This means knowledge of the human being that enables us to correctly understand nascent, developing human beings; to understand children correctly and the way they each develop with their own individuality.

Through this we learn to become part of life in such a way that we develop correct, lasting relationships, relationships that can really become fruitful for life. This comes about through the correct karmic effects within us, when because of karma we come face to face with a person with whom we are supposed to have a particular relationship. Practical knowledge of the human being, a practical, effective interest in humanity, is what this depends on. Humanity today has still not come very far at all in this way; it is still very limited in its progress. So how do we react when we meet a person today? We may react with sympathy or antipathy to the person. Go anywhere in the world, and see how this is the only reaction in most cases. Even when we meet many people, our reactions are completely controlled by this one point of view. "I like him, I don't like her." Or, "I like that about her; I don't like that about him." Preconceived notions! We imagine that a person should actually be a certain way, and when we see anything different in a person, then we make a judgment about the person. Until this sort of thinking stops—of thinking of others as sympathetic or antipathetic based on our prejudices, on certain personal preferences that we have about human nature—and until the attitude spreads of taking people as they are, we will not be able to make strides in true, practical knowledge of human nature.

Just think how very often today two people come face to face under these circumstances and some antipathy arises in one of them;

one does not like the other, then everything that the one person does in relation to the other is colored by this dislike. Through this a karmic relationship is very often totally wiped out, completely put on the wrong track, and it can be put right only in the next incarnation when these people come together again. Sympathies and antipathies are the greatest enemies of true social interest but this fact is seldom even noticed. Those who know what true social understanding means for the advancement of humanity observe (at times with a terribly heavy heart) the effect teachers can have in a school. Because of certain prejudices, teachers may think from the outset of one pupil as nice or not nice, compared to another. That is often terrible, whereas it is really about taking every person "as is," and making the very best from it.

However, it is the attitude based on sympathy and antipathy that enters our institutions. Our institutions, our social rules, which often extinguish teachers' individualities, are already such that in reality individuality cannot even be addressed. True understanding for spiritual science must take such effect that practical psychology and practical knowledge of the human being become part of the common interest. These are necessary for social understanding, so that we can create the polar opposite of the difficulty of understanding each other.

This is what must appear most particularly in the fifth post-Atlantean era for humanity to fully develop the consciousness soul. To a certain extent, people must experience everything through tests, where counterforces stand in their way. Thus the feelings of sympathy and antipathy will spread, and only through battling, conscious battling of superficial feelings of sympathy and antipathy, will the consciousness soul really be able to be born. In the same way, person-to-person social understanding will more and more overcome nationalistic feelings and perceptions that now exist. Nationalist feelings, which essentially first got out of hand in their current form in the nineteenth century, most significantly oppose social understanding, true person-to-person interest. And so these national "opposites," national feelings of sympathy and antipathy, arise today. They represent a difficult, terrible test for humanity because well-being can come only from overcoming them. If the feelings of sympathy and antipathy that come from national perspectives were to get further out of hand, as they have started to do, humanity would dream away the evolution of the consciousness soul. This is because national feelings go in the opposite direction. They do not let human beings become self-sufficient, but make us so that we appear only as a poor imitation, a reflection of a group nature or nationality. The first thing we must contemplate practically when we put this otherwise abstract thought before our souls is that especially the consciousness soul must particularly begin to evolve in this fifth post-Atlantean era.

Something further must begin in this era if the consciousness soul is to truly develop. If religious life will not adapt to the fifth post-Atlantean era but chooses, rather, to remain as was correct for the previous period, a certain stultification, a true deadening of religious life will begin as we become more and more individual. Group religions had to come about during the fourth post-Atlantean era because people were more invested with the group nature. Commonalities in dogmas, commonalities in religious principles and religious thought had to be, as it were, poured out by force over groups of people. However, because the impulse to individuality will become ever stronger by means of the consciousness soul in our present era, what is expressed through group religions will no longer penetrate to our hearts, to the individuality of each soul. People will simply not understand what comes from group religions. In fourth post-Atlantean times, people could be taught about Christ in groups; in the fifth post-Atlantean age, Christ is, in fact, entering into individual souls. We all carry Christ in our unconscious or subconscious already. But He must first be brought again to consciousness within us. That does not happen when established, rigid, lifeless dogmas are imposed upon people. It happens, rather, when everything possible is attempted to make Christ understandable to all people and to foster religious knowledge for all. Thus more and more tolerance must come about, directly in relation to the thinking of religious life; it must come about in this fifth post-Atlantean era. The situation in the fourth post-Atlantean age was still such that those who worked for religion imparted a certain number of dogmas, of set principles to their fellow human beings. This must become much different in the fifth post-Atlantean era. It is quite a different matter now. Now, because people are becoming ever more individual, religious life should support the attempt to become completely free from dogma; should really bring before people the things that can be explained, can be described to others, without dogma. This will come about more from personal inner experience, so that people can individually develop their own, free religious thought life. In reality, the religions with dogmas, with specific set dogmas and tenets, will kill religious life in the fifth post-Atlantean era. Thus the correct way to begin in this era is to make it more understandable to people that whereas in the first centuries of Christianity, dogmas and tenets were especially suited to people, something else has become appropriate in the centuries that followed. But there are also other religions. One attempts to describe the nature of other religions, and one attempts to clarify various views concerning Christ. In this way we bring to each soul what will deepen it. But we do not try to shape their souls ourselves; we allow them have their freedom of thought, particularly in the field of religion, in order to further develop this freedom of thought.

Just as social understanding is necessary on the one hand, as I have described it; so, on the other hand, freedom of thought in the field of religion is a basic requirement for the development of the consciousness soul—social understanding in the field of social existence; freedom of thought in the field of religion, of religious life.

What we are attempting to do is to increasingly understand religious life, to penetrate it, and thus be able to get along with our fellow human beings, even if each person develops their own religious life. This must be considered ever more because it is one basic requirement for the fifth post-Atlantean era—something that humanity must consciously acquire for itself. Specifically in the age of the consciousness soul, the ahrimanic forces directly attack this freedom of thought most of all. We see how denominations everywhere antagonistically regard the foundation of the spiritual-scientific stream—the spread of freedom of thought. We see how much slander and libel are directed at spiritual science for the simple reason that spiritual science is trying to examine the birth of the consciousness soul with full, light-filled understanding. Spiritual science does not want to spread the sort of religious life that is still built on the spreading and promoting of the intellectual- or mind-soul, as was the case in the fourth post-Atlantean era. The forms of Christianity in that era were based on the needs of the Greco-Roman culture. Those forms are already unsuited as forms for churches now; and they will become increasingly unsuitable for allowing freedom of thought to arise, as this freedom must emerge.

At the same time when the need for freedom of thought first began to stir out of modern life, an opposing power also set to work immediately. This could be called the "Jesuitism" of the different religions (though much is included in this term that must be described in detail, separately). This was actually brought to life in order to provide the strongest resistance to the freedom of thought that is a necessity of life in this era. And it will become increasingly necessary to eradicate this Jesuitism, which is opposed to freedom of thought in all areas in our era, because the freedom of thought radiating from religious life must continue to develop in all areas of life. But since this freedom of thought must be acquired independently, humanity is essentially being put to a test, and the greatest difficulties crop up everywhere. These difficulties become that much greater because the people of our epoch must also develop clarity of consciousness. At first, people experience the need for freedom as uncomfortable, and then anesthetize themselves in many ways.

Thus we see that an intense struggle exists between the burgeoning of freedom of thought and the authority from former times that is still holding on in our time. The anesthetizing obsession of abandoning ourselves to deception through faith in authority is present! Faith in authority has grown immensely and has become very intensive. Under its influence, human beings have developed a certain helplessness in regard to exercising their faculty of judgment. In the fourth post-Atlantean era, healthy understanding was provided to humanity as a natural gift; now we must acquire it, develop it ourselves. Faith in authority holds us back. But we become completely caught up in this faith in authority. Just think how people appear helpless compared to creatures that have no power of reason! Animals have many instincts that lead them in beneficial ways from sickness back to health;

whereas, humanity today works hard against common sense regarding sickness and health. In this way, humanity today submits completely to authority. It is not easy for modern humanity to even form an opinion regarding healthy living conditions. Certainly, all sorts of organizations, and such, make laudable endeavors. But these endeavors must all become much more intensive. Above all, we must understand that we are continuously moving toward a faith in authority, and that entire theories are formed that are themselves the foundation of views that strengthen this same faith in authority. In the field of medicine, in the field of jurisprudence, and in all other fields as well, people declare themselves incompetent from the start in acquiring an understanding, and they simply accept the word of science. This is indeed understandable given the complexity of modern life. But people will become increasingly more helpless under the influence of the power of such authority. Systematically cultivating this authority, this disposition for authority, actually is the principle of Jesuitism. And Jesuitism in the Catholic religion is only one specific example of the results, which also appear in other fields but which we simply do not notice. Jesuitism first began to uphold the power of the papacy in the field of ecclesiastical doctrine, which carried over from the fourth post-Atlantean period into the fifth. But the papacy is no longer suited for the fifth period. This same Jesuit principle, however, is also carried over again and again into other areas of life. Today we can see Jesuitism looming even over the medical field, which is essentially nothing other than Jesuitism transferred from dogmatic religion. We see how from a sort of medical dogmatism doctors strive for an increase in the power of their status as doctors. And that striving for power is the essential thing about the Jesuit-like aspiration for power in various other fields as well. This will become ever stronger. People will become increasingly more constricted by what authority imposes upon them. And well-being for our fifth post-Atlantean era will consist of asserting the right of the consciousness soul, which wants to develop, against this ahrimanic opposition—for this is indeed what it is. This can take place, however, only when people really desire to develop understanding and a healthy ability to exercise judgment. In our time, we do not receive—as we do our two arms—natural understanding at birth, which was comparatively still the case in the fourth post-Atlantean period. The development of the consciousness soul requires freedom of thought, but this freedom of thought can thrive only in a very specific aura, in a very specific atmosphere.

I have pointed out to you the difficulties present in our own era because it is moving in a very specific direction of development—toward the development of the consciousness soul. But this consciousness soul, precisely because it must develop as a consciousness soul, must have opposition; it must endure tests. Thus we see that great opposition arises to both social understanding and freedom of thought. Today, people do not understand at all that this opposition exists. In many circles, the opposition is regarded as exactly the right impulse, which should very specifically not be counteracted but instead should be developed.

However there are many, many people who have an open heart and good understanding for where modern human beings find themselves, who have an open mind and a good understanding for what can already be seen today. They understand the karmic situation of the crisis I have just described: how children no longer understand their parents; parents no longer understand their children; siblings no longer understand each other; and different peoples no longer understand each other. There are already enough people today to confront this situation, which is necessary, but which can be turned to the good only through truly heartfelt understanding. For the impulse for this new work for the world must flow consciously from the blood of the heart. The estrangement of individuals from one another will come about independently. What will have to stream forth from human hearts must be sought consciously. For only in the overcoming of these difficulties will the trials arise through which the consciousness soul can be developed.

Today one hears many people saying: "Oh, I don't have a feeling for what I should make of myself; I don't know how I fit into the world." This is the result of their not yet having found the opportunity to reflect clearly on what is needed today and on how human beings are part of that. Many people today develop dependent relationships to the point of physical illness, to the point of physical instability. A real understanding of this is increasingly and ever more intensively demanded. This is due to that which will necessarily pour out over humanity in the fifth post-Atlantean era—the danger of soul poverty—soul poverty in the sense of what has been said today. Many people see what I have described and feel it is necessary, really necessary, for people to come to social understanding, on the one hand, and freedom of thought, on the other. But few are willing to take the correct measures; people often attempt to promote what is necessary for social understanding with all kinds of idealistic sounding phrases. So much is being written today on the necessity of individual treatment for the young, growing human being! What elaborate theories are being conceived in all possible pedagogical fields! That is not what this is about. What should be spread widely, and in an understanding way, are what I would like to call positive natural histories of individual human development—as many descriptions as possible of how a human being has developed. Wherever we can, we should say how person A, person B, and person C have developed, and enter lovingly into the details of an individual's development taking place before us. This is necessary above all: a study of life, the will to study life, and not simply to follow a program, because theoretical programs are the enemy of the fifth post-Atlantean cultural period.

When societies arise, they should arise in accordance with the fifth post-Atlantean cultural period, so that the people who come together in these societies are of main importance, and what can result from the mutual association of these positive-minded people can indeed come about. Truly individual effects will result from this if we pay attention to them. What do we usually do today? First, we pass statutes and regulations. Indeed, this can be a very good thing, and is maybe even necessary, since outer circumstances demand outer regulation. But we must be clear in our field that all talk of plans and statutes is only a concession to the world; that the issue is really that living together individually must arise from people with a positive attitude, so that mutual understanding is attained. Then the possibility will present itself in this fifth post-Atlantean era—we have hundreds of years ahead of us—that the understanding of individual development, of development that is full of life, will issue forth from the circle of those who understand it into the wider world, which today ties up everything into paragraphs like a Spanish boot[‡]—into sections or laws or something similar. Thus, teachings that sound as if they are healing are popping up everywhere from the pulpits and from other speakers' platforms, which are supposed to instruct us about life. We see teachings appearing everywhere that simply ooze with abstractions, and in which people are presented with all manner of ideas and ideals. This cannot be what genuine change is really about; rather, it is a matter of penetrating concrete, real life with understanding. Now, how can this be done?

Some argue, and of course absolutely rightly so, that we can't learn to judge everything that comes from authority today. Just think, they will say, what someone has to learn who wants to become a doctor! It is right that this person should learn it. We cannot learn that *and* learn what a lawyer learns and *also* learn what artists learn, and so on. We simply cannot do it! Of course we cannot do that, without question. But we do not need to be able to learn all of these things; we need only to be able to judge. We must become capable of leaving authority to its work, but also of judging authority. We will not learn to do so by really going into every single specialty, but rather by acquiring the ability to judge from a foundation that can develop our understanding, our power of judgment, comprehensively. This can never come from material understanding of each specialty, but rather, from comprehensive spiritual knowledge.

Spiritual science must be the central knowledge, because spiritual science will not only give clarity to the relationships in human evolution, it will also, because of the nature of its thoughts and ideas, develop healthy understanding in us, which today must be brought up from great depths, just as it had to be brought out in the Greco-Roman cultural epoch, the fourth cultural period. The way of developing concepts, developing ideas, which is necessary for spiritual science, is different from other sciences. It does not enable us to become an authority in every field, but rather to become discriminating. And we will realize more and more why that is so, because there are mysterious forces in the human soul. These mysterious forces will bond the human soul and the spiritual world by our delving into spiritual science, and by being discriminating when we encounter authority. We will not know everything an authority knows; but if the authority does a particular thing in an individual situation, we will be capable of judging that.

We must particularly emphasize this as something that must be brought about through spiritual science so that it does not just teach people, but also enables them to exercise good judgment in this regard; that is, it first gives them the possibility of freedom of thought, first fosters independent thought in them. Spiritual science does not make us into physicians, but if we penetrate spiritual science correctly, spiritual science enables us to judge what is brought into public life by physicians. Once people understand what I mean by these words, then they will understand much about the healing forces for this era. It is really significant when I say that spiritual science will transform human understanding so that people will become discriminating, and the power of understanding is freed up out of their soul-life. Only in this way can they truly achieve freedom of thought.

If I may now speak somewhat pictorially, I would like to describe these thoughts to you in a pictorial, imaginative form. In spiritual science, we hear of the true spiritual world, the concrete spiritual world, of elemental beings that surround us. We hear of hierarchies, angels, archangels, and so on. For us, the world is populated with concrete spiritual content, with spiritual forces and spiritual beings. These beings that live in the spiritual worlds—it is not insignificant that we know about them! In the fourth post-Atlantean period, these beings were more or less indifferent to the thoughts of human beings about them, but in the fifth post-Atlantean period they are no longer indifferent. Now when human beings here on earth know nothing of them, it is as if they are deprived of a kind of spiritual food. The spiritual world is absolutely connected to our physical earthly world. You will understand this best if I tell you something that may itself seem paradoxical to you, but which simply is true. After all, although many things cannot be said today, some truths must be spoken, because people should not live without these truths.

You see, a correct point of view for the people who live here on Earth is to know that Christ entered into earthly life through the

Mystery of Golgotha; and since then, he has been part of earthly life. And from a certain perspective, one can see Christ's coming as fortunate for earthly life. But now put yourself in the position of the angels. (And this position is no invention of mine; this position is what comes to light as something real for the true esoteric researcher.) Put yourself in the place of the angels. They experienced something different in their spiritual sphere: they had the opposite experience! Christ went away from their sphere to go to humanity; he left their sphere. They must have said among themselves, "Christ went away from our world through the Mystery of Golgotha." They have just as much reason to feel sad about Christ leaving their realm as human beings living in a physical body feel Christ's coming to them as beneficial. This is a real thought process. Anyone who really knows the spiritual world knows that there is only one way for the angels to find solace, which I have expressed like this: human beings down on the earth in their physical bodies live with Christ-thoughts and those Christ-thoughts shine up to the angels like a light. They have shone up to the angels like a light since the Mystery of Golgotha. Human beings say, "Christ has permeated us, and we can develop in such a way that Christ will live within us; 'not I, but Christ in me.'"‡ The angels, on the other hand, say, "Christ went away from within our sphere, but he shines up to us like so many stars in the Christ-thoughts of individual people. We recognize him there, he has shone from earth since the Mystery of Golgotha."

There is a real relationship between the spiritual world and the human world. And this real relationship is also expressed in that the spiritual beings that inhabit the spiritual world around us can look in with pleasure and satisfaction on the thoughts that we have about their world. Only when we are able to think of them can they help us. Even if we do not reach the point of seeing into the spiritual world with clairvoyance, they can help us if we know about them. Help comes to us from the spiritual world when we study spiritual science. It is not just what we learn, the knowledge, but the beings in the upper hierarchies themselves help us if we know about them. Moreover, when we face authority in this era, it is beneficial for us that we have supporting us not just our own human understanding, but also what the spiritual beings are able to affect in our understanding when we know about them. They enable us to judge with regard to authority. The spiritual world helps us. We need the spiritual world; we must know about it; we must take it in deliberately. This is the third impulse that must occur in the fifth post-Atlantean era.

The first is human social understanding, the second is attainment of freedom of thought, and the third is living knowledge of the spiritual world through spiritual science. These three must be the greatest ideals for the fifth era. Social understanding must come to the field of social life; freedom of thought must come to the field of religion and other areas of our life together, and spiritual knowledge must come to the field of knowledge. *Social understanding, freedom of thought, spiritual knowledge*—these are the three great objectives, impulses, of this era. We must evolve under these lights because they are the proper lights for our time. Many people feel intensively that such a thing is necessary, that another way of living together must arise for people today, that other concepts must appear; but out of ignorance or unwillingness they evade the consequences of this feeling-recognition. We can see this in the circumstances in which some people find themselves in relation to the intention of spiritual science or anthroposophy. We need not even think of the malicious slander and libel against spiritual science, theosophy or anthroposophy, or of what is maliciously pitted against them for whatever reason. We can think, rather, of the honorable will that is present in modern humanity; of the honorable will that aims to create impulses in people that are along the lines of the correct impulses for this era. Just think of how many "reform" people are appearing in various fields; how many social pastors, other kinds of social preachers, and still other kinds of social speakers from non-theological or non-religious circles. How all this occurs, and how it is often filled with the very best will! Life in our time pushes people to bring something forth! Goodwill is present frequently, and in those moments we want to look at what is goodwill, not what is ill-will. But so long as this goodwill remains only in general talk—even if it is borne by such fervent feelings—then it is of no use, and the knowledge that can come only from spiritual science is not filled with the life necessary for the three great ideals to be realized: social understanding (social knowledge of human nature), freedom of thought, spiritual knowledge. But humanity's understanding of this in our time has not even begun, except for the small group that has formed within the spiritual-scientific worldview.

Today we are able to see many beautiful, noble insights in this direction. I would like to give you a taste of what happened to me "by chance," as people say, but in reality through karma. I found a little book in a store window, which I bought because of the impression the title made on me.[‡] The book is about about modern humanity, about what we are seeking and under what impressions modern human beings grow up. It mentions how much there is in the modern world, in the modern outside world, that helps modern humanity, that makes life comfortable for us, that makes life easy, and how life is a delight under the influence of certain amenities brought about recently by steam power and electricity; all that is mentioned. But then something profound is emphasized: that although modern humanity has entered a more frenzied, more eventful life than was the case in earlier times, our lives have become richer. All of this is mentioned with a certain joy, with a certain ardency. Exceptional spiritual events of recent times are described, and how modern humanity has it better in comparison to the duller, sadder, more instinctive life of earlier times. Then, what I previously indicated as difficulties of the fifth post-Atlantean era are also correctly described. The only thing the author does not recognize is that this springs forth directly from the singularity of this era and its requirement—the development of the consciousness soul. There is not clear, lucid clairvoyance here. That is what matters. But the author senses with an open heart. He writes, "Strange: we were able to begin with *joie de vivre*, or joy of living, in describing the inner process of development of our time. But we must speak of penetrating, inner spiritual poverty at the end of this period. What we experience here on a small scale, our time is experiencing on a large scale."[‡] By "on a small scale," he means the specific place in which he lives. "A richness of culture without compare, a blossoming of life in power and beauty—as almost none other in history—and, at the same time, spiritual poverty that is mounting and that grips entire social classes."

And now, after having understood this correctly, this man explores possible causes that might have led to this condition, in order not just helplessly to present this spiritual poverty, but to find what is right, so that the recent impulses of humanity can be guided in the correct way. And among these various things, he also presents what he calls theosophy, and how he came to know about theosophy. Here, among so many antagonistic people, we come across someone who meets theosophy sympathetically, with the very best will, with the will to really get to know it. He did acquaint himself with it, and therefore we take him under consideration. I bring this up because it is really very important and fundamental that we also concern ourselves with such positive connections between our spiritual science and outer life.

After this man also speaks about what mysticism—which does not achieve actual "mysticism,"—means to accomplish in deepening life and alleviating mental anguish, he says, "In addition to mysticism, there is theosophy.[‡] There are some who see it only as a guise, out to put surrogates in place of proven forces, or who find only a penchant for syncretism and eclecticism in it"—that is, a penchant for aggregating all sorts of religious denominations and worldviews. Those who do not go any more deeply into spiritual science talk about how warmed-over Gnosticism is part of it, and so on. But this man goes a step further. He says to those "...who find only a penchant for syncretism and eclecticism in it, corresponding to their individual tendencies, and throw it together with less lucid concomitant phenomena in contemporary life, with superstition, spiritism, visionaries, symbolism, and similar expressions of spiritual child's play that put people on edge with their secrecy"—that this is not true. "It wrongs this movement when one does not acknowledge the deep inner connections and values that come to expression in it." Thus, here is a sympathetic person. He says, "We must attempt to understand in it, at least in Steiner's circle, much more than one of the religious movements of our contemporaries; even if it is not of the original, but only the syncretic kind, but which is directed towards the basis of all life..." I hope he will also come to the originality of it, given how much goodwill this man has. "...We may judge it as a movement to fulfill humanity's suprasensory interests; and thus as a surpassing of realism, which clings to the sense aspect; we may recognize in it, above all, a movement that points out to people the moral problems they are confronted with for the purpose of self-consciousness, and that aims to work toward inner rebirth from a painstaking attention to self-education...." As I said, I am not reading this out of some foolish sentiment. It is not insignificant, given what else is said about anthroposophy, for us also to become familiar with such judgments. "...One need only read Steiner's introduction to *Theosophy* to see how seriously one is shown the work on moral purification and self-refinement. Further, it is a reaction to materialism in its speculation directed at the suprasensory; admittedly..." (and here is something to which I ask you to pay particular attention) "...it loses its footing in reality a bit, and goes beyond its capacity into hypotheses, clairvoyant fantasies, a dream realm, so that there is insufficient force left for the reality of the individual and social lifestyle. But all the same, we want to record theosophy, and must, as a corrective phenomenon in contemporary educational development."

Thus the only thing this man does not like is the ascent to spiritual knowledge, to concrete, real spiritual insight; that is, he wants to have the impulses for human moral perfection that can flow from Theosophy in his view as well, but he does not yet recognize that this can come, here in the fifth post-Atlantean era, only from true, concrete spiritual knowledge. He does not recognize the roots. He wants to have the fruit without the roots. He does not recognize the whole interrelationship. This man is extraordinarily interesting because he studied my book *Theosophy* with dedication, as one can see, but he failed to see that the one does not exist without the other. He would like to chop the head off this book but keep the body, as he sees the body as something of value.

This is connected with what I described to you earlier. Such people already understand that social understanding and freedom of thought are necessary, but they do not yet want to acknowledge that the third ideal, spiritual knowledge, must form the basis for our era; that is what they cannot yet come around to. To inspire understanding for spiritual knowledge is one of the most important tasks of the stream of the spiritual-scientific worldview. Many people call ascending to the spiritual worlds fanciful; they do not recognize that loss of knowledge of the spiritual worlds has been brought about directly by materialism and the lack of social understanding associated with it, by the materialistic life and life ethos of recent times. It is precisely those who are sympathetic whom we must study to see how it is still difficult for people today to recognize the necessity of definite spiritual worlds. Thus we must try all the more to gain understanding for such impulses as those of which I have spoken in today's lecture.

The little book I have been talking about is *The Thought World of the Educated: Problems and Questions*; it had already been published in 1914 in Hamburg by the Rauhe Haus Agency. It reproduces a lecture given by Professor Dr. Friedrich Mahling at the Thirty-Seventh Convention for Inner Mission in Hamburg on September 23, 1913. As I said, it came into my hands entirely by chance a few days ago when I saw it in the window of a bookstore, and I can only wonder that that no one in our circle noticed it. It could have fallen into someone's hands, since it has been published since 1914. It is actually necessary to concern ourselves specifically with the various threads running back and forth between many different fields. It is necessary to concern ourselves with one issue that we find so often, that of the vile railing against and ridicule of our movement, but we can also concern ourselves with the cases when honest understanding is sought, as in this case, when we can learn directly from the difficulties that people who are seeking honest understanding have today.

This is exactly what I wanted to base today's lecture on, to show what the three great ideals should be, the concrete ideals for the fifth post-Atlantean era: concrete social human understanding, freedom of thought, spiritual knowledge. The three concrete ideals must give direction to the sciences in the future. They must purify and cleanse life; must give impulse to morality; must provide orientation and direction; must penetrate life, must foster life in the widest scope within modern humanity. But the first two challenges will not be fulfilled—social understanding and freedom of thought—if spiritual knowledge is not added to them as the third aspect, because the consciousness soul must be developed. The spirit self, which must be developed in the sixth post-Atlantean cultural period, is the highest level of this consciousness soul. It will not be developed if human beings do not prepare inner independence, which is achieved through the developing of the consciousness soul. This is what we must also take into consideration in our spiritual-scientific pursuit—that what we recognize as abstract truths really have magic powers, which we must unleash only in order to shine a bright light on all life. And wherever people find themselves in life (whether they are in a branch of science or some field of practical work, even in the smallest job), they will take part in the great tasks of our time if they can give life to the abstract facts we talk about at our gatherings, in the sense that they should have life. Then cheerfulness will enter into people's souls; cheerfulness that is not just carefree superficiality but that is also connected to the seriousness that supports life, that increases our powers, that does not just enable us to enjoy life but makes us into competent workers in life.

In this sense, the three social and cognitive ideals I have talked about will also give the consciousness soul the ability to understand the Mystery of Golgotha, the ability to receive Christ into ourselves in a new way in this era. For we must establish a real bond with the spiritual worlds by coming to know how these worlds relate to this central impulse of earthly evolution and to the Christ impulse. Only then will the Christ impulse become an influence on the thoughts that have been able to shine into human souls in Earth-existence from the spiritual world since the Mystery of Golgotha, thoughts that can light up in human souls as bright comforting stars, as I have described; thoughts that themselves light up the world of the angels, who have lost the Christ from their spheres, so they see him shining back to them from the sphere of human thoughts.

No, spirit-knowledge is not something that may be described as fantasy. Spirit-knowledge is what is striven for in order to find what can remedy the soul poverty that is necessarily linked to the fifth post-Atlantean era. That is what I wanted to speak to you about today. I hope we will see each other again in this city in the not-too-distant future. Until then, I hope that we remain connected in thought, and also continue our work here in the spirit of our movement.

Lecture 5

Karmic Effects

Zürich, October 24, 1916

What spiritual science has to say about life and about the structure of the spiritual worlds is to be found through knowledge of the objective facts into which human beings can be led by corresponding capabilities. We are indeed familiar with all of this. Thus, if the issue is to justify or defend spiritual science in the world today, we cannot base our defense on anything other than indicating how people come to insight in the spiritual worlds by developing certain capacities and then explaining how these capabilities arise from a corresponding formation of living relationships in the spiritual worlds. An objection based on human wishes or desires can never be made in relation to the facts that come to light in this way (although it is often almost a matter of course, it is still good to point this out). Just as little could an objection be made in relation to the facts of the physical world, which are observed with the senses. Although this is obvious, one often hears objections to certain spiritual-scientific statements, objections that stem directly from human wishes or desires. Something along the lines of, "if spiritual science has that to say about the spiritual worlds, then I do not wish to become familiar with spiritual science because if it really were so in the spiritual worlds I could never get used to such a form of the spiritual worlds." As fundamentally absurd as such an objection is, it has been said. But it appears not only in this very obviously absurd form, it also appears masked in all sorts of dismissive attitudes that are held in relation to spiritual science. Even if some insight or other of spiritual science could never be supported by the claim that the world had only one meaning, that the spiritual world were like such and such—one can nevertheless know how things really are in the spiritual world. One can never say anything about the structure of the spiritual worlds based on such assumptions, but on the basis of real insight, one can turn it upside down and indicate what spiritual science and its results can mean for human life.

Two weeks ago,[‡] I demonstrated for a particular subject what the spiritual-scientific *ethos* means specifically for our time in relation to the great challenges of this age. Today I would like to make a few other points that will go somewhat more deeply into what spiritual science can be for humanity and, in particular, what it can be today for those who will study it more deeply. I would also like to point out the resistances spiritual science can meet from today's culture; and which resistances one must be armed against. The spiritual abilities that lead spiritual scientists to see into the facts of the spiritual world develop gradually, in a way that has often been described, in a way such that one first comes to know the major facts of spiritual life—those that are the essential facts with respect to the evolution of earthly life, to repeated earthly lives, to life between death and rebirth, and so on. Then, it is absolutely possible to speak correctly not only of these general, major viewpoints, of these general truths, but also to speak of certain special truths. And when we become more and more familiar with such special truths, then spiritual science becomes more valuable for the individual, concrete human life. Human life must at first be an enigma for outer physical view, because if it were not an enigma, human beings would not be subject to a development that makes us ever more capable. Our abilities, which are produced especially in connection with the soul, must come from our own efforts; they grow out of our efforts. In the spiritual realm, our efforts make us mature through the energy that we devote to solving the riddle of the world. By devoting energy to solving this riddle, our strengths are fortified; we become ever more capable in life, and we truly become perfected also within humanity's evolution. We need not worry that life will lose its interest for us when someone partially solves the riddle posed by the physical world and is able to look into the spiritual world, because life poses riddles in every realm. Upon entering the spiritual world, one finds still other riddles of life. We also gain something in relation to the physical world specifically from the experiences we have solving certain human and life riddles from within the spiritual world. We gain trust and experience through the solving of the deeper human and world riddles that are revealed only in the spiritual world itself.

One particular riddle is what human beings experience between birth and death as destiny. A great deal is packed into this word "destiny." Yesterday in the public lecture we were able to touch on how the matter of destiny is resolved through repeated earth lives.[‡] Those are general viewpoints. But we can also talk of specific circumstances. Let us take as an example someone losing a dear relative. Let us say that the relative dies at a young age, so that the one who remains behind has a long time on earth to pass through without this relative. By quickening such a thought within ourselves, we see at once before our spiritual sight that this is a matter of destiny for many people. Now, the point is that spiritual science can truly shed light on such a matter of destiny. Certainly, each case is fundamentally different. But precisely by studying individual cases in a spiritual-scientific way, we can have a glimpse into the mysterious course of human life. One could, for instance, consider the following experience. A person dies young, is taken away from his or her relatives. Yesterday, I said that the relationships that have developed between these people by their coming into contact with one another here through their physical bodies are much more extensive than what is expressed through those physical bodies. A much wider circle of unity develops when two people have lived together ten, twenty, thirty, or forty years; a much wider circle of forces develops between the two people than can unfold within the physical world in those years. When we turn a spiritual-scientific eye to such relationships, we then often see that what connects with the relationship requires through its inner nature a continuation. The one who remains behind here must bear the loss. If we express it abstractly, this person has physically lost sight of a dear human being unexpectedly, and the hopes for a life together here in the physical world are torn away as a result; the foundations for life together have been cut off. This is all part of life experience, but it is also part of what is, as it were, added to the experiences we share together in the physical body. The fact that sorrow and pain follow our experiences together in the physical body affects in the relationships that could have begun only in the physical body. Just as what we experience of each other daily when we face each other in physical bodies pours forth into the karmic line, into the advancing stream of evolution; so, too, is what we experience under the impression of loss added to what we experience daily. All perceptions and feelings we experience are added to the accumulation of experiences we have in life in the physical body. This is looking from the viewpoint of the one who remains behind in the physical world.

The viewpoint of the one who has crossed into the spiritual world is somewhat different. After crossing into the spiritual world, the one who has crossed is no less present with the person who was left behind. Indeed, it is clear to those who are truly able to investigate the spiritual worlds in specific cases such as these that, for the one who has crossed over, the conscious togetherness with those who have remained behind is a more intensive, more inner togetherness than could have existed in the physical body. But one sees that very often, this increased inner togetherness is there to properly complete the circle of changing relations that formed here in the physical world. Through true, positive investigation, one often makes the following discovery: One sees that people have met here in physical life, and through this a certain circle of unified interests has formed under the threshold of consciousness. Given the conditions of their lives, if these people had been together here in the physical world for a longer time, their relationships that would have developed on the basis of karma would not have been able to be deepened intensively enough. For those remaining behind, with whom the departed had been close, the one who passes through death's gate can often bring about a karmically necessary deepening during their remaining time on earth; a deepening that could not have been brought about through circumstances of life had the departed soul not passed through death's gate. The one who has passed is now with the thoughts of those souls on earth; penetrates, flows through the thoughts of those souls. Thus correct fulfillment of karma often involves pain borne on this side and, on the other side, an intensive togetherness with the thoughts of the ones who remain behind.

One other thing results if we follow the second soul—the one who will pass through the gate of death at a later time—as that soul enters into relationship with the one who died earlier. We notice that much is arranged differently according to the difference in time between the two deaths. When we enter the spiritual world, it is not the same to meet a person who died at the same time we did (to take this extreme case) as one who died fifteen years earlier. If the one we meet has already spent a certain time in the spiritual world, then the experiences he has had in the meantime are now in the soul that we meet, and so that soul affects us in a different way. A karmic bond is made accordingly that could not have been made in the same way through other conditions. We must see all of what we experience in this way with a person who is close to us as being completely based on our karmic relationship. I have said many times that, even if this knowledge cannot assuage sorrow and pain, for us to know what happens when everything fits together, what happens when everything interacts, it still must be said from a certain viewpoint that life takes on its true meaning only when seen as a whole in this way.

The point is that we develop all the relationships in which we find ourselves during a human life so that not only this life "comes into its own," so to speak, but also all the contributions that we must make in the following earth-lives for this earthly evolution, come into their own. What is begun with the painful loss of a relative or a friend or any other person close to us, will appear in its continued effects in the next earthly life. And in a certain way, all of these effects are already contained in their causes. No loss occurs in human life that does not correspondingly put us in the correct succession of earth-lives. Perhaps this will not give relief from our pain in specific cases, but from this viewpoint we will become able to reclaim an understanding of life.

By talking about such things, we can learn something directly from looking at actual cases. Another specific case that I would like to mention is the ending of a person's life through misfortune. One can presume from the outset that there is a great difference between the case of a life ending by a person's being run over by a railway train or dying of unnatural causes in some other violent way and the case of a life's being complete at an old age or ending because of illness. One can further make the presumption that there must be a difference between a life ended early by illness and a life that ends at an old age.

Now of course each detail of these cases is different, but we can also find certain clues in them. Above all, we can ask ourselves what a violent death is. This question can be answered only if we look at death not from here, from physical earth-life; we must look at it from the other side, where those who have passed through the gate of death look at it. I have mentioned in lectures, which have in fact already been published,[‡] that seeing death from the other side, from the side the dead enter through death's gate, is the most important experience, and shows the disincarnate person how life triumphs evermore. The direct vision of death from the other side, which is sublime, which is grand, which is always there, also means that a constant I-consciousness exists in us between death and rebirth. As our memory, which brings us back to a certain point in physical life, gives us I-consciousness here, so too does the vision of death from the other side, the spiritual side, give us I-consciousness between death and rebirth.

Now, how is it when this vision of death is affected by the fact that a violent end of life caused the death? Seen from the other side, a violent end of life is an experience, a perception, of the most far-reaching kind. As strange as it may sound, when one investigates these things, the following emerges: The ways in which the circumstances of time affect the experiences of the soul are much different in the spiritual worlds, which we enter through death's gate, than they are here; though some conditions here are reminiscent of what occurs in a much more extensive way between death and rebirth.

In order to explain what this depends on, I will resort to a comparison that results only when one knows the corresponding facts from the spiritual world. You are certainly aware that we can have experiences in a short period of time here in physical life, perhaps in the course of a day or a few hours, that mean much more to us than other experiences that we have had over a long period of time. Many can recall such an event from their own lives here in the physical world, one that happened in perhaps a very short amount of time, but brought more consequential inner experiences than the events of entire months or years. People often express it in this way: "I will never forget what I experienced then." Very often, what I have just characterized is hidden behind this simple phrase.

Now, it is true that the impression of their earth-life that disincarnate souls receive from a death caused relatively quickly, or perhaps in an instant, by the outer world—that had nothing to do with their own organism—compresses itself for the life between death and a new birth, and becomes just as rich as what could be achieved in a longer earthly life, perhaps even in decades of earthly life. I do not mean everything that was experienced in earth-life, but certain things that are important as forces for the life between death and rebirth. For those things, what would usually be distributed over a longer period of time can in fact be compressed into an instant, one can say. It is really a much different experience if with one's subconscious one sees death coming because inner forces assert themselves that cause death from within the organism, or whether death is caused by forces affecting one's organism from outside, having nothing at all to do with the organism itself. Such a death finds its true, real explanation only in the fact that we view it in connection with the entire course of human life through repeated earth-lives. You can very easily infer from what I said about the connection between the I-consciousness after death and the vision of the death that the perception of the death itself is something very meaningful for the strength and intensity we have in the I-consciousness between death and rebirth.

Circumstances that appear to be coincidental from here, from the perspective of physical life, are absolutely not coincidences; they are, rather, contained in a world of necessity. It may appear to be a coincidence here that someone is run over by a railway train; but seen from the other side, from the spiritual side, it is not coincidental. If the question is posed from the other side, from the spiritual side—if I may do so, though of course it can be only for purposes of comparison—"How does such a violent death appear in the totality of a human earth-life?" then we will always find that in the past this person has experienced, through the lives between death and rebirth and through various circumstances in repeated earth-lives up until the unfortunate event, that the I-consciousness developed for the purely spiritual world needed strengthening, invigorating. And this invigoration occurred by the person's physical life having been ended, not from within, but from without. So, we must reckon with the fact that we are not only related to our surroundings through connections that are caused by conscious forces in the soul. Only in the rarest cases can we know—ordinarily we cannot know—how our subconscious thinks. I have often pointed out to you that thought life does not end at the threshold of consciousness, that human beings continually lead a thought life in the sub- or one could also say, in the supra-conscious. People cannot think through and assess what this more encompassing consciousness could be for them. One could ask every single person, "Why haven't you had a mishap today?" There would have been the possibility for every single one to have had this or that mishap. Sometimes you might halfway realize why a mishap did not occur, but you see the connection only in the rarest cases. One time you may have a certain disinclination to do something and go somewhere a half hour later than expected, and later notice that something happened along the route that could have happened to you had you gone that half hour earlier. The subconscious was working here, and it delayed you. Such effects of the subconscious are constantly present; they are just not perceptible to human beings.

For anyone able to observe the circumstances of the world from a spiritual viewpoint, it is completely clear that those who meet with misfortune were not protected from it by the good genius that takes effect in the subconscious; rather, they meet misfortune by being driven to it through the necessity of karma. If this misfortune had not occurred, what I described would not have been able to happen: the strengthening of the I-consciousness in the way I indicated, which was necessary for them. People live into the circumstances in a certain earth-life into which they are placed through birth. However, they live into these circumstances after having observed during the last life between death and rebirth that in a certain way their I lacks strength. A drive to strengthen the I lives within them, and leads them to those circumstances that cause their misfortune. You must see the matter in this way; you see from these examples that life gains meaning when we look at it from this viewpoint of spiritual-scientific awareness.

As I have often pointed out, people do not think enough about the changes that have taken place comparatively recently in our soul evolution. Most, and in particular those who are infected with today's erudition, simply picture the soul life of centuries ago to be the same as today's soul life. That is a completely erroneous idea, as we know. In every detail the expression and attitude of human soul life has changed significantly. What spiritual science must bring up today from various sources about such life understanding, as I indicated, was present in souls in more of an atavistic-clairvoyant way not so long ago at all. People then had ideas to some extent about the connections in life; but human evolution is pushing forward, and such ideas are dying out. However, because humanity has already partially lost this old connection with the spiritual world in the course of evolution, and will continue to lose more and more of it, it will also be increasingly necessary for people to inform themselves again about their connection to the spiritual world through direct spiritual research. That is why spiritual science has appeared precisely in our time. People did not need it in the past because humanity was not on such a level of soul evolution. From this time on it will be necessary, for the reasons I gave, and will become ever more necessary.

Let us substantiate this assertion, as well, with certain concrete facts. Today there is only a small number of people who take spiritual science into their souls during life between birth and death. I say "spiritual science" rather than "spiritual research," meaning the imaginations and ideas provided by spiritual science. Through spiritual science, people experience something of the spiritual world here in this life between birth and death. This is not meaningless for the life that we enter when we pass through death's gate. And in addition, we have a consideration that first came to be true in our time, which I will now address. If we go back to earlier times, we still find an old inheritance of humanity in relation to the connection with the spiritual world. Human beings went through death's gate, and because they already had a certain connection to the spiritual world through ideas, through atavistic clairvoyance and such things, they had some commonality between life in the physical world and the life they entered after they went through death's gate. The fact that people while on earth knew something instinctively about the spiritual world caused them to have more than a mere accumulation of the thoughts that were memories of earth-life on the other side of death's gate. From our time forward, the singular aspect that will appear more and more in human souls is that people will go through death's gate and remain connected to the earth only through their memories. They will remember their earth-life here, to some extent; and only by having this earth-life in their memory after death, are they still connected to earth-life. In the strictest, most radical sense, this is the case for modern human beings who cannot take in any ideas about the spiritual world from spiritual science. If we take in such ideas, these ideas will provide something after death that will enable us not only to remember our life, but also to see into our earth-life. When we acquire ideas about the spiritual world here, windows from the spiritual world open onto the physical world after death, in a manner of speaking, onto everything that is here in the physical world. Thus we carry certain outcomes from this spiritual science through death's gate.

What we acquire from spiritual science is not simply a dead knowledge, but rather life substance; something that lives on when we pass through death's gate. Yes, this spiritual science, in the sense that I have often mentioned, has powerful life substance by virtue of the fact that because the dead live consciously in our thoughts, we can do something for them because we are part of spiritual science. This is related to what I have often said about reading aloud to the dead. The dead are in our thoughts, they see our thoughts. When we cultivate a spiritual-scientific train of thought, that is, when we read something to the dead in thought or tell something to the dead that we know or think about the spiritual worlds, then the dead are with these thoughts that we address to them through spiritual science. By addressing our thoughts to the dead, a bond of attraction is formed between here and there. Thus, because spiritual science is living, we can effectively send up living strength that gives living nourishment to the dead who are close to us.

Thus we see that in this inner way spiritual science can truly conquer death and transform it into life. A community among the living and the dead, which could otherwise not be formed in such an intensive way in this age, can be formed by filling ourselves here with thoughts taken from spiritual science and extending these thoughts to the dead. Spiritual science is precisely what intervenes in life in a living way, whereas the knowledge that is gained of the physical world through conventional science consists only of thoughts that have meaning for the time between birth and death. Such thoughts will be only memories in the life after death without having any living effect there. We must really contemplate this difference.

One more thing must be taken into account, specifically when we wish to think about the meaning of spiritual science for present and future human spiritual evolution. Not only does what we acquire of spiritual science here, or extend to the dead, make its way from the physical world into the spiritual world, but the spiritual-scientific knowledge we attain on earth and carry through death's gate works back, in turn, upon the earthly world. We should not lose sight of the fact that this earth-world is being impoverished little by little of forces which come from the earth itself, and which people develop only during life between birth and death. If no more forces flowed from the spiritual world down to the earth than have already flowed until now, then this earth-life would be depleted. It is a grim experience to see how thoughtlessly people already live today, not noticing that earth-life is being impoverished little by little.

That thoughtlessness, incidentally, is a phenomenon that is a reality not only of human intellectual and cultural life, but also of physical life, which is still so abundant on earth. I have already pointed this out, too, in other places. If you read the wonderful geology book *The Face of the Earth* by Eduard Suess,[‡] you will find an explanation of how the earth used to be much different in terms of its physical surface, and how the forces that were present many eras ago are no longer present today. The earth's surface is crumbling. What takes place in physical life also takes place in spiritual life. And, as I said, the way people look at the earth, without having any consciousness of it, often seems grim. For spiritual life, when we characterize the path that humanity is following, one has to say that despite the arrogance that infiltrates our time, it turns out that people's thoughts are becoming increasingly lifeless, ever more dead; ever more and more disjointed. People are of course proud of their thinking today. And how very learned school teachers often think they are when they explain Plato to their students! Mind you, the wise poet Hebbel wrote in his diary[‡] that he wanted to write a drama (which, however, was not completed), in which the hero was to have been Plato reincarnated. Plato is punished in school by his teacher because while reading Plato he cannot understand Plato at all.

People will encounter to a certain extent a discontinuity in their system of thought if a renewal of this system of thought does not come via thoughts that are born of spiritual-scientific insight. As strange as it sounds today, it is true. The intensive power that people need to correctly form thoughts so that they have the constancy of truth, weakens, because people are supposed to become independent, to attain their own power. Thus I could say that, in a manner of speaking, the gods have withdrawn the spirits that earlier inspired our correlation of thoughts; we must bring life back into our thoughts ourselves. But we will bring life into our thoughts only if we are not too arrogant to take up within ourselves the life that can flow from spiritual science.

Just as it is with thinking, so it is with feeling; and so it is with the impetus to will. This human impetus to will is going to become more and more obstinate—we could almost use this word for it—separating ourselves more and more from shared humanity if this great, encompassing impetus of the soul is not inoculated, this impetus of soul that can come to be only through seeing the spiritual connection of physical things. With this I am telling you serious truths about the development of humanity's future. These truths must be penetrated by those who deal with spiritual science. Spiritual science should not just be dead material that satisfies our curiosity; rather, spiritual science should be something that aims to intervene in the constellation of things that human beings will encounter in the future. But in this we must see which systems of forces must weaken and be replaced by others. I said that humanity's earthly forces would weaken if no influx of life comes from the spiritual worlds. What we gain from spiritual-scientific knowledge and carry with us through death's gate gives us not only the power to shape our life between death and rebirth, but also the power to enable spiritual forces to come to earth. More and more, people who are living on earth must be able to receive what comes down from spiritually permeated souls after they have gone through the gate of death—what they have taken with them and has been transformed in the spiritual worlds.

Thus one way to affect the spiritual world from the physical world, that is, to have an influence on the dead, is by reading aloud to the dead, by directing thoughts of spiritual science to them. In contrast, a way to affect the physical enrichment of Earth-evolution is to be receptive to what has been achieved by those souls during their sojourn in the physical world, carried through death's gate, and come down transformed from the spiritual world. This can happen because it is a singular fact that spiritual substance gained in physical life creates a form that undergoes metamorphosis in the spiritual world. The physical world can then receive what has been acquired in this changed form, which flows into the physical world in this metamorphosed form.

We work on our own karma for ourselves, so that this karma is fulfilled in repeated earth-lives, always between birth and death. But shared human karma is made up of both the currents of life that flow here on earth and the currents of life that stream from the spiritual world. Between death and rebirth, we work on this shared human karma with the powers that we develop beyond our own needs. Thus we see how spiritual science is necessary; how it is necessary that human souls work on it, not for the healing of individual human souls alone, but for the healing of the entire progress of humanity on earth as well. We work on our future earth-life from the spiritual world, as I said in the public lecture yesterday, by settling into our hereditary connections through the generations before our birth. But we also participate in preparing for future earth-lives what concerns not only ourselves, but also all of humanity. We should very specifically penetrate the thoughts that I am expressing in this way. We should meditate on them because they are the kinds of thoughts that transport us into a vital spiritual and soul relationship with the surrounding world.

And now, as a counter-image, I would like to show you how the world today judges what spiritual science discloses; and how the world sides with the disposition that brings about what I described as thoughts drying up, becoming discontinuous, becoming disjointed.

(This would look different in other areas.) Precisely those who often have big words to say today about various issues and who, through their arrogance, reject every connection with the spiritual world as these are imparted through spiritual science, contribute directly to this hopeless situation that we already see approaching today, and specifically in regard to the world of thought. Allow me to give an example.

Again a new popular collection has been published—so many popular collections have been published today—through which humanity can experience what people have uncovered in the way of wisdom. They say, "It is a great delight to put oneself in the spirit of the times" and "we have made such great progress."‡ There is a great deal of such material today. I want to point out to you a small volume from the collection on the questions of religion today.‡ These questions of religion are treated quite peculiarly. First, arrogantly claiming all today's wisdom, they show how people cannot be satisfied if they are able to believe only what natural science investigates, if they thus have only a naturalistic philosophy; and then they show how people cannot declare themselves to be satisfied with reaching what the editor of this little book calls their religious philosophy, if they have a purely moral philosophy. This religious professional criticizes in a very sharp way the pure philosophy yielded by moral demands. He claims that the pessimism into which much in our time is degenerating, is not ungrounded. It comes from a living tragedy of life itself. This was actually experienced in every time period, and this religious professional calls attention to the way that pessimism has asserted itself over knowledge in different time periods. People believe that through their thinking they can come to realize that one cannot know anything, that striving for knowledge can basically never be satisfied.

As an example, he actually cites important sources that we should certainly listen to, such as Pliny the Elder, the great Roman natural scientist, who said, "Humans are beings full of contradictions, the unhappiest of all creatures; other creatures have no needs beyond the limits of Nature. But humans are full of infinite wishes and needs that cannot be satisfied. Their nature is a lie—the greatest misery along with the greatest arrogance. In the face of such ill, the best that God has granted humans is the ability to take their own lives."‡

Such sayings can be cited from many, many people. Seneca, the wise Seneca says, for example, "Many learned people are tired of always seeing and doing the same things; they don't exactly hate life, but they have a feeling of disgust about it, which is increasingly gaining ground under the influence of philosophy. They ask how much longer will it always be the same? This unbearable inevitability of getting up and going to bed, of being full and getting hungry, of being cold and becoming warm again. Nothing has an end; everything is part of an unending circle. Everything is fugitive and pursuer at once. Day follows night, night follows day. Summer flows into fall, fall must give way to winter, and even winter's might is broken. Everything goes, in order to come back. I see nothing new; I do nothing new of which I do not become weary."‡

So said the wise Roman philosopher Seneca. Our religious professional believes some truth to be in it, but this is less interesting to him. Then he calls attention to the pessimism that has come about by people's surrendering more to their feelings. For example, he claims that is where Buddhist pessimism comes from: "Life is suffering." They look at life and add up the suffering and pain, the ill, and on the other hand add up the happiness and joy. The former is greater; thus they are pessimists. They look at life overall as an evil. Schopenhauer and Eduard von Hartmann did so as well. Again, our religious professional believes that people have good reason for this; but that, too, does not interest him further. He is more interested in ethically-based pessimism; he says that it is completely warranted to look at life without being able to penetrate it with what we call "God's kingdom"; with what we call the essence of religious confession. And thus our religious professional states two things. One is that human beings select the challenge of being bound to follow a moral law, either in the sense of Kant or Schleiermacher; a law that is very seriously obligating. But on the other hand, human beings are subject to their nature, their drives, tendencies, and desires. And now our religious professional states that human beings can never completely overcome these drives and desires; but they should follow moral law; moral law gives strict commands. A conflict will inevitably ensue. It must be present in life, and it is. This is warranted pessimism. One must interpret life pessimistically if it is looked at only from the standpoint of ethical challenges. This is life seen from the standpoint of ethical challenges, how humans are situated between these ethical challenges and their natural life. But even when we look at individual ethical obligations, we will see how pessimism is warranted, because—according to this religious professional—people often feel that they are in the middle of ethical conflicts in decisive situations. Our professional cites such ethical conflicts for important personalities.

Allow me to read just one example. "Luther,"[‡] says our religious professional, "who recognized his destiny as no other has, and saw right before his eyes the path he had to follow for the reformation of the church and of people, got into this dilemma"—he calls the incompatibility of obligations a "dilemma"—"at the moment when he was confronted with the question of whether he should approve or reject Philip I of Hesse's double marriage. You see, this was the most difficult of all conflicts for him. If he rejected this marriage and acted in the pure interest of human dignity, then he would have to abandon one of his most important achievements on the path to fulfilling his reformative destiny"—because if he had not approved this double marriage, the magnanimous ruler would not have accepted him anymore and, according to this religious professional, nothing would have come of the Reformation—"however, if he allowed the marriage and thus left this one way open, then he must have said to himself that it would be a thorn in his soul that he would always feel. This was a difficult dilemma, and whoever has no understanding for such struggles, and instead moralistically passes judgment on them, is no just writer of history." Such struggles, however, when obligations collide, cannot be avoided in the important issues in human life, according to our religious professional. That accounts for the warranted pessimism. Thus, for our religious professional, if we see it clearly, the world absolutely appears in such a way that from the standpoint of nature and from the standpoint of morality pessimism is fully justified.

Our religious professional now turns in his way to religion, and says that he must turn to religion so that all false paths that could be followed will be avoided. Buddhism, he says, tried to avoid the conflicts in life by actually overcoming existence, overcoming physical and spiritual existence; tried to remove them, as our religious professional believes, to unreal Nirvana. Plato wanted to remove life conflicts by overcoming matter with knowledge. Our religious professional says that Buddhism wants to do away with all existence, and Platonists want to do away with matter. Mystics, he says, reject individuality. Our religious professional counts as mystics all those in the world—besides those whose ideas have gotten into his head—who assert that they strive to reach the spiritual world. In summary: Buddhists reject existence; Platonists reject matter; mystics reject individuality.

None of those are viable paths for our religious professional. Instead, he turns to the path that he naturally sees as the only Christian one. And he says that one must turn away from the earth to the kingdom of God. Then a sort of description follows of this kingdom of God. For those who are able to think in a logical, consistent way—I will make no other demands—for those who have not yet fallen into what I have called discontinuity, the disjointedness of the system of thinking, this description of the kingdom of God by this man of the church brings nothing short of deep pain because of the emptiness, absurdity, and disconnected thinking in it. After this man, like so many people today, has dismissed everything "mystical"—that is, everything *he* counts as mystical—he finds a way to fairly "cram words into people's mouths" (forgive the trivial expression), because you get the biggest applause today when you give lots of lectures on things that people do not need to understand. You can say to people that everything else is nonsense, and then they listen to the way you "prove" to them that it is nonsense and that no one needs to bother with it. Then finally you say—as long as they are still there—true, real existence is love. And then you talk plain nonsense, which has no substance, but which repeats the word love, love, love, over and over, repeats it in such a way that in truth, no love can come into the world from it.

That is more or less the way people of religion speak today. Many people speak that way. And then our religious professional moves on to all kinds of insights, grandiose insights, such as this one for example. "Because love is the highest thing, God is love." Certainly, within certain limits, this is first of all not at all new; and second, one can agree with it. But the idea that this has to involve a being that loves and that can be called "love" because of loving so intensely is not really something that causes our religious professional any concern. But now he wants to speak for real Christianity. First of all, "God is love" means something very impersonal because love, as such, is simply impersonal. But our religious professional has no difficulties at all with this because he says, "The center of this reality is God. 'God is spirit' and 'God is love'... In reality, spirit and love are one." We can, in reality, declare everything to be one, if we continue in his way of thinking! "Because love is the highest form of spiritual living."‡

In truth, spirit and love are one, but at the same time love is the highest form of spiritual life. Spirit and love are one, but then love is the highest form of spirit, that is, a part of it, and the part is the same as the whole!" There you have the worst disconnection in thinking! Now everything that he assumes is based on God being love. Thus he must also say, "When we speak of the wrath of God and his punishments, in the end we must be able to understand it all as an expression of his love."‡

Now, furthermore, we have the possibility to understand God as love, because the wrath of God is also love, if it is understood correctly. God is spirit; only God is love—spirit and love are one. Wrath is also love, thus wrath must actually also be spirit. Thus we see that the terms are just jumbled in this disjointed thinking. But people will still be Christian, so he finds the need to write in his way, "Thus God can be nothing other than love, because He must be the highest form of spirit. What unfolds here is wisdom that cannot be outdone; even the highest philosophy cannot go beyond it. God is absolute freedom, the abolition of every conflict, the spirit coming into its own, love. Thus God is a person."‡

So: God is love, this love is the spirit coming into its own, and thus God is person!

"When God is given the 'characteristic' of a person, people often dispute it philosophically and religiously because they say the idea of person comes from the earthly realm and represents humanization when applied to God. But that is a great misunderstanding."

And so on. You see, what people achieve, which has already fallen into ruin—what one can call disjointedness of thinking—will become widespread as people in their arrogance resist the renewal of the world of thought through the adoption of spiritual science.

I would like to quote one more quaint excerpt for you. In order for this religious professional's audience to become completely clear about the fact that they do not need anything other than his lectures, and certainly nothing like science in order to refer to spiritual life, he says to them, "It is therefore foolish and senseless to expect from science an answer to the question of life after death. The excited people who have done so, and are still doing so, have never realized what will become of science if it gets involved with such questions; and what religion loses by borrowing certainty from science."‡

This man achieves what I have described to you. And at the same time this man is in the position to say to people that this is such high philosophy that he would lose face if he even admitted that science also has something to say about spiritual life.

This is the beginning of everything that is to come, only the beginning. We must also contemplate what I said here two weeks ago.‡ But the man I'm talking to you about is a man who "knows how to think." He accused Buddha of trying to help people get beyond existence; he accused Plato of trying to help people get beyond matter. He accused mystics of trying to help people get beyond individuality because through them personality would be destroyed, through them people would be taken out of their physical bodies in which, as our religious professional says, they would need to remain between birth and death. These redeeming religions cannot be valid. But what does Christian religious belief bring about if it cultivates right love (that is, what the religious professional calls love)? Here we read, "In other words, in the spiritual sphere of life of the kingdom of God, awareness is shut out from moral will and action, which takes away the freedom from even our best acts within the realm of our experience."‡

So, Plato is trying to free people from matter, Buddha from existence, mystics from individuality; and our religious professional is trying to free people from awareness through love so that they can settle into the kingdom of God without intentional consciousness. When one comes across such people, one says, "The Lord is with his own in sleep."‡ This could be something of a revelation for our religious professional. One sees that this man can look at life, and draw experience from life. But he suffers from disjointed thinking; one can see this when reading painful statements such as these. He turns against people's becoming mystics because such people want to overcome individuality, but they must stand in physical life directly within Nature. We must not have misconceptions with regard to life's uncertainties: "In earthly life, they cannot and may not be shaken off."‡

Things have gone so far with this disjointed thinking that someone with a healthy intellect can say, "In earthly life, they cannot and may not be shaken off." In earthly life, they cannot and may not be shaken off; but that is nothing more than saying, "You cannot fly to the moon, and you may not!" This is the way he combines "can" and "may" here! We must be able to see the great corruption of such thinking in details such as these.

Or when the man speaks of inner life, he says that he wants to confine Christian life only to what he calls the kingdom of God. Nature should not be conceived in a spiritual way, because human beings are placed within Nature—but they do not know how—and so human beings should stay in nature, though not knowing how they came to be there. Thus he says, "That is for Jesus, the kingdom of God, provided that all symbols and images are stripped from it."‡

What Jesus said in the form of meaningful symbols and images about the kingdom of God is repugnant to the religious professional; he gets rid of them. "The highest world is the one Jesus places above the moral world order. It is the one he speaks of unceasingly; people can enter here without giving up their relationship to the order of Nature, but also without abandoning their affiliation with the moral world. Everything is transfigured here; the conflict that has arisen between the world of Nature and the moral world ends here. It is resolved by love. The relationship of humans to Nature is a necessity that we cannot change, and no moral resolve helps here. Human beings must enter the kingdom of Nature through birth; no one is asked if he or she wants to be born."

This is the way a religious professional assists people in understanding the world. And then he goes on to say, "They"—human beings—"become forces of a mechanical necessity, forces of a highest mandate, which they do not understand, born into the fate of this physical reality."

That is Christianity! Human beings become "forces of a mechanical necessity, forces of a highest mandate, which they do not understand," born into the physical world. For this man, mechanical necessity, necessity of the machine, is the same as "forces of a highest mandate." That is expressed, that is spoken in the world today by those who feel called, and who are called by the world, to bring true Christianity to the people. And that enters the world in such a way that we can read straightaway in the forward, "This little book consists of twelve speeches that I gave last winter to more than a thousand attendees."[‡] (He declined to name the city.)[‡]

It is truly necessary for those of us who seriously wish to study spiritual science to turn our attention to what is actually alive in our time. If the necessity of spiritual science is sometimes alluded to with serious and intense words, it is because the people who are able to, must become conscious in the present day of why spiritual science is a requirement of our time, and of what kind of spiritual state exists in the camp where the antagonistic voices come from.

Today I quoted a person to you as an example of a general phenomenon of our time. The little book is not explicitly directed against our spiritual science. Spiritual science is not mentioned in it, because it is something highly insignificant to this man (whom I also know personally). Spiritual science is not alluded to, but is just generally lumped in with mysticism. Here we see a person, well known as one of the top authorities in his field, who, in his system of thinking, binds humanity to such nonsense. This is not noticed by thousands upon thousands because people simply do not look at things in the correct manner.

However, individual truths about the spiritual world should not be the only things to permeate us; we must also be permeated by the consciousness of how important this is for living knowledge, living words, to gain ground in the evolution of humanity. People will see that the dead end or impasse into which humanity has come with regard to social life and other areas of life is the karmic result of thoughtlessness. Thoughtlessness is much more extensive in our time than people believe. The task of spiritual science, of understanding in the correct way according to human sensibilities, will depend on people looking at the world with open eyes and really taking pains to form a healthy judgment of the world. Thus it was necessary today not only to say something to you in the first hour of my presentation directly out of the content of spiritual science that can bring enlightenment about important aspects of life, but also to illuminate the counter-image that results if one examines what spiritual science should be brought into. You will hear many voices such as the one described yesterday, coming from camps of all colors—whether religious, academic, or others—who regard spiritual science as an absurdity, as fantasy. Despite being famous people in our time, they demonstrably cannot think at all, and spread this lack of ability to think to the detriment and harm of the evolution of humanity in the world. We must be able to see these things in the correct light. And we are certainly obliged to see them in the correct light if we are to truly connect with spiritual science in order to do what we are able, according to our place in life that we have been given through karma; and to provide spiritual science in the appropriate way with the validity it requires, not for itself, but for the evolution of humanity. One can see that this is necessary by describing such a counter-image. Many such descriptions could, indeed, be given.

Lecture 6

The Great Delusion of Contemporary Culture

St. Gallen, October 26, 1916

Rich, detailed material is available to us today in our literature from which we can learn facts that spiritual science is able to bring down from extrasensory worlds, and our branches are able to work with this material. Thus it would be advisable, when we have the opportunity to meet in person, to talk about how this material can be positioned in relation to our spiritual life; how we can bring it into our life; how we ourselves can feel refreshed, uplifted, and strengthened through it in life. In short, it would be advisable if we consider the matters of our spiritual movement more, while we have the opportunity, because indeed we can only rarely meet in person given the nature of circumstances in these times.

Many of you will note that you still have a variety of difficulties as you immerse yourselves in spiritual science or anthroposophy today. Is it not true that we first come to terms with spiritual science through the needs of our souls because our souls pose questions about the most important riddles of life? We come to terms with spiritual science when we look at life today, with everything it can involve, and see how few of the various spiritual trends, whether religious or scientific, can really give satisfying answers in a deeper sense to the great enigmatic questions of life. And then, when we have come to terms with this spiritual-scientific movement through our thirst for knowledge, our yearning for knowledge; when we have immersed ourselves for a time in the knowledge that has been elicited until now from the spiritual worlds, we often encounter difficulties—difficulties of the most varied kinds. These are different for each person, and that is why they are not exactly easy to describe in a few words. Our friends often say that by immersing themselves in spiritual science, they have gained something extraordinarily valuable, something meaningful for life. But it has also isolated them; it has uprooted them from the community of other people. It has also, in a way, made life difficult for them. Those who are by nature dependent on the opinion of the outside world in their spiritual aspirations feel this particularly intensely, and the most varied difficulties result from this.

For other friends, something akin to a state of worry, one might say, occurs after they have immersed themselves in spiritual science for a time; something that frightens them, that makes them frightened by all sorts of questions: how to cope with life, and so on. Many of you have had to ask yourselves similar questions. Such questions are often questions of feeling and perception. I would like to begin today's contemplations with such difficulties of the inner soul life.

We sometimes do not correctly understand the true connection between these perceptions, which can be different for each person; the real connections. We must always bear in mind that those of us who feel attracted to anthroposophical truths make up only a very small handful of people today. We are in the middle of the struggle for existence that is waged outside of our circle with means that are sharply different from ours. And those who reflect even just a little on all that anthroposophy is trying to be for life will be able to observe how entirely different the goals of thinking, feeling, and willing under the influence of anthroposophical ideas are from the goals that the great majority of people set for themselves today. Because thoughts and feelings are actual facts, we should understand that our little handful of people, that is every single one of us, is thus part of a comparatively small life-group that is—one can say in most cases—completely opposite to the thoughts, sensations, and feelings of the rest of humanity. Even if the life difficulties that arise for us take on the most varied forms and do not immediately show connections to what I have just described, they are indeed connected; and we must attempt to bring before our souls the way we can cope with such difficulties; with the difficulties that arise when we remain true and devoted to the cause of anthroposophy but collide with the rest of the world.

As I said, things become blurred, and they do not always show their true colors. We have to effectively introduce to our own souls a remedy in order to find greater inner harmony despite the opposition of the outer world; and with this remedy we must make our souls strong so that they grow and overcome what often arises in our souls in the form of frightening things, disharmonies. The remedy is a clear, true understanding of the relationship to the rest of humanity that those who declare support for, or are interested in, anthroposophy find themselves in; our relationship to the rest of humanity. To think clear, incisive thoughts about this purifies our souls in such a way that we can also be strong when contradictory outer forces plague us. If one thinks about the matter within a limited horizon, one could say, "But what good does it do me to become really clear about what divides anthroposophy from the rest of the world? My life conditions will not change by doing so!" To think in this way would be a mistake. Although life conditions may not change from one day to the next through clear thinking that produces understanding; nevertheless, the strength that we gain from such clear thinking, in the way I just indicated, gradually strengthens us in such a way that our life conditions do, in fact, change. It is just that we sometimes do not find the opportunity to develop really clear, incisive, and therefore strong enough thoughts of this kind.

With regard to what we would like to gain for ourselves through spiritual science or anthroposophy, and what we would like to gain not just for ourselves but for the world, we must bring before our souls as one of these clear thoughts that in today's culture humanity lives in a terrible, more or less conscious or unconscious lie, and the effect of this lie is immense. This is actually saying something very meaningful, and I want to bring more clarity precisely to this point.

As a truly thinking person, with a fully healthy understanding, one can hardly look at what exists today in the form of general culture in the so-called cultivated world without being clear that much is missing from this culture; that, above all, this culture lacks sufficient impulses for life. Instead, in our time there are many widely dissipated ideals, as people call them, for which all sorts of societies and associations are founded that put on programs through which this or that ideal is supposed to be expressed! It is all very well-intentioned, such that one can say that those people who form associations, large or small, from all the circles and strata of life, under the impression of this or that ideal, want what is good from their viewpoint. And the convictions of these people should be respected fully. But for the most part, these people live under the restrictive influence of a certain constraint that comes from unconscious timidity, unconscious spiritual cowardice in regard precisely to the most important thing that humanity needs today. We say: *the* most important! What humanity needs today is spiritual knowledge, and the introduction of certain spiritual insights into our lives.

That was, in fact, a major question in the course of the nineteenth century. As you know, there are spiritual laws, laws governing the spiritual worlds. Certain people in every time have known about these, and of course these were also known in the so-called occult societies in the course of the nineteenth century, when spiritual science had not yet appeared in the form in which it is present today. These occult societies, which were more or less deserving of the name, wanted to cultivate occult truths in the most varied ways, and also had a certain insight into what spiritual truths mean for the world. Right in the middle of the nineteenth century, a crisis arose regarding the deepest impulses in the recent evolution of humanity. This crisis existed during a particular upswing in materialism in all fields; in the field of knowledge, in the field of life. Materialism had reached high tide. Indeed we see that numerous people emerged who wanted to found a comprehensive worldview from scientific materialism.

But this theoretical materialism was not the most corrupting thing; rather, it was practical materialism, the materialism that settled into ethical and social life and into people's religious feeling that led humanity to a crisis in the course of the nineteenth century. And, as a result, from the middle of the nineteenth century on, those who knew something about these occult societies directed their attention to how they could remedy this spreading materialism. In certain circles, people had spiritual-scientific insight, just not insight of the kind that can be effective on its own, nor in the form that, in all modesty, we strive for. Those who had a traditional, or in some other way outmoded spiritual-scientific insight into the evolution of humanity asked themselves, "How can we remedy what is dawning over modern humanity like a disaster as a result of materialism?" And they said to themselves, "We will remedy it by giving people proof that, just as sensory facts surround us, so too do spiritual facts and spiritual beings." But people were accustomed only to experimental thinking, and to outer experience and perception. And so these people, with spiritual-scientific insight and concerns such as those I mentioned, did not know what to do other than to prove the spiritual world in the same way that we prove natural processes of the outer sensory world. They tried everything. And we saw movements arise in the nineteenth century that focused on convincing people of the existence of a spiritual world. The most primitive of these movements was the spiritist movement. Although scholars today have difficulty coming to terms with the comparatively transparent methods of our spiritual science, truly brilliant scholars of the nineteenth century studied spiritism very seriously.

Spiritism has the characteristic of having an outward effect through something that can be placed before the outer senses, such as a chemical or physical experiment. For the most part, this method, which attempts to reproduce natural science as spiritual science, is already bankrupt today (I say, for the most part). And we will see more and more that it must become bankrupt because you cannot show people how to grasp spirit with their hands, figuratively speaking. Thus, much of what has been done by all sorts of occult machinations of certain so-called occult societies in the course of the nineteenth century, and up until the present time, has actually brought disrepute to spiritual-scientific study rather than supporting it. Therefore we see that, even in the most well-meaning people who have insight, namely in a social respect, but also in other ways in regard to practical aspects of life conduct, there is still much that needs to happen from the present onward, and into the future. For people who have such insight, we see how they almost feel a certain shock when someone says that the most important impulses needed in the present and near future must come from true spirit-knowledge, from the insight that true spiritual forces and spiritual beings surround human beings, just as sensory facts and sensory beings do. The people who mean well in regard to humanity's progress get a real shock. Let me give an example. We can learn quite a lot from examples that have to do with overarching life phenomena. If we turn our attention to a large movement, then we can clearly see in this large movement the things that we all come across daily on a smaller scale.

A quite important man, one who was truly serious-minded in regard to humanity's impulses toward social progress, was murdered in Paris on the day before the outbreak of this disastrous world war: Jean Jaurès.[‡] Jaurès was surely one of the most serious personalities directly active in the social efforts of our time. He was also one who strove to achieve insight through earthly knowledge into current life conditions and into the reasons for which these conditions are driving humanity further and further *ad absurdum*; further and further into impoverishment and hardship in the spiritual and material realms. And he strove with all of his strength to find ideas and thoughts to convey to people, so that through collective efforts the great life questions of our time could, in some degree, come closer to being answered. We can learn much specifically from such personalities as Jaurès because we learn the most when we consider the great deficiencies (which one must see from the spiritual-scientific point of view especially in our time, and about which one must have clear thinking) not of insignificant, but of great personalities. We learn the most, if we are sure of their primarily honorable convictions and serious efforts at realization, and also of a certain capacity for contemporary insight. We gain so much more when we analyze people whom we respect and highly esteem in regard to the damages of our time, rather than people for whom we have less respect because we cannot ascribe to them goodwill and good dispositions in the highest sense.

Now for such people as Jaurès, who devoted all of their thoughts, feelings and will to the service of humanity, to the service that must be provided in raising humanity to a higher social level, it is extremely difficult to talk about something such as our spiritual science. And he is truly no exception; we see the best people of our time in this difficulty. And precisely these very talented people would be able to effect what they wish to effect for humanity only if they could say, "Everything that I can achieve with my usual cognitive and scientific means provides me only with impulses that are too weak to really be able to seize life. I must recognize that all these impulses that I wish to convey to humanity as I go along are without a base. I must first create a base for myself; I must penetrate and permeate what I have believed until now with the more solid foundation of spiritual science. I must recognize spiritual facts, true spiritual facts."

You see, for someone who thinks all sorts of thoughts and forms ideals of how to assist human progress today, but does not recognize such spiritual facts, it is the same as for someone who is in a garden with many plants that are beginning to show signs of death, and who does this, does that, does a lot, and makes an effort the whole time; but achieves nothing. Oh, one plant gets a little better, another a little worse, but overall the plants don't get better. Why don't things get better? Maybe some sickness has taken hold of the roots, which this person does not check or consider. That is exactly the case with the social efforts of people such as Jaurès. They make an extraordinary effort and they find a great many splendid things on the surface, but they do not penetrate into the roots because the roots of human life today are missing the recognition of a true spiritual world. And people establish so many seemingly well-founded social insights that will in truth be fruitless for humanity if they are not based on the insights that can come only from spiritual science. Thus a real advance for today's humanity will only be possible if the most important part of spiritual science for our time can be recognized: namely, the reality of spiritual beings and spiritual forces. The acknowledgement of this, however, presents people with a real difficulty—especially the best-intentioned of people. Let us think clearly about this fact that these people, those with the best intentions, have difficulties precisely with the most important aspect of our subject: the acknowledgement of the spiritual world as such.

Over in Zurich I pointed out an example that illustrates this particularly well.[‡] There is a man who has spoken very positively about our spiritual science, and also had what he said printed.[‡] This man once had the courage to speak in front of a very learned audience that looks upon what lives within our spiritual movement as no more than pure foolishness. But this man cannot help but stop right before the most important aspects: before accepting the spiritual world. What does he say?

> We must rather try to understand it [this spiritual movement], or at least the circle around Steiner, as a religious movement among our contemporaries, even though it is not original but rather syncretic; but even so is directed towards the basis of all life. We may judge it as a movement for the satisfaction of people's extrasensory interests, and thus as surpassing realism, which clings to the sensory. Above all, we may recognize in it a movement that points people to personal reflection for the moral problems they face; and that aims for working toward inner rebirth out of a painstaking attention to self-education. One need only read Steiner's introduction to *Theosophy* to see with what earnestness people are pointed toward the work on their moral purification and self-refinement.[‡]

I am reading you these words because I want you to see with a truly clear awareness how the outer world relates to our endeavors. You see that this is a well-meaning person who, even so, sees our movement as syncretic; he does not recognize, does not know, what a completely new movement it is; that it is based on something new to the world: on the new natural-scientific movement, which is its foundation. He has a well-meaning attitude toward our movement, but cannot give any information about it because he does not understand it. And if we really take in this whole lecture that he gave, "The World of Thought of the Educated," we see that this man thinks that spiritual education of the human being is necessary in our time; and he sees in our movement an attempt to promote this spiritual movement for humanity. But then he says, and this is characteristic, "Further, in its speculation directed towards the suprasensory, it is a reaction to materialism; however, in doing so, it loses touch somewhat with reality and goes as far as hypotheses." He believes that true spiritual insights are hypotheses, not knowledge. "It goes ...as far as clairvoyant fantasies, a dream world, so that it no longer has adequate power remaining for the reality of the individual and social art of living."

And later he says, "But after all, we want to, and must, note Theosophy as a corrective phenomenon in current educational development." You see, even though he judges it in such a well-intentioned way, he feels compelled to stop before getting to all of the things without which our movement cannot even be imagined; and before the primary thing we contribute: suprasensory facts. Without human beings achieving a relationship to suprasensory facts, humanity cannot be saved from the dead end in which it finds itself today. But even well-meaning people believe that this movement leads to a dream world; that it does not have "adequate power remaining," precisely in relation to the social art of living, even though our movement specifically seeks to have solid ground under it, and without which all other social ideals have nothing to stand on. As I said, this is not ill will based on mistrust; rather it is mistrust sprung from unconscious timidity, unconscious despondency in relation to the acknowledgement of spiritual facts. This is a clear lack of insight; and it is clear that it is this lack of insight that spiritual science specifically can do something about in laying a foundation for social striving. And so, people such as Jaurès, because of the thoughts they assimilated from their upbringing and education, find themselves in life today without the possibility of recognizing that everything that occurs physically is dependent on the spiritual world. They cannot see that human beings can intervene in life within the sphere in which they work—for example, in relation to social life—that they can really intervene only if this is made possible for them by knowledge of the spiritual laws with which the spiritual world can be brought into the physical. And the fact that such people are faced with this impossibility; that this is truly a contemporary phenomenon widespread among the most enlightened people of our time, brings significant—though unconscious, but no less significant for it—delusions into our time. These grand delusions can be found everywhere.

Let us take the case of Jaurès, since his is a typical case. There stood a person before the rest of humanity who sought an improvement with all the means of social awareness; and he correctly recognized that it would only lead people to a dead end. There stood a person before the rest of humanity who, in order to attain the necessary insights in this field, had really made himself familiar with all the historical facts. He had studied history and wished to learn from the facts of earlier times what could happen in the present, and thus how errors could be avoided. Now Jaurès in all of his striving becomes unable, as others do, to recognize a spiritual world in a truly real way; to recognize in a truly real way that streams of spiritual life flow perpetually from the spiritual world through human beings into this world.

One of the best articles that Jaurès wrote deals with the relations that exist, according to him, between socialism and patriotism.[‡] Jaurès tries to show how historical events intervene in the evolution of humanity and have an effect on the evolution of humanity. After he has brought before us details about what had an effect on the Roman Empire in order to learn from that how things should be effected in the present, and after he brings various other things before us with an extraordinarily thorough thirst for knowledge, he then presents us with a new chapter from more recent times. It is a strange chapter in Jaurès' book, which concerns the proletariat and patriotism; and it is interesting to examine specifically this little chapter to see what is actually taking place in the souls of the most knowledgeable people around us today.

It is crucial to Jaurès to show in this chapter that ownership of property is not what is foremost in recent social progress, but rather industry, and so on—but we will not get involved with these things; the important thing is that he is compelled here to make reference to Joan of Arc, the Maiden of Orléans.[‡] Now just think, a man who lives completely in the ideas of the present refers to the Maiden of Orléans. Anyone who has studied recent history knows (those who look at the facts objectively will have to admit this) that the map of Europe would simply be much different today if Joan of Arc had not intervened. Of course Jaurès also recognizes this. He says:

> Joan of Arc completed her mission and sacrificed her life for the salvation of the fatherland, in a France for which property no longer represented the only life force. Communities already played a very important role; Saint Louis IX had sanctioned and solemnly proclaimed the organization of trade and guild rights;

> the Paris revolutions during the governments of Charles V and Charles VI‡ had seen the trading bourgeoisie and the crafts associations come on the scene as new forces. The most clairvoyant among those who wanted to reform the kingdom dreamed of an alliance between the bourgeoisie and the farming community against lawlessness and despotism. Into this modern France, which would soon be ruled by the 'People's King'‡ (the son of the poor ruler whom Joan of Arc was about to save); into this diverse, thoroughly educated and refined country, which was affected by the delicate literary pain of this Charles of Orléans,‡ whose imprisonment moved hearts in good Lorraine—into this society that was anything but rural, came Joan of Arc. She was a simple country girl who had seen the pain and hardship of farmers around her, for whom all of these torments only represented a closer example of the more solemn and greater suffering the plundered kingdom and the attacked nation had endured. No place, no property was important in her soul, in her thoughts; she ignored the Lorraine fields. Her farmer's heart was greater than all the farming community. It beat for the far-off good cities, which surrounded the stranger. Living in the fields did not mean necessarily being wrapped up in the questions of the field. In the noise and bustle of the cities, Joan's dream would surely have been less free, less bold and comprehensive. Loneliness protected the boldness of her thoughts, and she experienced the great community of the fatherland much more intensely because her imagination could fill the quiet horizon with a pain and a hope without confusion, and that went beyond it. She did not feel the spirit of rural revolt; she wanted to free the very large country of France in order to consecrate it to the service of God, to Christendom and to justice. Her goal seemed so high and holy to her that she later even found the courage to oppose the Church in order to reach it and to refer to a revelation that she said was superior to every other revelation.‡

Here [in Jaurès] we see a person who is doomed to think based only on materialistic principles, so to speak, because he is part of today's materialistic thinking, but at the same time is compelled to point out this strange phenomenon of the Maiden of Orléans because, to the high degree we can discern from his words, he wants to be historically honest, and to take her seriously. Thus Jaurès is confronted with the entire historical meaning of Joan of Arc. But now we ask ourselves: For such a person who holds a social view like that of Jaurès, what else, in the end, can Joan of Arc actually be?—other than someone who came to her impulses through a sort of religious ecstasy, which people should not aspire to do, likewise, if they want to remain reasonable. This may even be taking it too far personally for Jaurès if we suggest this; but for many others who act in the spirit of Jaurès, it is certainly not an overstatement. These people will certainly not recognize what must be clear to us from spiritual science: that in those earlier times the spirit-knowledge we have today—which has developed in modern times—was not yet achieved. Spiritual life streamed from the spiritual worlds and had an effect through individuals more or less subconsciously, such as with the Maiden of Orléans. These people will not acknowledge that she was a medium—one that took action not for people who, as in recent times, misuse mediums in so many ways, but rather for the divine-spiritual world that was attempting to affect the physical earthly world. We must recognize that what came from the Maiden of Orléans had more value than what her contemporaries were able to communicate from their human insights. Of course, our contemporaries cannot acknowledge that the spiritual world spoke through Joan of Arc. Nevertheless, if they are speaking of true facts, they must speak about people such as the Maiden of Orléans; they must acknowledge her. That is, they must credit what takes place—just think of it—to individuals whose spiritual lives they do not recognize, and whose spiritual lives they certainly do not wish to aspire to.

Here is nothing but the greatest delusion—though people do not want to admit it even today and can anesthetize themselves to this fact, too. I will describe just one case to you of the great delusion, which is pulsing through all aspects of our social life today, and which is the cause of people not recognizing what is true, what is the absolute truth, but having to look at it as a fact, nevertheless, given what recent spiritual development has brought forth. Lies are now accepted as facts, too, and they have a corresponding effect. And if thoroughly well-meaning, earnestly striving, important people such as Jaurès are caught up in a great delusion such as this through the circumstances of our time, what comes from them cannot have a liberating effect for humanity.

Yes, we find ourselves in this present moment, which must be allowed to effect our souls clearly and distinctly. We must have the courage to examine great delusions such as this with clear insight; and from this clear examination, find the strength to keep ourselves going in the face of what is streaming in from all sides. What streams in from this great delusion, from one side or another, sometimes comes in a very masked and hidden way. What true inner insight into the connections of human life can people who find themselves in a great delusion such as this actually gain? They might think that the odd characters who pop up, such as the Maiden of Orléans, who want to have a connection to the spiritual worlds, must be ascribed historical significance, but that in truth this should not be presented as an example anyone should aspire to as a way to somehow bring spiritual forces into the physical world! A great deal more water will flow down the Rhine before other circles realize and recognize the entire profound fact that we have talked about.

Today natural scientists have taken on the same airs that the theologians took on in regard to the Maiden of Orléans back then. The last thing Jaurès points out is part of the deep tragedy of the arrival of the Maiden of Orléans. The theologians said back then, "What she has unearthed in terms of her spiritual world-knowledge is not consistent with what we know through our theology!" It is out of the same opinion that existed in the theological field then that, after only a short period of time, the natural-scientific people speak today. The Maiden of Orléans answered those who judged her on the basis of their theology, and who said she must justify her miracles and her mission using religious texts, with these words: "More is written in God's Book than in all your texts!" That is a historical quotation. But it is also a quotation that is still applicable today because all objections—all theological and natural-scientific objections—can be responded to from the standpoint of spiritual science. More is written in the book of the spiritual worlds than our adversaries think possible. And Jaurès adds to these words, "A wonderful word that is contrary in a certain way to the peasant's soul, whose faith is primarily rooted in its origins. How far it all is from the vague, narrow-minded, and limited patriotism of the landed class! But Joan hears the divine voices of her heart as she looks up to the radiant and gentle celestial heights."‡

Yes, such recognition sounds very good coming from the mouths of our contemporaries, but what is this really—to even the most learned of our contemporaries? An acknowledgement of something that they take more or less as fiction; a fiction that to some extent can make life better, but to which they accord no reality. This is what the great delusion does!

Thus we see that we need clarity about the existence of this great delusion. Its effects confront us everywhere, and it is preventing spiritual science from having the influence today that it should really have. More and more, people will have to gain not only theoretical insight into spiritual science, but also potent inner strength in order to bring spiritual science into every area of life. This is true in the many different areas of life. But again it can be said that the true facts are masked in this case, because an objection could seemingly be made to everything that spiritual science says.

Let us take an area of life that is most appreciated by human beings for the simple reason that it is quite closely connected to their outer well-being. You see, spiritual science would have an incredibly beneficial effect on university medical departments, medical science, and pharmacology, if they were allowed to be influenced even a little bit by spiritual science. Modern natural-scientific development has caused medical science itself to take on a materialistic character more and more. Certainly, this materialistic character has also been very beneficial. One need only mention the extraordinarily great progress that has been made in surgery to find some justification. Even if what I am saying has been said again and again, we must marvel at the recent progress made by natural science. But there are other sides of medical knowledge and the art of medicine that are no less important. They suffer tremendously from this materialistic trend and will be able to meet a beneficial future only if spiritual-scientific knowledge is introduced to their research.

Through spiritual-scientific insights, connections in the human organism are discovered, whereas current medical science knows only isolated details. Certainly, such things are often sensed instinctively by more insightful researchers, but progress cannot proceed quickly enough in this way. If such a wide-spread rejection of everything that is spiritual science did not reign, specifically in the medical field, and if medical science did not strive to become monopolized into one power by medical authorities and governments, immense things could be accomplished for the healing of humanity in the field of medicine through spiritual science. You may say, well, nothing is stopping a spiritual scientist from bringing this progress about! Here again, things are masked, because this is actually not true. The materialistic mode that reigns today in fact prevents spiritual science from intervening. It is a thoroughly false belief that spiritual scientists today can help a person in all cases. They are prevented from this by the outer materialistic mode of medical science, and will be prevented more and more if the materialistic mode of medical science continues still longer. We cannot say to spiritual scientists in the medical field, "This is Rhodes; dance here"‡—because their legs are not free to dance.

There are indeed all sorts of commendable efforts being made against the reigning materialism in medical science; but these efforts are insufficient. Most of all, the insight is lacking that although it is necessary to oppose materialistic medicine, at the same time we must work with what modern medicine has acquired, with the means that are needed outwardly in this field, but in a spiritual-scientific sense. People would be astonished at what would result if the spiritual-scientific view were brought into clinics and dissecting rooms, as well as to all of the other resources and sources of aid in the medical establishment. This is the direction in which our endeavors must go. Our endeavors must go not toward disregarding materialistic medicine, but rather toward bringing spiritual science to the materialistic mode. And before this is accomplished, we will not be able to help even in individual cases. The situation that makes it impossible cannot be discussed in such a short lecture, but it is so. Thus, if there were less prejudice against spiritual science, an immense amount could be accomplished precisely in a field that is so natural to physical human healing.

And concerning the burning social questions, it would come to light that the many attempts being made to improve things in the social field, to improve various living conditions, will fail. For only when people come to base social insights, as well, on spiritual-scientific axioms—like mathematics or geometry are based on their axioms—only then will truly effective means be found.

And so we live in a world that must, if we are moved by spiritual science or anthroposophy, stand across from our own souls with radically different thoughts and feelings. We live in an atmosphere, so to speak, that demands a potent development of strength, a powerful perseverance. Those are the deeper reasons why one can often become disheartened and feel lonely; why perhaps a few, here and there, although declaring support for spiritual science, cannot cope very well with life. But when we have clear insight as to how great is the thing that we are part of in the whole human nexus, and how it seems like a small thing today only because we are still at its beginning, we can find this strength; then we can really find it. Every great thing in the evolution of humanity must begin small.

Here, too, as I did recently in Zurich,[‡] I would like to point out how limitation, illogic, and disjointedness live in the whole way of thinking of our contemporaries. This is the result of a blinding effect that natural science seems to have on contemporary humanity. Natural science has produced magnificent and admirable results with reference to the outer sense world; and in this context the people who had administered to the spiritual heritage of humanity felt driven back, more and more driven back. It did not go well, especially for certain theologians. It is incorrect to simply reject from the outset what humanity evolved through time as theology. There are deep, important basic truths in this theology, including about the human soul. Although these teachings must first be more clearly illuminated in many respects by spiritual science, still they contain basic truths. Only because these truths are not represented in a way that meets the needs of humanity today, the yearning for an answer to the spiritual-scientific question must arise now in thinking people and feeling souls. But the theologians who did not want to be part of such spiritual-scientific efforts found themselves in a strange situation. They had truths, but these truths were not applicable to anything because the other sciences had taken the objects of these truths from them. The theologians had truths about the soul, but the soul was taken from them by natural science. And now perhaps theology proclaims truths with words, but it does not concern itself with the objects. It will even let the objects be investigated by natural science, because theologians are too comfortable in many respects to really take up natural science now. And that is what we must see as important in spiritual science: that this spiritual science takes up natural science completely; that it becomes involved in all that natural science has acquired and joins in by adding spiritual-scientific principles to the natural-scientific mode. The theologians did not want to do this; at times they are filled with a very strange conviction, precisely when it comes to retaining the objects.

A person who is seen as quite an extraordinary theologian in certain circles—both as a professor, which he used to be, and as a pastor—wrote a little book in which he gives an account of his religious talks.[‡] And in this little book he expresses thoughts through which we can, in an odd way, eavesdrop on him; we can see into the soul of an important person in our time. Indeed, however, I cannot say anything else but that one is stunned now and then by the kinds of thoughts an important person can promote! For instance, right away in this famous, important man's first lecture, he says that we must tackle natural science and give it back to open, rational people; one may keep only people of freedom as theologians. But even freedom becomes just a word in this sense! Does he not then say that he will have all of the contents of the soul transferred to natural science? Now he has not retained anything, except clever words, and he even gives a quaint reason for having this conviction; he simply says very dryly that he has this conviction. So a theologian who wanted to describe to his audience the most modern form of Christianity in these lectures says right away in the first lecture:

Human beings, as we encounter them in zoology—two-legged

> *Homo sapiens* that evolved to standing, with a finely equipped spine and brain—are just as good as any other organic or inorganic form that is part of nature; are constructed of the same material, the same energy, the same atoms, with the same strength in effect and at work. The entire bodily life of human beings, however complicated it may still be, is determined by natural science in its entire composition, lawfully ordered as are all other animate and inanimate beings in nature. In this respect there is no difference whatsoever between human beings and a jellyfish, a drop of water, or a grain of sand.‡

Theological lectures, lectures by a theologian, a pastor! But this theologian talks in this way not only in regard to the body. He continues: "The *soul* functions, which are accessible through natural-scientific observation, are subject to laws just as strict as bodily processes; the feelings that we have and the ideas that we form are imposed on us by nature as well"—please, the feelings and ideas!—"as the nerve processes that lead to feelings of willingness or reluctance. They are mechanical presentations just like a steam engine."‡

You see, the soul thus slips over to the natural scientists and this theologian retains only the old theological word-husk for which he finds sentences. The last pages, the last lectures, consist only of empty phrases to wrap what he talks about in theological word-husks. But then he explains the conviction of why he is so generous today in his devotion to objects. And here we catch a very strange conviction—just think, he says that theologians must act as he acts, must go even further—he says, "This certainty in the laws of nature in human beings applies not only to their bodily but also their *soul* functions. This is what we theologians never wanted to admit."‡ Only he is the exception, he has gone beyond this, he now admits it, "because we confused the natural-scientific concept of soul with the theological one, and feared unpleasant consequences for faith as a result."

But now he has come so far that he admits he no longer fears any unpleasant consequences for faith! Then he says, "These come about precisely when we do not let science come to its full conclusion,"‡ that is, he now says, "We should give in to science now; otherwise it will have unpleasant consequences! Otherwise, this science will have horrible consequences." And then we catch him in his truly strangest splendor: "because then we forfeit the trust of thinking people."

There you have what this great theologian is striving for today! People—the most accomplished—have come, in all the ways that I have described to you today, to the feelings with which they turn their trust to us when we speak of the spiritual; we must not forfeit this, and thus not use the true inner soul strength that could be the basis of a spiritual insight! We see that if, when we detect what runs through people's innermost being today, if we do not thoughtlessly pass over such things, then people today reveal themselves to be quite strange. We must have clear insights about this. We must not be surprised, given these clear insights, that if such thoughts are cultivated by those officially engaged in the religious and spiritual education of humanity today, we find it difficult to adapt to the world, considering all those who are radically opposed to us.

We must hold up for ourselves again and again the matter we are actually serving in the world by opposing the tempting thoughts that come today from such quarters with the only thoughts that can be fruitful. Such thoughts may always lift us from even the deepest depression again and again, and give us strength once more. Such thoughts are extremely important in every second of our lives. It is important that we conduct spiritual science in such a way that we show spiritual science outwardly as little as possible, but take it into ourselves so forcefully and intensively that we ourselves have the strength in the face of the tests it imposes on us to say to ourselves, "These tests must exist!" Because our karma has led us to spiritual science, we willingly take on what it imposes upon us in the form of tests. The conflicting forces contrary to spiritual science in the world today are terribly difficult, and people basically do not know this at all. Of course this man [A.W. Hunzinger] has no clue about the nature of thought and feeling. This can be revealed only when we have a clear view, through spiritual science, into the whole perniciousness and destructiveness of such thinking. This man has no awareness whatsoever of any of that! However, he cannot be assigned any blame because of this, nor be disregarded; and such a fact must be taken quite objectively, like an earthquake, like a volcanic eruption, which also have destructive effects on humanity, though in a small area through outer physical means. But this man really cannot think.

And he is only one example of the most important people of our time who cannot think. He cannot think! Just imagine, he says that we of course give the human body to natural science; it does not work any other way because what should we theologians do with it? We cannot investigate the body, after all. This man has no idea of the fact that the spirit, when we really investigate it, is co-builder of the body, that the body simply cannot be separated and given away in this manner, as I explained yesterday in the public lecture.‡ This man gives away the body, but he also gives away the soul. Because it experiences in the same way as a steam engine, he retains, as he says explicitly, only the "person of freedom"—what is free in the human being—for theology. He magnanimously gives away the "person as nature";‡ he retains the "person of freedom." But now, after he has kept the person of freedom, he openly says, "'human beings as nature,' as a part of nature, lose their independence and freedom; everything they experience is suffering; they must suffer absolutely according to the law of nature."

Thus human beings lose their freedom through their nature. And now just think what else this theologian is keeping! First, he says, he gives people as nature to nature, and retains the person of freedom; but then he states that the person as nature is such that people lose independence and freedom as a part of nature, and "everything they experience is suffering; must suffer absolutely according to the law of nature." Now he has nothing more at all! Thus we cannot be surprised that Hunzinger speaks only in empty phrases from here on. But the good man does not notice this at all, and he is a typical example of how the most important people today notice nothing of the discontinuity of the thinking that has influence now. Humanity has arrived at a stage of evolution in which the thinking that should take place about physical life must be fructified by the thoughts that also have to do with the spiritual world; otherwise these thoughts will break apart at all the points where they correspond to the physical world, because the people who have a say today are not familiar with the simplest facts regarding world conditions.

We know that people are in a transitional period today. We do not mean this in the superficial sense in which people now speak of transitional periods, but in another sense. We are in the transitional period in which the old atavistic-clairvoyant instincts have died away, and in which conscious entrance into the spiritual worlds must be achieved. That is an obvious fact for spiritual scientists. The old atavistic-clairvoyant abilities that people had also gave them powerful thoughts. History tells little of these powerful thoughts, which greatly influenced human life in the Chaldean cultural epoch and the Egyptian cultural epoch. However little they stand up today in our estimation, they did stand up in that time. Influential thoughts—our time must recover thoughts again that are capable of influencing reality! But they can do so only if they are also fructified by the spiritual world, as thoughts were in ancient times. But people today are not made fruitful by way of the unconscious. Thus consciousness must arise if people are to really accept spiritual-scientific knowledge.

And even this man, in whom we can detect so easily the fact that he is deeply affected by the worst damage from the thoughtlessness of our time, and the fact that he causes immeasurable damage by infecting so many people with his thoughtlessness—even he is not a malevolent person. He is actually an insightful person. He is a person who does have the insight that people can have in our time, even if they are not able to progress in a certain way to the true spiritual world in the sense that I have talked about. Even people such as Jaurès cannot make such progress. But such people as this man who gave these religious lectures, even such people know that humanity has come to a dead end in a certain way; that we cannot continue with the thinking, feeling, and willing of the old convictions, the elements of the old worldview. And he also knows that this has led to materialism in recent times, and he knows that things must change. He is actually fundamentally quite radical because he talks about nineteenth century culture causing people to have concepts such as the craze for sports, convenience, and material possessions. This man speaks of all of these things, which are shadow sides of materialism; he speaks of all of them, and he is absolutely ready to say that the craze for sports, convenience and possessions as they appeared in the nineteenth century must be combated.

But he has only empty phrases for what he says here, because the following, "we believe our eyes; we do not believe our powers of knowledge," is found at the end of the first lecture. And so, an important, famous man today says the following. First, he says, quite correctly, that all things that happen here must be given another assessment; "they should no longer be the ultimate goal. There must no longer be salesmen for whom earning money is the end in itself; the enjoyment of life must no longer be the substance of life; there must no longer be people who live only for their health."

Thus he is very radical. We will certainly not claim such radical things to be from the spiritual-scientific standpoint; rather we will leave people their own freedom, and we know that if they understand karma and reincarnation and the rest that spiritual science contributes, they will find their way in the world. But this man who knows that people have gotten themselves into a dead end, says quite radically—it would be quite different if he took up spiritual science—that people should not earn money anymore, should not enjoy life anymore, should not live for their health anymore. Once I visited a sanatorium for people suffering from nervous diseases. It was run by a well-known man. I could see whole droves of patients marching past as they went to lunch. It appeared to me that the sickest, most fidgety person suffering from a nervous disease was the noted director of the hospital himself! (This is one case in a thousand.) Our theologian, however, is radical: he says that the substance of life must be different; no one must live simply for health anymore; and so on. But then he ends his lecture with the following lines: "That means everything we have been doing until now must still be *done*, but we must *think* differently while doing it."‡

This is reforming life! Imagine! This is reforming life for a person who looks so deeply into what is necessary: Everything must become different; that is, nothing itself needs to change, but our thinking about everything must change. "These things must not represent the most inner aspect, the goal, the highest value. We must *strive* for them with the same energy; we must *judge*"—that is, think of—"them on a different scale than before."‡

Now, one need add nothing to these things! It is necessary that we direct our attention to these things because they are present not only in one person, they are present today in our whole civilized world. And what people experience in their destiny comes from nothing more than this deficiency of thought and feeling; that is the karma of this deficiency of thought and feeling! We must first turn our attention to this, and as spiritual scientists must find the way not to listen to what soars and surges through the world today and what is accepted as being "of the highest value" by other impulses. We must really be able, rather, in this context to examine these main things, because they do have influence. We must do this without letting ourselves become befuddled by all sorts of other feelings that rule the world today and under whose influence today so many lies are told. We live in such a climate—I have said this before in Zurich—that this man, who hands down such rubbish to people so that by listening to him "these thought-beasts" enter into hearts and minds, is allowed to say, "This little book consists of twelve speeches that I gave last winter in..."[‡]—and now comes the city, which I do not want to name[‡]—"to more than a thousand attendees."

But—which city is quite trivial—this is happening now by the thousands! This must be understood. And it is necessary that we really lay the whole gravity and meaning of such a view before our souls.

After we have taken much from the spiritual world, we must realize what it should be to us, and through this also realize that we are to a certain extent looking at the counter-image of the worldview that is much more dominant in people today than we believe. Sadly, people live much too thoughtlessly today! That is what is such a hardship for the soul: to have to examine—forgive me for having to say this, but we must recognize it clearly—the mindlessness so widely spread in the world, the stupor in which humanity lives in relation to what has an effect and control in the evolutionary process of humanity. We must also retain the necessary nuances of feeling for the sort of truth that is in spiritual science by asking for these nuances of feeling through our examination of the counter-image. What is important, therefore, is not the search for all sorts of beautiful words that sound good, as if they came from high ideals, to be presented to humanity. Rather, of primary importance is the recognition of what our best contemporaries cannot recognize: that it is the spiritual world that must be opened up.

There are good reasons—and these reasons cannot be explained here because it would take too long—there are good reasons that for centuries humanity has resisted understanding Christianity in the spiritual sense. There was gnosis in the first centuries of Christianity. You all know that our spiritual science is not a revival of Gnosticism. Gnosticism made the first attempts in those days to arrive at a spiritual science;‡ but it was driven back because people did not want to see Christian truths in a spiritual light. This same bias continued and has become part of the natural-scientific method. Humanity has learned something from this, and has fought the possibility of understanding the spiritual for centuries.

But today the time has arrived when it is the most difficult for those who are very much part of contemporary culture (which is actually materialism, even though people do not admit it) to recognize a true spiritual world; that is, not just to talk vaguely about the spiritual world, but to recognize the spiritual world through examination. We must get it clear in our minds, however, that the recognition of this spiritual world is one of the most important things. Only then can the rest of it come—what must come in the form of a new basis of the ethical, social, and other practical orders of life—when we lay the groundwork through spiritual science and the knowledge of true spiritual facts and spiritual entities.

It was a great satisfaction to me that we could be together once again here in St. Gallen after a long time;‡ and I therefore saw it as my task specifically on this day to add to what you can learn from our literature, something of what must be talked about within our movement, perhaps personally from soul to soul, so that it can be understood correctly. Because within our movement it matters that we do not simply take up this or that idea from spiritual science in a catechism-like way; rather, it matters that we find the correct relationship of our souls to the knowledge from the spiritual world. Then spiritual science will be not only a science to us, but it will also truly become a way of life for us; it will be soul sustenance for us. It will be a soul sustenance that does not undermine our spiritual health and spiritual refreshment. Rather it will stimulate us in a way that we can still adapt harmoniously to the world, despite all the resistance from the outside world, which we have sought to understand to some extent today. I wanted to speak to you today about how we should interact on a soul level with spiritual science. If it was necessary to present contemporary phenomena, which can perhaps be illuminated by spiritual science only in this way, it was because only clear and plain insight into the course and development of the world in which we live will lead us as adherents of the anthroposophical worldview to the correct inner attitude and harmony. And from this inner harmony, harmony will arise in our lives. Indeed, our spiritual-scientific ideal is for this harmony to affect our lives through spiritual science more and more. I wanted to give you a small contribution today according to the spirit of this ideal.

LECTURE 7

The Connection between the Living and the Dead

Bern, November 9, 1916

THE GOAL OF OUR SPIRITUAL-SCIENTIFIC EFFORTS is to form ideas of how we as human beings can live together with spiritual worlds in a way similar to the way we relate to the physical world through our physical body with experiences and perceptions. Through our observations we are already able to take up knowledge that has come before our souls over the years. We know that the world that lies just behind the world of our sensory perceptions is the elemental world. Our impetus to will, conveyed through the physical body and our actions in the physical world, are directed to this elemental world. We could also give it a different name. We receive clear ideas from these suprasensible worlds only when we get a little bit involved with their characteristics; when we try to know what they mean for us as human beings. Our entire life between birth and death, and also the life that then proceeds between death and rebirth, depends on our connection with these various worlds spreading out around us.

For us, the elemental world should be the world that can be perceived through what we call imaginations. Thus we may also call this elemental world the imaginal world. For ordinary human life, under normal circumstances, human beings cannot bring the imaginal perceptions from the elemental world to consciousness. It does not mean that these imaginations are not there, or that we do not have a connection with the elemental world and receive imaginations from it at any moment of our sleeping or waking life. These imaginations flood continually through us unnoticed. And just as when we open our eyes or ears to the outside world we have sensations of color and light and perceptions of sound, so too, we have continuous impressions of the elemental world, which cause imaginations in the etheric body. These imaginations differ from ordinary thinking in that with ordinary, everyday human thinking, only the human head is involved as an instrument that processes and experiences; whereas, with imaginations, on the other hand, almost our entire organism is involved, but especially the etheric organism. These imaginations—we could call them unconscious—are continuously running through our etheric organism, and they become conscious only with trained esoteric perception.

Even though these imaginations do not directly and immediately enter our consciousness in daily life, they are not without significance to us. They are actually much more important in our entire life than sensory perceptions, because we are much more intensively, much more intimately connected to our imaginations than to sensory perceptions. We do not receive many imaginations from the mineral kingdom. We receive more imaginations from what we develop in our coexistence with the plant world and the animal world. But by far the greatest part of what lives in our etheric body as imaginations comes from our relationships with our fellow humans and from everything that results in our life from these relationships. Indeed, our whole relationship to our fellow humans and the way we stand by them is basically founded on the imaginations that are always a result of the way we encounter another person. These do not assert themselves, however, as imaginations to ordinary consciousness, as I already pointed out. Rather, they assert themselves in the sympathies and antipathies that play such an extensive role in our lives. We develop these sympathies and antipathies, to a lesser or greater degree, to what is close to us as human beings in the world: in indefinite feelings; in inclinations or disinclinations only hinted at; in all that develops into friendship; into love that grows in such a way that we believe we cannot live at all without this or that person.

All of this is based on the imaginations that are continually brought up in our etheric body through living with our fellow human beings. And we always carry in our life something that cannot exactly be called memory, because it is something much more real than memory; we carry within us these, let us say, heightened memories—these imaginations that we have received from all of the impressions of the people we have been with, and that we receive continuously. We carry them all in us, and they basically form a major part of what we call our inner life; not the inner life that remains as clear memory, but the inner life that asserts itself in a general feeling, a general mood, a general view of the world and of our coexistence with the world. We could only pass coldly by what is in our world if we did not develop an imaginative life in togetherness with other beings; that is, with other people.

What we call the interest of our soul in our surroundings is something that asserts itself and that we must particularly heed as especially belonging to the elemental world and our etheric life. What is advantageously present in the powers of our etheric body asserts itself when we are immediately captivated in certain cases by an interest in another person. Such an interest, in the way it develops between one person and another, is based on very specific relationships that appear between the etheric of one person and the etheric of the other, and that cause the playing back and forth of imaginations. We live with this imagination and these interests (their effects, their strength, and so on, we are often not able to account for, or are able to account for only vaguely), which we do not notice at all, because our life is not ordinarily inspired, but rather proceeds in a more or less dull manner.

We are part of the elemental world with all these things. We are part of this elemental world in such a way that we truly have our own etheric body from this world, which is the instrument for relating with this elemental world. Through our etheric body we are developing relationships, not only with other etheric bodies that are part of other physical beings; but through our etheric body we are related also to spiritual beings of an elemental nature, and specifically to those that can arouse imagination—unconscious or conscious—for us human beings. People differ from one another by their relationships, one with certain elemental entities, another with other elemental entities. This can also happen in such a way that, for example, a person's relationships to certain elemental entities can coincide with the relationships of another person to the same elemental entities.

But we must hold fast to the fact that whereas we always have a relationship, to a certain extent, with a great number of elemental entities, each of us has a particularly strong relationship to an elemental entity that is more or less the counter-image of our own etheric body. One could say that our own etheric body has an intimate relationship with a certain etheric being. Just as our etheric body (what we call our etheric body from birth until death), by being integrated into the physical body, develops its own relationship to the physical world, so this etheric being (which is in a way the counter-image, the opposite pole, of our own etheric body) conveys our connections to the entire elemental world, to the surrounding cosmic-elemental world.

Thus we see an elemental world that we ourselves are part of through our etheric body, with which we relate to, and have concrete connections to, specific elemental entities. Within this elemental world we come to know entities that are actually just as real as people and animals are here in the physical world, but which have not reached physical incarnation; rather, they have reached only the etheric state, and their closest corporeality is in fact etheric corporeality. Just as we move among physical people here, so too, do we continuously move among such elemental entities. Some are not connected to us, but have connections to other people instead. But a certain number are particularly close to us, and are related to us in the most intimate way, and mediate our contact with the cosmic-elemental world.

We ourselves are beings such as these elemental entities right after we go through death's gate, when we still carry our etheric body with us for a few days. We ourselves have become such an elemental being, to a certain extent. Now and then, I have described this process of going through the gate of death. The more specifically we examine this process, the more specific the imaginations it produces, because the impressions we receive immediately after passing through the gate of death live in imaginations, assert themselves as imaginations. Now, more specifically, it turns out that a certain interaction occurs immediately after death between our etheric body and its etheric counter-image. The fact that our etheric body is taken from us some days after death is based mainly on the fact that our etheric body is to some extent attracted and absorbed by its etheric counter-image and then becomes one with it, so that we in fact lay aside our etheric body some days after death; consign it, so to speak, to our etheric counter-image.

When our etheric body is taken from us by our cosmic image, quite particular relationships come about from what is taken from us in this way and the other elemental entities with which we have had relationships in life. What comes about is an interaction between what our etheric body has become, together with its counter-image, and the other elemental entities that accompanied us from birth until death—a kind of interplay that could be compared to the one between a sun and its planetary system. Our etheric body creates a sort of sun, so to speak, with its cosmic counter-image, and the other elemental entities surround this sun like a sort of planetary system. And when this interplay takes place, the forces are created that add what our etheric body can bring to the elemental world in the correct way through a gradual becoming. This process, which we usually label with the abstract word "dissolving," is fundamentally the effect of the forces that arise from this sun-planetary system we leave behind. What we have achieved for our etheric body, what we have acquired for this etheric body, in the course of our earthly life, gradually becomes part of the spiritual world, weaving itself into the forces of the spiritual world; and we must be completely clear that every thought, every idea, every feeling that we have on earth, even though they remain hidden, are important to the spiritual world. They will go with our etheric body and become elements of this spiritual world when the coherence of our etheric body is torn apart upon passing through the threshold of death.

We do not live in vain. The fruits of our life and how we integrate them into the thoughts we acquire and the feelings we experience are assimilated into the cosmos. This truth is something we must take into our feeling, into our perceiving, if we want to conduct ourselves correctly in the spiritual-scientific movement. One is not a spiritual scientist by simply knowing about certain things, but rather by feeling into the spiritual world through insight; by feeling oneself to be an element of the spiritual world in a very specific way; by knowing that what you now cultivate as thought has meaning for the whole universe because it will be given over in its corresponding form to the universe upon your death.

We can interact in one way or another, as I have described, with what is committed to the universe after a person's death. And some of the ways in which the dead are present to those left behind in earth-life is due to the fact that the etheric individualities, who are now actually isolated from their true human identities, send their imaginations back to the living. If the living are sensitive enough, or are in some extraordinary state, or have prepared themselves in a normal way through appropriate spiritual training, then the effects of what is given to the spiritual world by the dead can also arise for the living in a conscious way as the effects of an imaginal nature.

A connection remains after death, however, between what is the actual human individuality and the etheric aspect from which it has just separated—a connection that is an actual interaction. This can be seen most clearly by the fact that through spiritual training one can have real contact with one and another person who has died. A certain kind of communication may then take place. The dead person conveys to his etheric body what he himself wish to transmit to us while we are still here in the physical world. For only by transmitting it to the etheric body—inscribing it, so to speak, into the etheric body—only by this means can we who are here in the physical have perceptions of the dead in terms of what we call "imaginations." As soon as we really have imaginations of the dead person, the etheric body of the one who has died acts as the "change-over switch" (if you will allow me to use this simplistic, much too mechanical expression.) One must not think, however, that we thus will have less warm-hearted relations with the dead because a "switch" must be present.

Just as those who we encounter in the outer world let their character be conveyed through their physical image, which is called up in us through our own eyes, so too the conveyance through the etheric body is something very similar. We see what the dead person wishes to have approach us by receiving it along the roundabout way through their etheric body. This etheric body is outside of them, but they have a deep connection to it in such a way that they can inscribe what lives within them into this etheric body, and we can read it there as imagination.

Of course, if someone who is spiritually trained wishes to come into contact with the dead through their etheric body in this way, that means that connections have been established either in the last life between birth and death or in previous incarnations. These connections have moved the soul of the person still living here on earth to the point that this imagination can make an impression on him or her. And that can happen only if a direct soul interest was present in a very specific, intensive way for the dead themselves. Soul interest, whether it is noticed or not, must be the mediator between the living and the dead if contact is to take place. (We will discuss the latter instance in a moment.) The soul interest must be such that we truly carry something of the dead within us, so to speak; that the dead constituted at least a part of our own experience.

Only when we train spiritually can we create a substitute for this; for example, by letting the handwriting, or something else in which the individuality of the dead lives, affect us; this seems external at first, but it can be transformed into something more internal through spiritual training. And it will be possible to the extent that we have acquired a practice of coming into relationship with the individuality, and to the extent this individuality has put himself or herself into the handwriting, has settled into the handwriting. Or, we must have the opportunity to engage ourselves with active interest with the feelings of the physical survivors, take part in their pain and in the whole interest that they have in the dead. By taking these up into ourselves with our interest, we can make our own souls ready to read into the imagination I have spoken of, the concrete feelings from the dead that are flowing over and living within their dear family members.

Now we must be clear that noticing this imagination, which flows from the etheric body, depends to a certain extent on spiritual training or on specific relationships; and that just because people do not notice it does not mean that it is any less present. We can say that people living here in the physical world are not only surrounded by elemental forces in the form of imaginations, which originate from the physical body of a living person, but that our etheric body is also continuously filled with imaginations that we take into ourselves, even if we do not notice it, which originate from those who have some kind of connection to us and who have passed through death's gate before we have. We can say that just as we have a connection with the air around us as physical bodies in physical life, just so are we in relationship to the entire elemental world of the dead. We do not get to know our human life if we do not gain knowledge of these relationships. These relationships are, however, of such a subtle kind that they go completely unnoticed by most people. But who would deny the fact that people do not always remain exactly the same between birth and death?

If we take just one look back at our life, we will notice that we have gone different directions at various times in our life. Even if we imagine our life has taken such a seemingly consistent course, numerous events have occurred. Although these events may not exactly have led our lives in very different directions (which could also have been the case at times); they still have enhanced our lives through joy or suffering, in one way or another, and brought us into other relationships, in one way or another. We know that when we go to a new place, we can have a different sense of well-being, even from the different composition of the air. These differing soul moods that we move through in the course of our lives originate from the influences of the elemental world; and they come in no small part from the influences that come from those dead with whom we previously had a relationship on earth. If someone meets a friend or someone else in life with whom a relationship is formed, for whom a favor must be done or perhaps also some reproof or criticism given, this is due to the influence of certain forces. Whoever recognizes the occult order in the world knows that when two people are brought together to perform a task, sometimes one, and sometimes several, of those who passed through death's gate earlier were involved with this coming together.

Our life does not become less free as a result. No one who does not want to look foolish would say, "How can people be free when they have to eat?" It is just as incorrect to say that we become less free when our souls continually receive effects from the elemental world in the way described. But truly, just as we are connected to warmth and cold, to what becomes our food, to the air around us, so too are we connected to the elemental world, but primarily with what comes to us from those who died before us. We can truly say that human beings' effects on their fellow humans do not stop when they pass through death's gate; through their etheric body, with which they themselves remain connected, they send their imaginations to those with whom they had a connection. Indeed, this world that we are speaking of, though it remains unnoticed in daily life for good reason, is a much more real one for our human life than the one we usually call "real." So much for this elemental world today.

Another kingdom that is continuously around us, and to which we also belong as we do the elemental world, can be called the soul world. The name does not matter. We are always connected to the elemental world in a waking state. When we are sleeping—when the I and astral body are outside the physical and etheric body—the physical body lying in bed and our etheric body are indirectly connected to this elemental world and we have the most direct connection with the higher soul world that I am talking about, we just do not have conscious awareness of it. The connection is there during sleep when our astral body is free around us; it is also there when we are awake, though then the connection is mediated by the forces that the physical body has attracted to itself; that is, it is not a direct connection.

We find beings (we call them soul beings; philosophers of the Middle Ages called them heavenly beings) in this soul world that are just as real, indeed even more real, than we are during our life between birth and death. These beings do not need to be incarnated in a physical body nor even incarnated in an etheric body. Instead, they live in what we are accustomed to calling the astral body as their lowest corporeality. We are always in very close connection to a great number of such pure astral beings during our life and after our death. People differ from one another in that different people have a connection to different astral beings. Thus, two people can have relationships with the same astral beings—and each of them, in turn, with others—but both have relationships in common with one or more astral beings.

From the time that we lay aside our etheric body after passing through the gate of death, we human beings are part of the world in which such astral beings exist. Then we are with such beings in the soul world with our individuality, and our immediate surroundings are those beings of the soul world. Thus we are in relationship to what is contained in the elemental world in such a way that we can cause within it what elicits imaginations in the way I described. But the elemental world is then outside of us in a certain way; we could also say that it is now "below" us. We use a part of it to interact with the rest of the world, but we ourselves belong directly to the world that we have just described as the soul world. We now have contact with the beings of the soul world, and thus also those who have gone through death's gate and, after some days, have laid aside their etheric body. Just as we continually receive influences from the elemental world, even if we do not notice it, so too, we continually receive influences directly into our astral body from this soul world that I am now describing. Only these direct influences that we receive from the soul world can be inspirations. (Of the indirect influences via the etheric body we have already spoken.)

Now it will become clear to us what sort of influence the soul world has on us if I first, with a few words, touch on the way in which this influence appears to the spiritually trained who are in a position to receive inspirations from the spiritual world. They appear to them in such a way that they can become aware of these inspirations only when they can take something into themselves from the being that wishes to inspire them; something of the characteristics, the life tendency and life direction of this being. Should the spiritually trained wish to develop a conscious relationship with a dead person—not only via the etheric body, but also in this direct way through inspiration—it is necessary for them to carry more in their soul than what can be generated through interest and sympathy. The spiritually trained must be able to transform themselves in a certain way, at least for a short time, so that they take on something of the habits, of the behavior of the being—let us say the human being—with whom they wish to communicate. They must be able to settle in so that they can say to themselves, "I have taken on the habits to such an extent that I could do what this person could do; feel what this person could feel; sense what this person could sense; will what this person could will." It has to do with "could"! The possibility must be there. We must be able to be more intimately together with the dead. For the spiritually trained there are many ways if the dead themselves allow it. We must simply be clear that those beings, who are part of the world we are calling the soul world, actually are in relationship to our world in a completely different way than we humans are here in the physical body. There are, thus, very specific conditions for interacting with these beings; and very specific conditions also exist for interacting with the dead as long as they are in the astral body, that is, as astral beings. I can draw your attention to particular examples. What we human beings develop here for our life in the physical body through relationships to other human beings, which occur directly during earthly life, holds another kind of interest for the dead.

Here on earth we develop sympathies and antipathies. Let us be very clear that the sympathies and antipathies that we develop here in the physical life are influenced by the physical body and its relationships; they are influenced by our vanity, our egotism. Let us be clear about how many relationships of a certain nature we develop to various people out of vanity and egotism; and out of other things that are based on our physical earth-life here. We love some people, and we hate some people. In most cases we think very little about the reasons for our love and hate, our sympathies and antipathies; indeed we often avoid thinking much about these sympathies and antipathies, for the simple reason that highly unpleasant truths would usually emerge. Were we to pursue what is actually expressed within our not loving a particular person, for example, we would sometimes be compelled to attribute to ourselves so much prejudice, so much vanity, or other qualities, that we are afraid to do so. And thus we do not become clear about why we hate this or that person. But, indeed, with love it is often quite similar. With love, however, interests and sympathies and antipathies develop that, in truth, have significance only for our earthly life. Yet it is out of all this that we act. We arrange our lives according to these interests.

Now it would be quite wrong to believe that the dead could have the same interest in what we take up on earth in the form of ephemeral interests and sympathies and antipathies that are under the influence of our physical life on earth. Truly, the dead are obliged to see these things from a very different perspective. And if we question ourselves further about how we are influenced in judging our fellow human beings by our subjective feelings and by what results from our interests, our vanity, our egotism, and so on, we may not believe that the dead would have an interest, either in our relationships of this nature to other people or to every behavior that then results from such interests. But on the other hand, we also may think that the dead do not see what lives in our souls, because it really does live in our souls. The dead see it; the dead take part in it—but the dead see something else; the dead have completely different judgment than the living do. They look at human beings much differently—and that is a very particular main point: how the dead see the people who are here on earth. We had better not believe that the dead do not have an active interest in human beings. They do, because the human world is part of the whole cosmos; our life is part of it. And just as we are also interested in the subordinate kingdoms in the physical world, so, too, are the dead intensely interested in the human world. They send their impulses into it; they affect the world through the living. We gave an example just a short while ago of how the dead have an effect after they have passed through death's gate.

But the dead see one thing, first and foremost. They see how a person is who follows impulses of hate—who hates this or that person based on purely personal intentions. The dead see this. But the dead also observe clearly, according to their way of seeing and knowing, the part Ahriman plays in influencing people to hate. The dead see Ahriman influencing people in this way. They also see how Lucifer influences people when they are vain here. That is what is significant, that the dead see the human being in connection with the ahrimanic-luciferic world. Thus, what often colors completely our human judgments is omitted for the dead. We see this or that person, whom we inevitably judge one way or another; we blame them for whatever we find reprehensible about them. The dead do not immediately blame people for these things; rather, they see how we are tempted by Ahriman and Lucifer. That perspective causes (for them) what we can call a "damping down" of the sharply differentiated feelings we have for certain people in our physical earthly life. For the dead, it is much more a sort of general human love. But do not think that because of this the dead cannot criticize evil—that is, that they cannot recognize evil. They do see it, but they are able to trace it back to its source, to see its inner connections.

But all of this that I have described to you also means that trained people can consciously come near to the dead only by really freeing themselves from personal feelings of sympathy and antipathy in relation to individual people; by not letting themselves become dependent on personal feelings of sympathy and antipathy in their soul. Just imagine that a trained clairvoyant wishes to approach someone who has died, whoever that may be, so that the deceased's inspirations can become part of the clairvoyant's consciousness; but the person living here on earth feels very particular hatred for someone else—a hate that originates from personal relationships alone. Indeed, as our hands avoid fire, so the dead avoid such a person who hates in such a way for personal reasons! The dead cannot come near because hatred affects them like fire. In order to come into conscious relationship to the dead, we must be able to make ourselves independent from personal sympathies and antipathies, as they are in our life.

Thus, you will also comprehend that the whole connection of the dead to the living depends on our inclinations here in our life on earth. This is true insofar as the relationship is based on inspiration—which is always there, even if it is not noticed, and always lives in the human astral body, so that humans are always in connection with the dead in this direct way. If you have a misanthropic disposition; if you do not take an interest in and have sympathy for our world; and, specifically, if you do not have open, non-judgmental interest in and sympathy for our world and our fellow humans, then the dead cannot access you as they would wish to. They cannot move into your soul in the correct manner; or if it does happen, it is made extremely difficult for them, and they are able to do it only with suffering and pain.

This coexistence of the dead with the living is quite complicated indeed. But you see from this that human beings have an effect after death, beyond time, including by directly inspiring living people on the physical plane. And it is absolutely true that those who live on earth at any given time are deeply dependent—specifically with respect to their inner habitual qualities, the way they think, the way they feel, what tendencies they have—on the people who died before them and who had relationships with them in life, or with whom they created some kind of connection even after death, which can occur under certain circumstances but is more difficult.

A certain part of the world order and of the progress of humanity is completely based on the dead having an inspiring influence on the life of human beings on earth. Indeed, in our instincts, there really is knowledge of this influence, the knowledge that it must be so. We can see this specifically when we observe cultural practices that were widespread earlier and are now dying away because humanity continuously advances to other, new forms of life in the course of its evolution. People knew earlier, when they sensed more of the actual reality of spiritual worlds, much more about the necessities that exist for life as a whole. They knew that the living need the dead; need the impulses of the dead, even in their habits.

Think back to earlier times, when it was the custom for the father to ensure that the son took over his business; that the son carried on in the same way. A connecting bond was formed through the physical world because the son had followed in his father's footsteps; a relationship was created between the activity of the son and the activity of the father, and the father continued to have an effect in the son long after the father had died. This was the basis of much in life then. And now, if whole communities place great value on various tangible objects being passed on within a class or within the families of this class, it is based on the knowledge of the necessity that the life habits of those who came before must extend to the life habits of those who come later. The life habits of those who came earlier have matured to the point that they come from them only after they have gone through death's gate; only then do they become mature.

These things are ending, as you know, as the human race progresses, and one can see a time approaching in which these inheritances, these conservative conditions, will no longer play a part. The physical bonds will no longer be present in the same way they were earlier. Instead, people must take that much more from spiritual-scientific knowledge of what will lift the matter into their consciousness, so that people can consciously take up the life habits and customs of earlier times that are still needed, so that life may continually advance. We are now living in a transitional time—since the beginning of the fifth post-Atlantean period—which has brought chaos. But relationships will come again later in which people will take up what comes before them in a much more conscious way through knowledge of spiritual-scientific truths. People have already done it unconsciously, instinctively. But what is still instinctive today must be transformed into consciousness. We do not pay attention to it; but those who study history in a spiritual way could notice (if they only went into the real connections, and not into the dreadful abstractions that dominate the so-called humanities today) that what is taught during an era carries the character of what goes unconsciously, instinctively, so to speak, into what the deceased send streaming into the present. If we know one day how to really study the great pedagogical thoughts spread by the bearers of pedagogy in an era—by the true bearers, not by those who are charlatans—then we will see that this fundamental pedagogical thinking originates from the shared transfer of the habits of those who died a while before, who send their habits streaming in.

Thus, having moved into the astral world, the dead have a much more intimate coexistence with people because what enters into the astral body reaches even further into our inner nature than what enters into the etheric body. The dead have a much more intimate coexistence with people than do etheric bodies or some elemental beings of another kind. But you can see from this that the time following human life is always determined by the preceding time; that the preceding time becomes more and more a part of the time following. Strange as it may seem, we become truly mature enough only after our death to affect other people directly by having an effect on their inner nature. What we should not do in earthly life—impose our own habits on another person who is mature (I mean spiritually mature, not mature in the customary sense)—is actually proper after we have passed through death's gate and fulfills the requirements for the continued evolution of humanity.

These things happen beyond all else that is contained in karma and in the laws governing incarnation. And if you ask about the secret causes of people's actions, you will find that many of them, though not all, perform those actions because certain impulses flow down from those who died twenty, thirty years ago, or even longer. These are the secret but real interrelations between the physical and the spiritual worlds. Something of what we carry through death's gate matures, not only for us, but also for the rest of the world. It is mature enough to affect other people only from a certain moment on; but it does become more and more mature.

Now please note that I am not speaking of outer phenomena but rather of inner, real, spiritual effects. When someone remembers the habits of a deceased father or grandfather, and then describes these habits in the physical plane from memory—that is not what I mean; that is something different. I mean the inspired influences not perceptible to conventional consciousness that assert themselves in our habits and in our most intimate nature. Much in our life is based on the fact that we see ourselves, at times, as forced to free ourselves from the well-meaning influences that come from the dead. Indeed we secure much of our inner freedom by having to free ourselves from influences coming from one side or the other. Inner soul conflicts, which we often do not know the cause of, become clear to us when we see them in the light that comes from such knowledge. If one were to use a trivial word, one could say that the past "rumbles"; the souls of the past really rumble within us.

These things are simply truths that we see through spiritual sight. But people today have a very particular relationship to these truths—that is, they are afraid of knowing the truth. It was not always so; those who study history in a spiritual way know this. People now have a terrible fear—not a conscious one, but an unconscious fear. And this unconscious fear of the knowledge that we are part of the spiritual world, that mysterious connections exist not only between souls here in the physical world but also between souls here and in the other world—this holds people back. That is one part of the fear that instinctively holds people back from spiritual science. They are afraid to know the truth. But they do not know that by not wanting to learn the truth, they interfere in a disturbing way with the whole evolution of the world and thus, of course, they interfere most of all with the life that then must be lived between death and rebirth, when these connections must be understood.

What lives in us becomes even more mature, when it is no longer only inspiration, but when it becomes intuition, in the sense that I use the word in *How to Know Higher Worlds*. But intuition can be a being only—above all, only—if it has, let us say, to use a paradoxical term, a "spirit body." Human beings can have intuitive effects on other beings in this sense (that is, on beings who are still embodied here in physical life) only when they have laid aside the astral body, when they themselves belong wholly to the spiritual world; that is, decades after their death. Then they can have an effect on other people through intuition, too, and not just through inspiration as I have described. In this way they first have an effect spiritually as an I that is now in the spiritual world in the I of one who is still on earth. Before, they had worked as inspiration into the astral body, or indirectly through the etheric body into the etheric body, of earthly people. One who has been dead for decades can, as an I, have a direct effect, which of course can also be mediated by the other bodies at the same time. Then the person's individuality has grown to be able not just to settle into people's habits, but actually into their viewpoints! This may be an uncomfortable, a quite unpleasant reality to today's prejudiced sensibility; but it is simply a reality. Our viewpoints, which originate in the I, are continuously under the influence of those who are long dead. Those who are long dead live in our views. But through this, the continuity of evolution is maintained by the spiritual world. This is a necessity; otherwise, the thread of viewpoints would be continually broken.

Forgive me for bringing in something personal at this point; but I bring this personal anecdote for purely objective reasons, because only through a concrete example can such a reality be completely understood. In fact, no one should express views as personal opinions, however honestly we come by them. Those who are quite honestly grounded in the esoteric, and who are experienced in the requirements of spiritual science, will not impose their opinions on the world. Instead, such individuals do everything not to directly impose their opinions on the world because the opinions acquired under the influence of one's personal temperament will be able to have an effect only thirty or forty years after one's death. They have an effect such that they enter the soul in the same way that the impulses of the *zeitgeist*, the archai, enter the soul. Their personal views have become so mature that they can really have an effect and correspond to the objective course of things. That is why it is necessary for those who are grounded in esotericism to avoid making personal proselytes or personally recruiting followers for their opinions.

The general custom today (that once people acquire an opinion, they can hardly wait to make propaganda for it) could not be striven for by a true, practicing spiritual scientist. And here is my personal anecdote. It is truly no accident, but rather something necessarily connected to my life, that I did not begin by writing down my own views and telling the world. Rather, I wrote *Goethe's World View*,‡ completely in the spirit and sense of Goethe's worldview, in order not to present the view of a living person. Even if that living person is oneself, we could never give true legitimacy to teaching spiritual science to the extent that I am trying to do here; rather, it is a necessary to put ourselves completely into the objective course of world evolution. So I did not write my own theory of knowledge but rather *Goethe's Theory of Knowledge*,‡ a theory of knowledge implied by Goethe's worldview. From this you can see how the evolution of the human being continues, in a certain way; how those things mature that human beings acquire here. This maturing is not just for a person's own life, advancing along the path of karma; it also becomes more and more mature for the world. We continue to have an effect on the world when we are mature enough after a certain time in the spiritual world to send imaginations into people's habits, and, after a longer time, inspirations. And only after a yet longer time are we ready and mature enough to send intuitions to the most intimate part of human lives—into their views. We should by no means think, here on Earth, that our views come out of nowhere, or that they develop anew in every era. They grow from the ground in which our soul is rooted, which is, in fact, identical to the influences of those long dead.

Through the knowledge of such facts, I believe that human life will truly experience the enrichment it needs, according to the whole character and sense of our current time and into the near future. Much of the old has rotted away, and the new must develop, as I have often explained. But human beings cannot enter this new era without the impulses that come to us through spiritual science. The perception of the universe and of the other beings in the universe that we acquire through spiritual science depends on our life being determined differently by spiritual science than it was before. What we are always part of, and what humanity will be called to realize as it develops further during the Earth-stage through the fifth, sixth, and seventh post-Atlantean periods, shall become living in us through spiritual science.

These things, which are connected to the enrichment and stimulation of humanity's world-feeling and deepened presence in life—these ideas I wanted to convey today. This is what I wanted to inspire in your hearts as we are able to be together again after some time. I hope that we can be here together more often to talk about similar things, so that through our souls we can contribute to the evolution of humanity that is striven for by spiritual science.

Lecture 8

The Relationship of Human Beings to the Spiritual World

Zürich, December 3, 1916

From the public lecture yesterday[‡] you could see how the spiritual world, where we exist between death and rebirth, and the physical world are intertwined; how the spiritual world and physical world also fundamentally intertwine in our so-called physical life between birth and death. We ourselves give direction, so to speak, to the manner in which we are born with such and such characteristics by having a relationship between death and rebirth to what happens here in the physical world; that is, with the hereditary stream that finally leads to our birth.

We examined evolution in a rather outward way yesterday; now we can examine it in a more inner way by attempting to bring before our soul the relationship of the human being to the spiritual world from another viewpoint. We live here in the physical world between birth and death. We are familiar with this physical world through our sense perceptions. Indeed, this is trivial, one hardly need say it: if we did not have our sense organs, we would not be aware of our relationship to the physical world. But everything of the relationship to the physical world that is conveyed to us through our sense organs, of course, breaks away from us when we go through death's gate. We can say that gaining knowledge of the physical world is our task between birth and death; we are integrated into this physical body in order to gain knowledge of the physical world.

Now, we are not members of the physical world only; rather, we are members of spiritual worlds as well. The closest spiritual world, which borders our physical world, so to speak, is the one that we have become accustomed to calling the etheric world, or also the elemental world. (Whether or not this expression is appropriate is not so important here.) This elemental world is initially unknown to people because we are living in the physical world. The elemental world is the first suprasensory world, but that fact does not make it less meaningful for us than the physical world, the sensory world. As soon as a sense for this elemental world arises in people, which happens when they are able to perceive imaginatively, it is clear to them that this elemental world is just as richly populated with beings as is the physical world. Human beings themselves, because they have an etheric body, are part of the elemental world. The relationships in the elemental world are only somewhat different than the relationships in the physical world.

First, I would like to comment on the fact that perception in the elemental world can take place only when human beings are able to free themselves completely from what makes them earthly humans. This disengagement from what makes a human being an earthly being is, generally speaking, not difficult. However, it is more difficult for human beings today than it was in prehistoric times. We all know of prehistoric atavistic clairvoyance. This was primarily so because humans could free themselves from what made them earthly humans. As earthly humans, we are composed of only a very small amount of solid matter. We are made primarily of fluid. In the moment when we can emancipate ourselves from what is solid in us, when we can just feel into the part of ourselves that is fluid, the imaginative aspect can begin to surface. Existing only in a solid state actually prevents us from knowing through imaginative perception about what is around us as the elemental world. This imaginative perception, which has been lost, will indeed return to humanity. The lost imaginative clairvoyance from the past was of an unconscious, dream-like nature; what will form more and more in our fifth post-Atlantean period is a fully conscious imaginative seeing that will incorporate itself into people through completely natural development.

I now come back to what I said earlier, that our relationship to the elemental world is different from our relationship to the familiar physical world. I would first of all like to give an example that will substantiate this for you. In the physical world we form our relationships to various beings, at least seemingly, out of free human choice:

we form friendships; we create other relationships to the beings around us. In the elemental world, in which we exist through the etheric body, this is not the case in directly the same way; rather, we are in close connection to certain other elemental beings more or less through our whole life. Thus we can really compare our relation as independent elemental beings (which we are because of our etheric body) to a number of other elemental beings, which in fact accompany us through our whole life, to the relationship of the sun to the planets orbiting it. Our own etheric body is a sort of sun-elemental being, and it is accompanied by a host of elemental beings, which belong to it as the planets do the sun, so that these elemental beings form a sort of sevenness with it, as the planets form a sort of sevenness with the sun, according to the old views.

Now, a continuous interplay between our elemental companions and ourselves exists during our entire physical life between birth and death. Not only does our state of health depend on the way in which our elemental or etheric body relates to its "satellites," but also our relationship to the outer world, to certain outer beings (namely, other human beings). Our health is regulated by the interplay of relationships between these companions and our own etheric body. A kind of medicine will exist in the future that will consider very specifically what I have just addressed. There will be a medical-physiological point of view that will determine how one or the other satellite stands in relation to the etheric body, and thereby we will be able to evaluate the state of illness or health. What is called illness today is, in truth, only the outer physical picture of what is actually there. In reality, in illness some irregularity is present in what I have compared with a planetary system, and the illness is only a reflection of this irregularity.

We could say that those who know such things should begin teaching theories on healing illnesses today. We could say *Hic Rhodus, hic salta!* ["Prove what you can do, here and now!"],[‡] and esotericism should show its skill here. Indeed, esotericism will do so the moment its legs are cut free, because one cannot dance if one's legs are bound; and the binding of the legs is the presence of contemporary materialism, which has occupied all of medical science. This cannot be improved by one or the other person performing isolated actions, but it will come about only by a large number of people who, through their common will, are strong enough to bring about such a system of medical practice, one that incorporates spiritual principles.

It is particularly important in this respect to recognize that it was not for nothing that Paul spoke his immensely important words—words which were actually never understood correctly because people believe themselves to be Christians when in reality they are not at all. Paul explained that sin came into the world by law; that is, sin is there by law.[‡] In a further sense, that which disturbs order, is there by law. These things can only be hinted at today since generally in our materialistic time whenever something is out of order, people cry out for a law without knowing that precisely what is out of order comes from the laws that are made. But, as I said, this can only be hinted at because much, much more is involved in understanding these things. I said that people only believe that they are Christians. Countless people read such a thing as this from Paul, but it is rarely understood.

By virtue of the fact that we are etheric beings, we exist in an elemental world, and a certain system is in close relation to us. This system of the elemental beings, etheric beings, which accompanies us, is also the system of beings that first extricate our etheric body from our physical body when we pass through death's gate. Because of their powers, because they are organized in a certain way, they can then move us into the elemental world. This elemental world, as I have already indicated, can be perceived completely through imaginative knowledge. In this elemental world there are a number of beings, which can be called nature spirits. But also all those are there who recently passed physically through death's gate just a short time ago, as we know, within just a few days. Then what we call the etheric body is given over to the elemental world. It is laid aside like a second corpse.

But we must not believe that this second body, which is laid aside there, is quickly destroyed in the elemental world. This is not the case; rather, the etheric body dissipates, as it were, into the elemental world. But this dissipating, this becoming thinner and thinner, does not mean it is not perceptible to other beings who can perceive imaginatively. Thus this elemental body, this etheric body, is primarily always perceptible to those who have stepped through the gate of death. The person lays this elemental body aside and now lives between death and rebirth but remains in connection to this cast-off etheric body. It is not as it is with the physical body, to which a person loses connection when it is laid aside. With the elemental body, the opposite is the case: the person retains the connection, and this connection that the person has to the elemental, to the etheric body, can extend down into the physical world.

Now if a person here in the physical world has made the soul receptive by acquiring imaginative perception of the elemental world, then the soul can also maintain a conscious connection with the dead in imaginations, which of course appear much more subtly than conventional imaginations. This is conscious connection with the dead. However, what becomes conscious was actually always present unconsciously if there was a relationship between the one who remained behind here in the physical world and the one who has entered the spiritual world. Let us suppose we have lost a beloved person to death. Whether we know it or not (those who develop imaginative perception can know it) the dead affect us when they send their will into the etheric body that was cast off, as into a mirror; and the mirror then sends rays to us. The dead person has an effect, indirectly through the elemental and etheric body, on the living person. This is the effect, which is indirect, so to speak.

If I would characterize how this indirect effect is expressed, I would say it is expressed within our ideas that we carry through the world. Indeed, people usually know, especially in our materialistic time, only the ideas that represent outer physical reality to them. But among the ideas that we carry thus through the world, there perpetually exist some that are subtle in a way; some that are not directly perceptible. People simply do not notice them. If we were accustomed to intimately take note of our soul life; and if we did not allow more gross ideas that flow from the physical world to predominate over the more subtle soul life, then we would see that more subtle ideas are, in fact, always present. And they come from those who had been connected to us, who went through the gate of death before us, and especially those who, shortly after they went through death's gate, were able to transmit their deeds, actions, and thoughts to us through reflection.

Thus, for a time we carry in our imagination and ideas the being of the dead, due to the fact that in the spiritual world we as etheric beings belong to the elemental world. If we speak of "monism," and wish to be down-to-earth about it, then we must speak primarily of the monism that I just mentioned; of the unity or union formed from the interaction of the living and the dead. In truth, those who have gone through the gate of death have not left us at all. They are much nearer to us than we think.

People develop more and more as they live through the time between death and rebirth, and they can also have a direct effect on the world here. We perceive after a certain time, as an effect of the dead who have gone on, that their rays of force permeate our soul life. But these rays, this direct effect, cannot settle into our imaginative life, into our thoughts directly; rather, it settles into our habits; into the way that we are, into the way that we live life here. What affects us from the spiritual worlds, and what comes to us from those who have passed through death's gate before us, stream into those things. Now we must be clear that such interaction of the dead with the living depends on various things. The dead are in an environment where similar beings are present—in other words, soul-beings; that is, all entities that belong to the higher hierarchies down to human beings. And because the cast-off etheric body serves as an intermediary, the dead can have perceptions of the people that are veiled from them, in a way, by the physical body; but they penetrate this veil with the help of their etheric body. Those who have gone through death's gate are subject to the conditions under which one lives in the soul world, in the spiritual world; they must comply with them. Now I need point out only one main point, and you will understand what I mean by this. We know that luciferic and ahrimanic forces have an effect in the most varied ways throughout the world in which we live. If these luciferic and ahrimanic forces did not exert their force of attraction on us, then what is expressed in humans as incorrect or evil actions would not exist in the world. The luciferic and ahrimanic forces must work upon human beings, must give human beings the opportunity to follow them.

If we picture this correctly, we will see that the essence of a human being is quite different from what we often make it out to be when we criticize a person. If we had the capability in the physical world always to see how the luciferic and ahrimanic influences affect people, we would judge them quite differently. Not that we need be less critical—for when we divert our adverse judgment from an individual, we must then confront Lucifer and Ahriman. We would then be much more tolerant of the person as a person. Those who live in the soul life in the period of time between death and rebirth practice this tolerance, both for those beings with them in the spiritual world and for those people who are still embodied here in physical life.

It is simply the nature of those who have passed through death's gate to acquire this tolerance, and to always see that part of a person has the luciferic or ahrimanic aspect. The departed do not see a bad person who follows evil desires; rather, they see that Lucifer is a certain part of the person. They do not see a jealous person; rather, they see that Ahriman is a certain part of them. That is how those who live between death and birth, judge. This tolerance is part of their being, just as it is part of our being to be naturally healthy and have healthy eyes. Because it is part of the nature of the dead, it is terribly painful for them when they maintain the connection they began in physical life and encounter another way of thinking here in us. Let us suppose that through our personal antipathies, we manifest hatred toward a person who is also in connection with the dead; this hatred represents terrible pain for the dead who try to approach us—as they indeed must because they are still connected to us. This hatred, which is drawn against them like a jagged sword, like a spear, must be overcome by the dead.

Thus, the way the dead wish to work into us and how they themselves experience this effect depend very, very much on the mood of our soul. They always work into us, but so much of the effect depends on the mood of our soul. These direct influences from the dead play a role, which I have described, in our customary ideas borrowed from our surroundings; in our perceptions, in our feeling tendencies, in our temperament, in our habits. But a continuous interplay exists between what transpires in the realm of those who have gone through death's gate and our own souls.

If you consider all this, then you will be aware that complicated effects are taking place within what we carry inside us as soul; and much is involved in comprehending all the enigmatic aspects that vibrate through a human soul. So much moves through it that the human soul itself is conscious of little of what pulsates there. But the overall mood of the soul—what we can or cannot do—depends on this. All of this, again, is largely determined by our karma; the fact that we were brought together here specifically with certain people who have an effect on us in the way in which I described naturally has to do with our karma in a larger sense.

As we bring this before our souls, we must be clear that our time, according to what spiritual science should bring people, has actual, real yearnings, but that these real yearnings are still often satisfied in the wrong ways. There are a number of people today who have overcome the prejudice that existed in the middle and last third of the nineteenth century that everything to do with the soul can be explained only in terms of physical and physiological effects. But half-truths or even partial truths often have much worse effects than complete errors. And one such half- or partial truth is the basis for what is variously called today analytical psychology, or psychoanalysis.[‡]

People search, but they search gropingly. They sense that various things are hidden in the depths of the soul, but they cannot resolve to really make strides into the spiritual world in order to find what is hidden there. What do psychoanalysts say today? They say that if they come across such a person as this, the overall state of being depends, in various ways, not only on what is in the consciousness but also on a whole array of factors that reside in the subconscious, beneath the threshold of consciousness. A person comes along who feels his mood somewhat constricted or repressed. An irregularity in the entire nervous system appears. He must then, according to the psychoanalyst, look into what was experienced perhaps years ago; what, in terms of experiences, was not completely worked through, but instead suppressed in the subconscious. But because it has been forgotten does not mean it is not there. The psychoanalyst senses very well that what has been pushed from consciousness is not thus pushed from reality; it is still down there in the subconscious. Now the psychoanalyst assumes that if the person loosens it up into consciousness by a sort of catharsis, then one gets to what eats away and feeds on it down below.

Staring from this point—of course I cannot explain psychoanalysis here in all its ramifications, but I want to indicate some of them—the psychoanalyst now searches for many things in the depths of the soul. Let's say that some years ago, a man had this or that ideal of life, this or that hope or plan, but he did not or could not carry it out. It is no longer in his consciousness because he is living in his present life, but it is not eliminated from the reality of his soul—it goes on gnawing away and consuming him. His whole condition of being depends on what is down there in his subconscious. Perhaps he had an unhappy love affair—this is what psychoanalysts most usually find, of course, because they are on the lookout for it. That is an isolated province of his soul consciousness; he fought it, and it is no longer in his consciousness, but it continues to have an effect. In particular, it continues to have an effect, according to the psychoanalysts, when feelings of love were present and the beloved did not reciprocate; when the feelings remained unfulfilled.

Then the psychoanalysts search down in the depths of the soul life; beyond the destroyed springtime hope of life, beyond what I just indicated: the "base animalistic mire" of life, what perpetually has an effect as the "base animalistic mire" of life. They search for the correlation with everything in the person that is animalistic, the animal nature, and which contributes to their psychological life. The analytical psychologists, who go farther, say that if one delves down, more and more deeply, one finally finds what contributes to races, nations, and so on. One finds what contributes to the soul in a more or less unconscious way. But finally, deep down, one finds the demonic aspect, the absolute undefined aspect that lies beneath the "base animalistic mire." Such people, who currently are particular followers of psychoanalysis, often quietly insinuate that in these *demonic* depths below lie the spiritual impulses that lead to gnosis, theosophy, anthroposophy, and such. Though this is sometimes insinuated in a somewhat hidden way, it is still insinuated. Read one of the recent pamphlets from *Knowledge and Life,* and you will be able to find such insinuations here and there, even if they are hidden between the lines.‡

Now, I said that half- and quarter-truths often have worse effects than complete falsities. There are half- and quarter-truths in analytical psychology; that is, in searching in the subconscious depths of the soul. But if we compare it to what we indicated today—that all the realities that exist there in the depths of the soul are affected by the realm of the dead—we will be driven to a much different approach. We will not search for the "base animalistic mire" of the soul,[‡] or for the closeted eroticism leading to this or that soul mood. On the contrary, we will often have to seek the underlying cause of an unhappy soul mood in a person who has passed on, for whom we are making difficulties through our own conduct. These difficulties find expression in dissatisfactions of one kind or another surging up into our consciousness. In short, we would do well to bring into our consciousness, in a reverential, sacred way, the correlation that exists not simply between our world and an abstract, pantheistically ambiguous spiritual world, but rather a correlation that exists with the real spiritual world in which those who have passed through the gate of death are real and are with us as they were in life. But how they affect us goes much closer to our souls than how they affected us in life, when we were always separated from them by our body and theirs, which stood between us like a barrier.

Now let us return to the description I began earlier of the soul's journey into the spiritual world. There comes then later in this journey a time in which a person has become fully free from the astral body, has laid aside the astral body completely. Sometime later, the person can have an effect on the physical world from the spiritual world in a much more intensive way as a result of being on a more inward path. Outward life on earth was oriented earlier in many ways toward such instinctively known truths, even if what came about in outward life was often derived from ordinary outward causes. But this outward aspect is the basis of an inner aspect (one often knew this only by instinct). I have said that the dead have a direct connection to the people they have left behind here, and to whom they are particularly connected by love after they pass through the gate of death; the connections are such that they have an effect on habits. At the time when people still felt such things quite instinctively, it was considered that sons should leave the circle of their parental home as little as possible. Then, access was easier. Learning the same trade, being part of the same profession, the whole conservative embrace of the same stream of life; these were all instinctive expressions of the fact that it was easier for those who had passed through the gate of death to work into those whom they left behind here if those left behind lived in circumstances similar to those in which the deceased themselves had lived. Then it was easier for these deceased to find their way to them. Someday we will be able to follow such subtle impulses and causes in the historical evolution of humanity.

If a person has been dead for a long while, the astral body has been completely laid aside. This happens only after decades have passed, because the movement that we complete in the spiritual world is much slower than movement in the physical world. Thirty years in the spiritual world corresponds to about one year in the physical world. We hurry here in the physical world; in the spiritual world we always have a revolution in a much bigger circle, so to speak, to execute than we do here in the physical world. In short, one year in the physical world corresponds to thirty years in the spiritual world; in thirty years in the spiritual world, we experience approximately the same piece of the world as in one year in the physical world; thus we experience that piece of the world in a more inward, intensive way.

What people undergo here has much to do with the large world, with the macrocosmos. What is experienced here, in the microcosmos within people, can also always be expressed in the relationships to the macrocosmos. For example, I would like to bring something to your attention. If we calculate the number of days of an average human life, we get the same number of years that the sun needs to go through the entire Platonic year, the Great Year. Thus, people live a lifetime of the same number of days that the sun needs in years to move the whole world sphere forward from one sign of the zodiac to the next. When the sun has gone through all the signs of the zodiac, it has taken about 25,900 and a few years to do it. People live about that number of days in a single life between birth and death (of course it is not the same for everyone).

And another interesting relationship is that people also take as many breaths in a day as the number of days they live, and as the number of years the sun goes around through the whole zodiac.[‡] You see, the world is truly ordered in the deepest sense, according to measure and number. And we must believe that this fine integration of humans in the world, this correspondence of harmonies, will lift the crass materialists of our time out of their worldview that chooses to see the universe as nothing but a mechanism. It would indeed be a peculiar "mechanism" that organizes the individual beings within it in such a wonderful, numerical, harmonically ordered relation to the whole.

And it is also very strange that we can really say, if we look at the world in a spiritual way, that people are slowly moving forward as they undergo the evolution between death and rebirth, in order to do everything in a more thorough way. That is, they move forward that much more slowly in the spiritual world, in the way that Saturn revolves more slowly around the Sun than around Earth. Saturn revolves that much more slowly around the Sun than around the Earth, as people move more slowly in the spiritual world than here on the physical Earth. For this reason (not because they knew less than today's astronomers), the ancients calculated Saturn as the farthest planet belonging to the solar system. This is astronomically correct, because the other planets we count as part of the solar system today, Uranus and Neptune, came to it later and affiliated themselves; they also revolve in a much different arrangement, even in a different rotation, than the other planets that belong to our solar system.

Now, at least *one* such spirit-year, that is, thirty earth-years, must have passed before the soul of the deceased (if a normal age in life of 70 to 80 years is reached) can enter the whole point of view, the whole spiritual life, and not just the habits, of those who remain behind here, those who are connected with them or who join with them of their own accord. But the dead also have a very comprehensive and detailed effect in this way in our lives. It is quite true that we carry within ourselves, with regard to the whole way we relate to the spiritual, the impetus of people long dead who work into us. The correlation of the future with the past is affected by this, when such a harmony occurs between the dead and the living. Just as the indirect revelation of the dead through the etheric body, which they lay aside, affects the imaginative perception; so what enters the habits in the way described has an effect on the inspirational perception. And what I just described can have effect only when the dead have gone through one spirit-year. It has an effect, if it should become conscious, on the intuitive perception. But it has a perpetual effect. We can find the meaning of evolution most correctly only if we consider such things consciously.

Forgive me for bringing in something very personal at this point; you know I don't like to, and thus do not often do so. Those who make the effort now to look at what I started writing decades ago will be able to see that I completely refrained from expressing my own opinion. I did not write *my* opinion on Goethe; rather, I attempted to express the thoughts that could have come from Goethe. I wrote *Goethe's Theory of Knowledge*, not *my* theory of knowledge. In such a way, we can join very consciously with beings long dead and can work out of their spirit. That is also what gives us a sort of credential to be permitted to work upon the living. The counterfeit credential many people insist on (especially in our time) is that anyone who has just barely formed a thought, immediately turns around and wants to pass it on to countless others—as many followers as possible. Those who know from the spiritual world the conditions of existence, the fundamental laws of existence, know that a person actually, as strange, as paradoxical as it is, may be permitted to have an effect on the depths of the souls of fellow human beings only when the individual has died; and even then, only after undergoing one spirit-year; that is, thirty earth-years. Prodigious gains would be made if the selflessness in the world could gain some further ground, so that those living at a later time would be able to join with the deceased, and attempt to maintain the continuity of evolution in a truly conscious way. Whether it is a relationship of free choice or a relationship of another kind caused by karma, the dependence on those who make an effort to send the rays of their influence out from the spiritual world is, when we live it consciously, profoundly significant.

I have tried to evoke a feeling in you of the combined effect resulting from interaction between the so-called dead and the living. However, we must realize that the conditions are much different in the spiritual world than they are here. You can find a good portion of these conditions and the conditions of experience in the spiritual world described in the lecture series that I gave some years ago in Vienna.‡ From these things alone, one can only glean some things that are important from one side or the other. It must be said here that something similar, and again something very dissimilar, to our physical life is present in the spiritual world. Before we enter this physical world in the fullest sense, we undergo the embryonic period, in which life conditions are much different than from the moment when we have fully entered the physical world as beings breathing the outside air. In a certain sense, the time we live through in the first spirit-year—which has so often been called the kamaloka period—is similar to the embryonic period. Just as people use another human being, so to speak, in order to be carried into the physical world over ten lunations, so are they carried into the spiritual world by all their wishes and desires, which hold them together and which they slowly shed. And the consciousness in this first spirit-year—thirty years after death—is still somewhat similar to the consciousness here in the physical world, even though the skills and so forth, which can be acquired only in the physical world, can only be indirectly conveyed by the etheric body.

But then other conditions of consciousness set in; a much higher consciousness than the one we are able to have here in the physical body sets in. You can see, if you remember some of what was said in the aforementioned lecture cycle, how this consciousness has a different character in the spiritual world. You must only consider how much consciousness depends on what can come into this consciousness. And when as ordinary people we move about here in the physical world, the phenomena of the mineral, plant, and animal kingdoms, and the physical human kingdom come into us with other soul experiences, cultural experiences, and so on. After death we are no longer aware of the mineral world as such; we are aware of only the general life in the plant world. You may read in my *Theosophy* how things are in ascent in the so-called spiritual world.

All of this is also linked to a very different experience in the spiritual world. There are really no words for all of this, as you can understand. Our language was basically made for the physical world; thus we always have difficulty correctly depicting these different relationships. That is why misunderstanding can arise so easily. Above all, we can express ourselves only in a comparative way. Here in the physical world, you are standing at one point of the whole universe; with your eyes, you look at your surroundings in all directions. It is not that way in the spiritual world. There, you are in the surrounding space and look from the surroundings, so to speak, into the inside of a hollow sphere. But this is comparative, as it is not a hollow sphere, because time has a much greater significance than space. So, from the surrounding space you look at everything—that involves very different conditions of perceiving, very different conditions of looking!

And within perceiving itself there are again very different conditions. Let us imagine that a person passed through the gate of death at sixty, seventy, eighty years old, or even earlier. Now this person distinctly feels an inner experience. If you feel hunger here in this physical life, you do not say that the hunger is here or there, but rather that the hunger is within you. That is how you feel when you look in from the great surrounding space on some place that you know has something to do with you. Now you must begin making the effort to do away with what is manifest there, what reveals itself! And only when you have done away with it, does the true manifestation appear. Thus we can say that as spiritual beings we have an image within us; but this image means nothing at all to us; it must first be done away with, and only when we have done away with it, do we find an angel or archangel within us revealed to us! Yes, as paradoxical as it sounds, it is true. We must first work to achieve perception of this being that announces itself behind the image. Thus understanding the spiritual world is tied to determined exertion, determined work. However, the souls who have stayed behind here in the physical body can more or less manifest themselves to the dead without going through this exertion when they really form their thoughts about the dead or present something to the dead by reading aloud to them or the like.

I only wish to make comprehensible to you through what I have said how very different the conditions of perception, of life, of experience are in the spiritual world. And if that is true, then you will not find it surprising that more or less thirty years of spirit-time equals one year of physical time; because in the spiritual world we stand in the surroundings and look in on the center. And it is very important to hold on to that.

You can see how difficult it is to talk about certain spiritual things from the fact that much looks quite the opposite; because we must cloak it in terms suited to physical perception, we are thus readily confronted with misunderstandings. People say, and rightly so because they first of all see the matter from the physical world, that human beings experience repeated earth-lives. That is correct. But why do they experience repeated earth-lives? While they live here between birth and death, they live through a certain period of time. Then they pass through the gate of death into the spiritual world and complete an orbit; but they come back in this orbit to the same point in time. And when we live through a life in the spiritual world, we are actually always at the same world-position or place. That is very interesting! In the kingdom of spirit, time does not rule; rather, duration does. We come back to the same place again. In fact we repeat life in the same relationship to what we have since experienced, at the same world-place. We always go back to the same starting point. We make actual orbits. You will say that is difficult to imagine. And it is difficult to imagine, and through some of the things I have presented today, which are somewhat easier to imagine, I want to make such a thing as this a part of your meditation in your soul life. Sometimes we must meditate on such things a long, long time, if we wish to understand their full scope.

I have made it my main task today to describe a bit the way in which the souls who have passed through the gate of death have an effect in the world, if people with whom the departed had been connected in the physical body have remained behind. And you have thus also seen from another perspective that the world is truly a connected whole; that the dead are, in truth, dead only to outer physical sight. In the instant that they pass through death's gate, they have another kind of access to our souls, and that is the entire difference. They now have an effect on us from within, whereas when they were living they affected us from the outside. Such things should more and more become not just external theories, but should settle into human consciousness; should become not just a world idea, but rather a worldview; indeed, I mean to say, a world perception. Then spiritual science will bear the fruits it should bear, and which it is capable of bearing.

One further remark in closing. Consider what it means that human beings during a certain time between death and rebirth must carry within themselves the feeling that they carry the hierarchies within themselves as their inner experience! That is true! That could lead people to the most terrible arrogance, which could live in the soul as a dark feeling when they are reborn. In ancient times, a barrier to this arrogance was made by the fact that people more or less knew that when they passed through death's gate and entered the spiritual world it was not they themselves who were seeing; but, rather, the highest beings of the highest hierarchies who were conveying sight to them. But people lost this connection in the spiritual world, just as they lost the old atavistic clairvoyance in the physical world here. It is because of this that what Paul spoke of with the words "Not I, but Christ in me," and what true spiritual perception achieves with the quotation "We are born of God; we die in Christ," must occur. If we learn in the greatest depth from the perception that can come to us from spiritual science that Christ is for Earth, we will prepare ourselves in the correct manner for this seeing from the surroundings.[‡] And if we experience the gate of death with the correct feelings of "In Christo morimur," then, looking in from the surroundings, we find our own I-being among those beings whom we see—who are part of the higher hierarchies and are also elemental beings; and also beings embodied here as human souls, or are even disembodied human souls. And we see from the outside, the relation of our I-being to the other beings, which I have just described. To be able to have these feelings after we have passed through death's gate is incredibly important because we are able to correctly come to terms with physical embodiment only if we can have these feelings for our own I. We can have them only if we know that they are due to correctly passing through the gate of death with the feeling of "We have died in Christ."

This being connected with Christ gives us the opportunity to see our relationship in the spiritual world with Christ's spiritual eye, so to speak; to see ourselves as an I-being among other spirit-beings.

With such observations as we made today I would like to achieve, not just the acquisition of a further piece of knowledge, but the transformation of this knowledge into sensing, into feeling. Even if all the ideas put forward today pass through us like mere dreams, and only a basic feeling remains with us—which I have tried to sum up in these concluding words—and leads us correctly into the spiritual world so that we are able to carry it through the physical world in the next earth-incarnation; if this feeling remains with us, then we are carrying the correct thing from such observations into the rest of our lives.

We also want to be at one with such feelings by considering them to be the most intensely connecting feelings. The close, invisible community of those devoted to anthroposophy will gradually bring this into the world: this holding together, this oneness, in the perceptions and feelings that are born out of the ideas of spiritual science. The world needs this invisible community of souls that is able to carry into the world the forces of such unity as has been characterized. In this sense, we will be together in the future in the spirit, though we are not together physically for a time. And thus it should be with us always: that our spiritual unity carries our physical unity evermore.

Notebook Entry for the Lecture of February 18, 1916

(notebook archive no. N.B. 530)

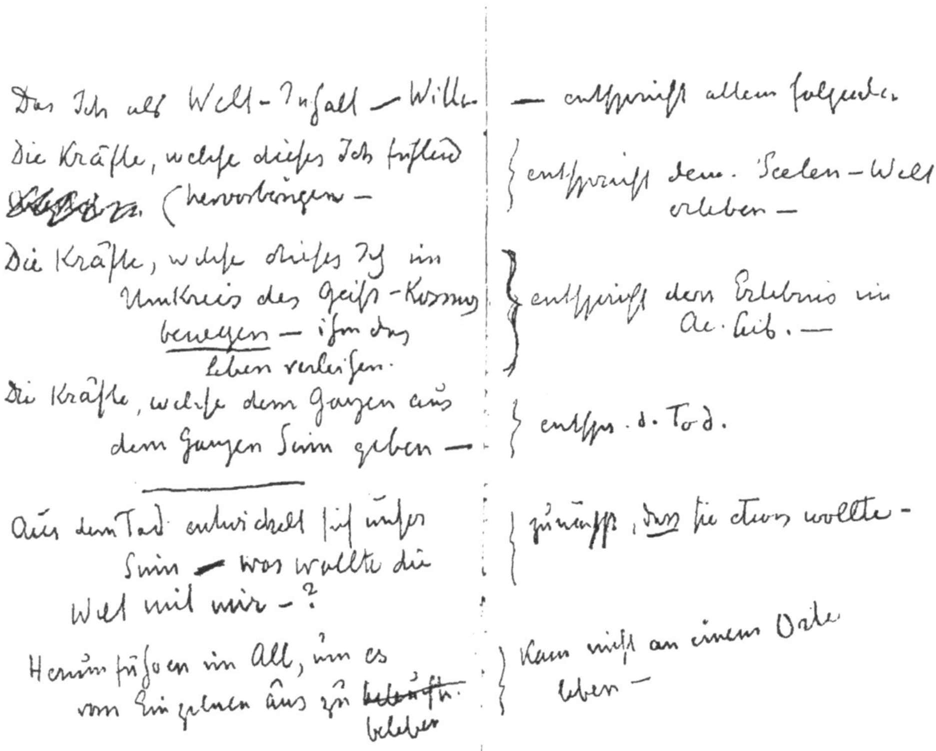
Das Ich als Welt-Inhalt – Wille – — entspricht allem folgenden
Die Kräfte, welche dieses Ich fühlend hervorbringen – } entspricht dem Seelen-Welt erleben –
Die Kräfte, welche dieses Ich im Umkreis des Geist-Kosmos bewegen – ihm das Leben verleihen. } entspricht dem Erlebnis im Ae. Leib. –
Die Kräfte, welche dem Ganzen aus dem Ganzen Sinn geben – } entspr. d. Tod.
Aus dem Tod entwickelt sich unser Sinn – was wollte die Welt mit mir –? } zunächst, dass sie etwas wollte –
Herumführen im All, um es vom Einzelnen aus zu beleben } Kann nicht an einem Orte leben –

The "I" as world—matter—will / —corresponds to all rest

The forces that produce the "I" sensitively— / corresponds to the soul world / experience —

The forces that <u>move</u> this I in vicinity of spirit-cosmos—impart life to it. / corresponds to the experience in etheric body.—

The forces that give meaning to the whole from the whole—corresponds to death.

Our meaning develops from death—what did the world want with me—? / first, <u>that</u> it wanted something—

Leading around in universe in order to bring to life from the individual / cannot live in one place—

Admission Ticket for the Lecture of December 3, 1916

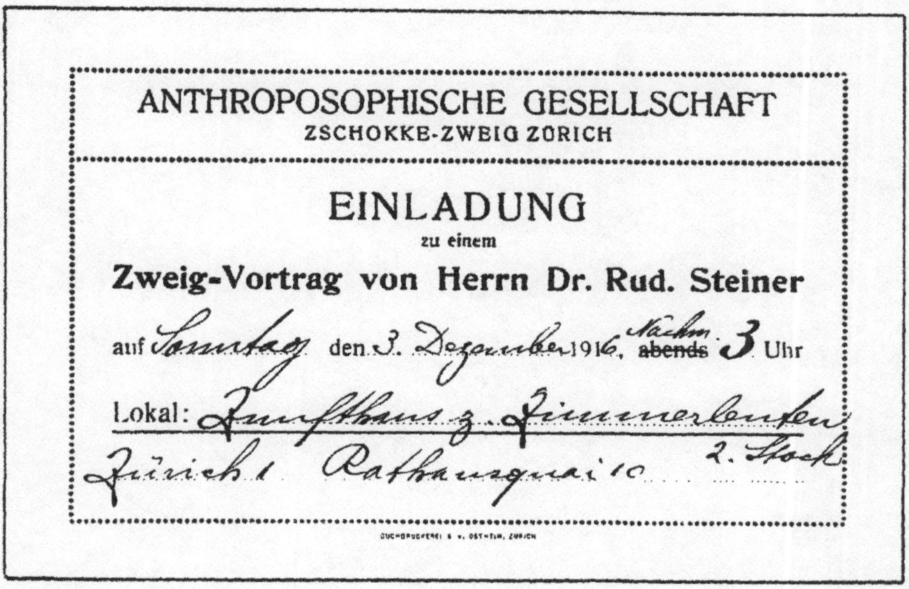
ANTHROPOSOPHISCHE GESELLSCHAFT
ZSCHOKKE-ZWEIG ZÜRICH

EINLADUNG
zu einem
Zweig-Vortrag von Herrn Dr. Rud. Steiner

auf Sonntag den 3. Dezember 1916, Nachm. ~~abends~~ 3 Uhr

Lokal: Zunfthaus z. Zimmerleuten
Zürich 1 Rathausquai 10 2. Stock

EDITORIAL AND REFERENCE NOTES

A note regarding the lectures

Rudolf Steiner originally did not wish the numerous free lectures and courses held in the years 1900 to 1924, both publicly and for the members of the Theosophical, later Anthroposophical Society, to be written down, as he intended them as "oral impartations not destined for print." However, after more and more incomplete and inaccurate transcripts were produced and distributed by attendees, he felt compelled to oversee their transcription. He entrusted this duty to Marie Steiner-von Sivers. It was incumbent on her to oversee the stenographers, manage the transcripts, and review the texts for publication. Since, for lack of time, Rudolf Steiner could only correct the transcripts himself on very few occasions, we must consider his qualification regarding all publications of lectures: "You simply must accept that there will be mistakes in the documents I have not looked over."

In his *Autobiography: Chapters in the Course of My Life* (chapter 35), Rudolf Steiner also wrote about the relationship between the lectures for members, which were originally available only as manuscripts for private use, and his public writings. What is said there also applies equally to the courses on individual subject areas, which were given to a limited circle of participants familiar with the basic principles of anthroposophy.

After the death of Marie Steiner (1867-1948), the publication of Rudolf Steiner's collected works was begun according to her instructions. This volume is part of that complete edition.

On this edition

All of the lectures collected in this volume were given to members of the Anthroposophical Society in 1916.

The main topic of this volume was greatly influenced by the history at that time: World War I had already lasted for two years. Victims were being mourned; many people were affected by personal loss. Do the dead remain connected to us? What meaning do the countless sacrificial deaths have? What is the fate of the so-called dead?—these were burning questions. Rudolf Steiner attempted to address them in his lectures and to show how those remaining behind could connect in the correct way to their dead.

But the lectures for members during this time address another topic as well, which could be given the name of the lecture called "The great delusion of modern civilization." Rudolf Steiner vividly shows the increasing disjointedness and thus the dishonesty of thinking, illustrating with examples from recently published books and brochures that were current at the time. At the center of these reflections is the lecture of October 10, 1916, in Zürich, "How

Can Today's Poverty of Soul be Overcome?" in which Rudolf Steiner clearly compares the ideals of today's cultural epoch and the current trends that prevail.

Text documents: All lectures were recorded and transcribed into longhand by the professional stenographer Helene Finckh. We can therefore assume a good, i.e., relatively authentic, textual basis with minimal discrepancies. Some corrections were made as a result of a new comparison of the longhand texts with the shorthand; changes to the 3rd edition are substantiated in a corrigendum at the end of the notes section in the German edition.

Regarding the individual lectures: In addition to these lectures to members, Rudolf Steiner also held one public lecture in each of the cities during his visits. These have so far not been published in the *Gesamtausgabe* (Collected Works). The member lectures in Zurich (October 10 and 24, as well as December 3, 1916) were held for the Zschokke branch; the lecture in Bern (November 9, 1916) was held for the Johannes work group.

The title of this volume was given—following the lecture in Bern on November 9, 1916—by the [German] publisher.

Martina Maria Sam oversaw the revision of the 4th edition for 1995. The table of contents and notes were expanded, and an index of names was added.

No original blackboard drawings are available.

References: See the following volumes of lectures by Rudolf Steiner on the life between death and rebirth, as well as the connection between the living and the dead: *Life between Death and Rebirth,* CW 140 (Anthroposophic Press, 1975); "Life between death and new birth in relationship to cosmic facts," GA 141; *How the Spiritual World Projects into Physical Existence,* CW 150 (Rudolf Steiner Press, 2014); *The Inner Nature of Man and Our Life Between Death and Rebirth,* CW 153 (Rudolf Steiner Press, 2013); *Spiritual Life Now and after Death: Forming our Destiny in the Physical and Spiritual Worlds,* CW 157a (SteinerBooks, 2013); "The mystery of death. The nature and significance of Middle Europe and the European folk spirits," GA 159; *Chance, Providence, and Necessity,* CW 163 (Anthroposophic Press, 1988); *The Influence of the Dead on Destiny,* CW 179 (SteinerBooks, 2008); *Dying Earth and Living Cosmos,* CW 181 (Rudolf Steiner Press, 2015); *Our Dead,* CW 261 (SteinerBooks, 2011).

Particular attention can be called to the lectures in *Death as Metamorphosis of Life,* CW 182 (SteinerBooks, 2008), held 1917-1918, which are thematically close to those of this volume.

Notes on the text

Lecture 1

Page 9, Goethe's *Theory of Color* (*Farbenlehre*)
See "Goethe's natural-scientific writings," published and with commentary by Rudolf Steiner in Kürschner's *German National Literature* (1883/97), volume III, section 6, p. 289-330, GA 1c, reprinted Dornach 1975.

Page 9, Jakob Böhme
1575-1624, German mystic and theosophist, originally shoemaker in Görlitz; first philosopher to write in German, hence also called "Philosophus Teutonicus"; great influence on German idealism and German Romanticism.

Page 9, "When humans see into the depths..."
Literally: "When you look into the depths and the stars and the Earth, you see your God..." (*Aurora*, 1612, chapter 23, line 9).

Page 11, Last year a young boy died
This is referring to Theodor Faiss, who died in 1914 in Dornach at the age of seven when he was crushed by a furniture truck that overturned upon him as he was running an errand for his parents. Cf. also the address on October 19, 1914 in *Our Dead*, CW 261; and the lectures on February 14, 1915, in "The spiritual background of the First World War," GA 174b and on February 22, 1915, in "The fate of people and nations," GA 157.

Page 17, Meister Bertram
1345-1415, German painter and carpenter. *The Fall*, part of the Grabow Altarpiece from 1397. See a similar representation by Hugo van der Goes, *The Fall*, in the Kunsthistorisches Museum in Vienna. Cf. also the lecture from December 13, 1916, in *Art History as a Reflection of Inner Spiritual Impulses*, CW 292, p. 164.

Page 19, Theodor Ziehen
1862-1950, professor of psychiatry in Berlin. *Guidelines of Physiological Psychology in 15 Lectures,* 2nd edition, Jena 1893.

Page 19, He gets to shades of feeling
In the 9th lecture of *Guidelines* (see above), he says, "Older psychology saw emotions almost without exception as expressions of a certain independent soul capability ...In contrast, our discussions thus far have already taught us that feelings of inclination and disinclination do not exist at all in this independence, that they appear rather as qualities and attributes of perceptions and ideas, as so-called feeling tones."

Page 22, Such an article
This could not be traced.

Page 23, Ernst Haeckel
1834-1919, doctor and natural scientist, professor of zoology in Jena. *Thoughts on Eternity [Ewigkeitsgedanken]*, "Eternity. Thoughts during the World War on life and death, religion and developmental theory," Berlin 1915 (see in particular foreword and first chapter ("World war and the law of nature").

Lecture 2

Page 31, the lectures I once gave in Vienna
April 6-14, 1914, *The Inner Nature of Man and Our Life Between Death and Rebirth,* CW 153 (Rudolf Steiner Press, 2013).

Page 32, There was a young child... at our building in Dornach
Cf. the note regarding p. 11.

Page 35, in the Vienna lecture series
Cf. the note regarding p. 31.

Page 37, A very thick book was written about Goethe
Presumably *Goethe in Light of Genetics* by Robert Sommer, Leipzig 1909.

Page 37, "I have my stature from my father..."
Literally from "Gentle Xenien" VI:32:

I get my stature from my father
Leading a serious life,
From mother dear my happy nature
And passion for spinning tales.

Page 37, in Kassel during a lecture series
"The Gospel of John in relation to the three other Gospels," GA 112, June 24–July 7, 1909; see in particular the lecture of July 5, 1909.

Page 38, There was a professor in Halle
Hans Vaihinger (1852-1933), philosopher. *The Philosophy of "As If." A System of Theoretical, Practical and Religious Fictions of Humanity Based on Idealistic Positivism*, Berlin 1913.

Page 38, Fritz Mauthner ... who wrote a philosophy of language
1849-1923, writer and philosopher of language. Since Mauthner considered the philosophers' dispute as only a dispute about words, he attempted to sort it out with a critique of language and terminology. Thus to him progress in realization was only possible if a word grew through "metaphorical use." See his works *Contributions to a Critique of Language* (1901/02); *Language* (1907); and in particular *Dictionary of Philosophy. New Contributions to a Critique of Language* (2 volumes, Munich and Leipzig, 1910/11). See also Rudolf Steiner's explanations from April 23, 1919, in "Spiritual-scientific treatment of social and pedagogical questions," CW 192, and in *Chance, Providence, and Necessity*, CW 163 (Anthroposophic Press, 1988).

Page 39, He said that when a raindrop...
In *Dictionary of Philosophy* (see previous note), volume 1, article "History" (in particular section V).

Page 41, He has analyzed many criminal brains
Moritz Benedikt (1835-1920), doctor, criminal anthropologist, professor of neuropathology, co-founded criminal anthropology with Lombroso. "On the psychophysics of morality and justice" (two lectures, held at the 47th and 48th assemblies of German natural scientists; in *Vienna Medical Press*, Vienna, 1875, page 26f.); "Anatomical studies of criminal brains," 1878. —Cf. also Rudolf Steiner's lectures from March 28, 1912 ("Darwin and extrasensory research") in "Human history in light of spiritual research," CW 61, and from November 24, 1915, in "The spiritual background of the First World War," CW 174b.

Page 43, *How to Know Higher Worlds*
(1904/05), CW 10.

Page 44, the day before yesterday to our dear friends
Cf. the lecture from February 16, 1916, in Hamburg in this volume.

Page 44, "Your eyes shall be opened..."
Cf. Mos. 1:3, 1:5.

Page 44, Meister Bertram
Cf. the note re: p. 17.

Page 45-46, what should imbue our path with a serious principle
In "Outline of the principles of an Anthroposophical society," 1912, it reads in the first of the three basic principles: "All those people can join together in a fraternal way in society who see a common spiritual aspect in all human souls as the basis for loving cooperation, however varied they may be in regard to beliefs, nationality, situation, sex, and so on."

Page 46, what has recently been written about us
Slander of Rudolf Steiner, including alleging that he was a Jesuit, in *The Theosophist*, February 1913 and December 1914.

Lecture 3

Page 49, overview... of the total person
On the elements of the human being, see especially the chapter "The Essential Nature of the Human Being" in Rudolf Steiner's *Theosophy. An Introduction to the Spiritual Processes in Human Life and in the Cosmos* (1904), CW 9.

Page 49, known by Immanuel Hermann Fichte...as well as Troxler and others
See I. H. Fichte's *Anthropology: The Teachings of the Human Soul, Based on Natural-Scientific Methods,* (Leipzig, 1856). For example, in the 2nd edition from 1860, on p. 272 (§118) it reads: "Thus the truly persistent thing—this *unifying* principle of the body—which proves to have an effect during our entire lives, cannot be found in elements of matter." (§119): "Thus we are shown a second, greatly *different* cause in the body. ... Insofar as [the principle] contains the actual persistency of metabolism, this persistency is the *true, inner, invisible*, but also completely visible materiality of the *body in existence*. The other, outer appearance of this, formed from ceaseless metabolism, may continue to be called 'the body', but it is, in truth not persistent and not unified, merely the effect or the image of this inner corporeity, which throws it into the changing material world just as magnetic force seems to create a solid body from pieces of iron filings but also scatters in all directions when its binding energy is removed." In I.P.V. Troxler's 6th edition of *Lectures on Philosophy: On the Contents, Education, Purpose and Application of the Same in Life, As Encyclopedia and Methodology of Philosophic Science* (Berne, 1835), he writes: "Even in the past, philosophers differentiated between a fine, sublime soul-body and the grosser body, or believed the body to be a sort of shell for the spirit; a

soul, which had an image of the body about it, which they called *schema*, and which to them was the inner, higher human being." — See also, among others, Gotthilf Heinrich von Schubert, letter of June 28, 1855, to Rudolf Rocholl (in Rudolf Rocholl, *Solitary Paths,* Leipzig 1881, p. 218): "The life force itself is a master not only of sense-elemental corporeity but also the forces of higher, extrasensory corporeity, which are the elements of the lower order according to laws other than these, which know our chemistry, elicit from the non-physical, and can change, connect and dissolve it. The ancient prelate Oetinger believed, as all of his fellow disciples in the deeply insightful so-called school of Alchemy, in the possibility of the creative effect of the forces of a higher corporeity on the elements of lower corporeity, and I believe this as well."

Immanuel Hermann Fichte, 1796-1879, professor of philosophy in Tübingen 1842-1863; co-founded the *Journal for Philosophy and Speculative Theology*, among others, with Chr. H. Weiss. Cf. also the chapter, "A Forgotten Stream in German Spiritual Life" in Rudolf Steiner's *The Riddle of Man* (1916), CW 20 (Spring Valley, NY: Mercury Press, 1990).

Johann Gottlieb Fichte, 1762-1814.

Ignaz Paul Vitalis Troxler, 1780-1866, doctor and philosopher; taught in Aarau, Lucerne, Basel, Berne. Cf. the chapter, "A Forgotten Stream in German Spiritual Life" in Rudolf Steiner's *The Riddle of Man*, CW 20 (Mercury Press, 1990), as well as the lectures on October 29 and 30, 1916, in "Inner impulses of evolution in humanity. Goethe and the crisis of the 19th century," CW 171.

Page 49, Saturn, Sun and Moon stages of evolution
See in particular chapter four, "The Evolution of the World and Human Beings," in Rudolf Steiner's *An Outline of Esoteric Science* (1910), CW 13 (SteinerBooks, 1997), on earlier and later embodiments of our planet Earth, as well as the corresponding chapter in his work, *Cosmic Memory: From the Akashic Chronicle* (1904-1908), CW 11 (SteinerBooks, 1987).

Page 62, *The Souls' Awakening*
1913; in *Four Mystery Dramas,* CW 14, scene 6 (SteinerBooks, 2015).

Page 66, how "wonderfully far" we have come today
Wagner in Goethe's *Faust, Part I* (night, V. 573).

Page 66, Lucifer and Ahriman
See, for example, The Influences of Luciferic and Ahriman, from CW 191 (Anthroposophic Press, 1976), as well as chapter four of *An Outline of Esoteric Science* (1910), CW 13.

Page 66, that Lucifer is symbolized in the Bible as a serpent
Mos. 1:3.

Page 67, Meister Bertram
See the note regarding p. 17.

Page 67, At our last gathering

Leipzig, March 7, 1915; lecture: "The intimate element of Central European culture and Central European striving" in "The secret of death. Nature and meaning in Central Europe and European national characters," GA 159/160.

Page 65, here on earth
Added by the editor to facilitate comprehension.

Lecture 4

Page 77, this or that form of socialism
In German: "Sozialismen"

Page 84, ties up everything... like a Spanish boot [Spanischer Stiefel]
After V. 1913 in Goethe's *Faust, Part 1* (Study, Mephisto to the student). The Spanish boot was a medieval torture device, which bound the legs, for the purpose of obtaining information

Page 87, "Not I, but Christ in me"
Paul in a letter to the Galatians (Gal. 2:20).

Page 89, I found a little book
"The World of Thought of the Educated. Problems and questions," lecture given at the 37th Convention for Inner Mission in Hamburg on September 23, 1913, by Prof. Dr. Friedrich Mahling, Rauhe Haus agency, Hamburg 1914.

Page 89, "Strange: ... with *joie de vivre*..."
Ibid p. 35f.

Page 90, "In addition to mysticism, there is Theosophy..."
Ibid p. 42f.

Lecture 5

Page 95, Two weeks ago
Lecture in this volume on October 10, 1916, in Zurich; see p. 70ff.

Page 96, Yesterday in the public lecture
"The human soul and human body from the point of view of spiritual science," Zurich, October 23, 1916 (not published, planned for GA 71).

Page 99, I have mentioned in lectures, which have in fact already been published
E.g. in the cycle *The Inner Nature of Man and Our Life Between Death and Rebirth,* CW 153 (Rudolf Steiner Press, 2013).

Page 104, Eduard Suess
1831–1914, professor of geology in Vienna. *The Face of the Earth,* 3 volumes, Vienna 1885–1909.

Page 105, the wise poet Hebbel wrote in his diary...
Friedrich Hebbel (1813–1863), *Diaries* (published by Theodor Poppe, no. 1336). The citation reads literally, "After the transmigration of souls, it is

possible that Plato was beaten up again on a school bench because he did not understand Plato."

Page 107, "It is a great delight..." and "... such great progress"
Wagner in Goethe's *Faust, Part I* (night, V. 570f. and 573).

Page 107-108, a small volume ... on the questions of religion today
A.W. Hunzinger, "Principle Questions on the Art of Living," in the collection *Science and Education,* Leipzig 1916.

Page 108, Pliny the Elder, ... who said
Pliny the Elder, 28–79; quoted in Hunzinger (see previous note regarding Hunzinger for p. 107), p. 80.

Page 108, the wise Seneca says
Lucius Annaeus Seneca (often known as Seneca the Younger or simply Seneca; c. 4 BC–AD 65) was a Roman Stoic philosopher, statesman, dramatist, and in one work humorist, of the Silver Age of Latin literature. He was a tutor and later advisor to emperor Nero; quoted in Hunzinger (see note regarding Hunzinger for p. 107), p. 81.

Page 109, "Luther..."
Ibid., p. 89f.

Page 111, "The center of this reality..."
Ibid., p. 126f.

Page 111, "When we speak of the wrath of God..."
Ibid., p. 127f.

Page 111 "Thus God can..."
Ibid.

Page 112, "It is therefore foolish and senseless..."
Ibid., p. 151

Page 112, two weeks ago
Cf. the note regarding p. 95.

Page 112, "In other words,..."
A.W. Hunzinger, "Principle Questions on the Art of Living" (see note regarding p. 107), p. 120.

Page 113, "The Lord is with his own in sleep"
Psalm 127:2.

Page 113, "In earthly life,..."
A.W. Hunzinger, "Principle Questions on the Art of Living" (see note regarding p. 107), p. 114.

Page 113, "That is for Jesus,..."
Ibid., p. 128f.

Page 114, "This little book consists of..."
Ibid., p. 5.

Page 114, the city
Hamburg

Lecture 6

Page 121, Jean Jaurès
Jean Jaurès, 1857–1914, French writer and politician; supported peace and international reconciliation, particularly between France and Germany.

Page 122, Over in Zurich
Cf. lecture in this volume from October 24, 1916, p. 94-115.

Page 122, "There is a man who... also had what he said printed..."
Friedrich Mahling, "The World of Thought of the Educated..." (cf. the corresponding note regarding p. 89).

Page 123, "We must rather try to understand..."
Ibid., p. 42.

Page 125, One of the best articles Jaurès wrote
"Fatherland and Proletariat," special printing of the 10th chapter of his book *The New Army,* Jena 1916.

Page 125, Joan of Arc
Joan of Arc (the Maiden of Orléans), 1412-1431.

Page 125-126, "Joan of Arc completed her mission...every other revelation"
Jean Jaurès, "Fatherland and Proletariat" (see note regarding Jean Jaurès, for p. 125), p. 98f.

Page 125–126, Saint Louis IX
Saint Louis IX, 1215-1270, Charles V, 1337-1380, Charles VI, 1368-1422, kings of France.

Page 126, the People's King
Louis XI, 1423-1483.

Page 126, Charles of Orléans
Charles of Orléans (Charles VII), 1403-1461.

Page 129, A wonderful quotation
Jean Jaurès, "Fatherland and Proletariat" (see note regarding Jean Jaurès, for p. 125), p. 99.

Page 130, "This is Rhodes; dance here"
In the sense of, "Prove here and now that you can!" After Aesop's fable ("The Leap at Rhodes"): A braggart was told *"Hic Rhodus, hic salta!"* when he claimed that he once made a great leap in Rhodes, for which he unfortunately had no witnesses.

Page 131, as I did recently in Zurich
Cf. lecture from October 24, 1916, p. 94ff.

Page 132, A person…wrote a little book
A.W. Hunzinger, *Principle Questions on the Art of Living*; cf. note regarding p. 107.

Page 133, "Human beings, as we…"
Ibid., p. 11.

Page 133, "The mental functions,…"
Ibid., p. 11.

Page 133, "This certainty in the laws of nature…"
Ibid., p. 11.

Page 133, "These come about precisely…"
Ibid.

Page 135, yesterday in the public lecture
"Anthroposophy and the Mystery of Human Life," lecture in St. Gallen, Switzerland, October 25, 1916 (unpublished; planned for GA 71).

Page 135, "the 'person as nature'..."
A.W. Hunzinger, *Principle Questions on the Art of Living*, p. 12 (cf. the corresponding note regarding p. 107).

Page 137, "That means…"
Ibid., p. 19.

Page 137-138, "These things … the most inner aspect, the goal…"
Ibid.

Page 138, "This little book consists of…"
Ibid., p. 5.

Page 138, the city, which I do not want to name
Cf. the corresponding note regarding p. 114.

Page 139, Gnosis made the first attempts…
Cf. Rudolf Steiner's lectures *Christ and the Spiritual World and the Search for the Holy Grail*, CW 149 (Rudolf Steiner Press, 2008), particularly the lecture of December 29, 1913.

Page 139, that we could be together once again here in St. Gallen
The last lecture in St. Gallen before the one printed here was held by Rudolf Steiner on December 19, 1912, published in *Esoteric Christianity and the Mission of Christian Rosenkreutz*, CW 130 (Rudolf Steiner Press, 2001).

Lecture 7

Page 158, *Goethe's World View*
Rudolf Steiner, *Goethe's World View* (1897), CW 6 (Mercury Press, 1985).

Page 158, *Goethe's Theory of Knowledge*
Rudolf Steiner, *Goethe's Theory of Knowledge: An Outline of the Epistemology of His Worldview* (1886), CW 2 (SteinerBooks, 1985).

Lecture 8

Page 160, From the public lecture yesterday
"The human soul and human destiny in relation to world evolution from the point of view of spiritual science," Zurich, December 2, 1916 (unpublished).

Page 162, *Hic Rhodus, hic salta!*
Cf. the note regarding p. 130.

Page 163, Paul explained...
Romans 7:7 and 7:8: "Nay, I had not known sin, but by the law... For without the law sin was dead."

Page 167, one such half- or quarter-truth
See also Rudolf Steiner's lectures on November 10 and 11, 1917, in *Secret Brotherhoods and the Mystery of the Human Double*, CW 178 (Rudolf Steiner Press, 2004), and on January 22 and March 12, 1918, in *Dying Earth and Living Cosmos*, CW 181 (Rudolf Steiner Press, 2015).

Page 168, one of the recent pamphlets from *Knowledge and Life*
Here Rudolf Steiner is referring to the article "Human Truth" by Adolf Keller. This was published in No. 3/1916 on November 1, 1916. It says, for example: "This effect, as it is expressed in moral perception, is direct, conclusive, absolute. Where then does the source of this direct responsibility come from, which cannot be detected in the consciousness? Frommel finds it in the unconscious and builds a religious-psychological theory from it..." (p. 103). And toward the end of the article (p. 114): "If the feeling of absolute responsibility is incontrovertibly found in the unconscious, from which the most valuable moral and religious forms of life were established, so too are those other soul tendencies found in it from which paganism and in particular the Gnostic religious forms emerged. Frommel does not succeed in clarifying with his assumptions why he believes the moral forces of the unconscious to be God's work but denies this characteristic in his other dynamic tendencies. If they are the psychic foundations for Christian theism and moralism, then these pure dynamic tendencies form the unconscious, soul root base for pantheism and for all forms of gnosis, whose primitive elemental forces are in turn very involved with all kinds of contemporary visionary sects."

Page 169, for the "base animalistic mire" of the soul
This term, which Rudolf Steiner often used, comes from the article by Adolf Keller just mentioned (see previous note). There it says (on p. 113): "Experience certainly encounters this feeling of an absolute responsibility in the subconscious, from which life's norms are then formed. But unfortunately much more as well: The remains and refuse of our past personage, the discarded and suppressed sketches of our life plan, the base mire of our animalistic nature, the collective character of the people, the race, humanity and their history, indeed a biological and cosmic mneme and, more than anything, the evil and demons that approach people not with this moral responsibility but with the power of temptation and the compulsion of hell, of blind destiny."

Page 171, that people also take as many breaths in a day
Cf. also Rudolf Steiner's lectures from February 13, 1917, in *Building Stones for an Understanding of the Mystery of Golgotha*, CW 175 (Rudolf Steiner Press, 2015), and from August 22, 1919, in *Practical Advice to Teachers,* CW 294 (SteinerBooks, 2000).

Page 173, lectures I gave some years ago in Vienna
The Inner Nature of Man and Our Life Between Death and Rebirth, CW 153, (Rudolf Steiner Press, 2013).

Page 175, more or less thirty years of spirit-time equals one year of physical time"
Cf. the note regarding p. 170.

Page 176, If we learn in the greatest depth...that Christ is for Earth, we will prepare ourselves in the correct manner for this seeing from the surroundings
Corrected in the 3rd edition after comparison with the original shorthand. In the previous editions, it read: "If we learn in the greatest depth from the perception...that Christ is for Earth, we will prepare ourselves in the correct manner for this seeing from surrounding space."

RUDOLF STEINER'S COLLECTED WORKS

The German Edition of Rudolf Steiner's Collected Works (the Gesamtausgabe [GA] published by Rudolf Steiner Verlag, Dornach, Switzerland) presently runs to over 354 titles, organized either by type of work (written or spoken), chronology, audience (public or other), or subject (education, art, etc.). For ease of comparison, the Collected Works in English [CW] follows the German organization exactly. A complete listing of the CWs follows with literal translations of the German titles. Other than in the case of the books published in his lifetime, titles were rarely given by Rudolf Steiner himself, and were often provided by the editors of the German editions. The titles in English are not necessarily the same as the German; and, indeed, over the past seventy-five years have frequently been different, with the same book sometimes appearing under different titles.

For ease of identification and to avoid confusion, we suggest that readers looking for a title should do so by CW number. Because the work of creating the Collected Works of Rudolf Steiner is an ongoing process, with new titles being published every year, we have not indicated in this listing which books are presently available. To find out what titles in the Collected Works are currently in print, please check our website at www.steinerbooks.org, or write to SteinerBooks 610 Main Street, Great Barrington, MA 01230

Written Work

CW 1	Goethe: Natural-Scientific Writings, Introduction, with Footnotes and Explanations in the text by Rudolf Steiner
CW 2	Outlines of an Epistemology of the Goethean World View, with Special Consideration of Schiller
CW 3	Truth and Science
CW 4	The Philosophy of Freedom
CW 4a	Documents to "The Philosophy of Freedom"
CW 5	Friedrich Nietzsche, A Fighter against His Own Time
CW 6	Goethe's Worldview
CW 6a	Now in CW 30
CW 7	Mysticism at the Dawn of Modern Spiritual Life and Its Relationship with Modern Worldviews
CW 8	Christianity as Mystical Fact and the Mysteries of Antiquity
CW 9	Theosophy: An Introduction into Supersensible World Knowledge and Human Purpose
CW 10	How Does One Attain Knowledge of Higher Worlds?
CW 11	From the Akasha-Chronicle
CW 12	Levels of Higher Knowledge
CW 13	Occult Science in Outline
CW 14	Four Mystery Dramas
CW 15	The Spiritual Guidance of the Individual and Humanity

CW 16	A Way to Human Self-Knowledge: Eight Meditations
CW 17	The Threshold of the Spiritual World. Aphoristic Comments
CW 18	The Riddles of Philosophy in Their History, Presented as an Outline
CW 19	Contained in CW 24
CW 20	The Riddles of the Human Being: Articulated and Unarticulated in the Thinking, Views and Opinions of a Series of German and Austrian Personalities
CW 21	The Riddles of the Soul
CW 22	Goethe's Spiritual Nature and Its Revelation in "Faust" and through the "Fairy Tale of the Snake and the Lily"
CW 23	The Central Points of the Social Question in the Necessities of Life in the Present and the Future
CW 24	Essays Concerning the Threefold Division of the Social Organism and the Period 1915-1921
CW 25	Cosmology, Religion and Philosophy
CW 26	Anthroposophical Leading Thoughts
CW 27	Fundamentals for Expansion of the Art of Healing according to Spiritual-Scientific Insights
CW 28	The Course of My Life
CW 29	Collected Essays on Dramaturgy, 1889-1900
CW 30	Methodical Foundations of Anthroposophy: Collected Essays on Philosophy, Natural Science, Aesthetics and Psychology, 1884-1901
CW 31	Collected Essays on Culture and Current Events, 1887-1901
CW 32	Collected Essays on Literature, 1884-1902
CW 33	Biographies and Biographical Sketches, 1894-1905
CW 34	Lucifer-Gnosis: Foundational Essays on Anthroposophy and Reports from the Periodicals "Lucifer" and "Lucifer-Gnosis," 1903-1908
CW 35	Philosophy and Anthroposophy: Collected Essays, 1904-1923
CW 36	The Goetheanum-Idea in the Middle of the Cultural Crisis of the Present: Collected Essays from the Periodical "Das Goetheanum," 1921-1925
CW 37	Now in CWs 260a and 251
CW 38	Letters, Vol. 1: 1881-1890
CW 39	Letters, Vol. 2: 1890-1925
CW 40	Truth-Wrought Words
CW 40a	Sayings, Poems and Mantras; Supplementary Volume
CW 42	Now in CWs 264-266
CW 43	Stage Adaptations
CW 44	On the Four Mystery Dramas. Sketches, Fragments and Paralipomena on the Four Mystery Dramas
CW 45	Anthroposophy: A Fragment from the Year 1910

Public Lectures

CW 51	On Philosophy, History and Literature
CW 52	Spiritual Teachings about the Soul and Observation of the World
CW 53	The Origin and Goal of the Human Being
CW 54	The Riddles of the World and Anthroposophy
CW 55	Knowledge of the Supersensible in Our Times and Its Meaning for Life Today
CW 56	Knowledge of the Soul and of the Spirit
CW 57	Where and How Does One Find the Spirit?
CW 58	The Metamorphoses of the Soul Life. Paths of Soul Experiences: Part One
CW 59	The Metamorphoses of the Soul Life. Paths of Soul Experiences: Part Two
CW 60	The Answers of Spiritual Science to the Biggest Questions of Existence
CW 61	Human History in the Light of Spiritual Research
CW 62	Results of Spiritual Research
CW 63	Spiritual Science as a Treasure for Life
CW 64	Out of Destiny-Burdened Times
CW 65	Out of Central European Spiritual Life
CW 66	Spirit and Matter, Life and Death
CW 67	The Eternal in the Human Soul. Immortality and Freedom
CW 68	Public lectures in various cities, 1906-1918
CW 69	Public lectures in various cities, 1906-1918
CW 70	Public lectures in various cities, 1906-1918
CW 71	Public lectures in various cities, 1906-1918
CW 72	Freedom – Immortality – Social Life
CW 73	The Supplementing of the Modern Sciences through Anthroposophy
CW 73a	Specialized Fields of Knowledge and Anthroposophy
CW 74	The Philosophy of Thomas Aquinas
CW 75	Public lectures in various cities, 1906-1918
CW 76	The Fructifying Effect of Anthroposophy on Specialized Fields
CW 77a	The Task of Anthroposophy in Relation to Science and Life: The Darmstadt College Course
CW 77b	Art and Anthroposophy. The Goetheanum-Impulse
CW 78	Anthroposophy, Its Roots of Knowledge and Fruits for Life
CW 79	The Reality of the Higher Worlds
CW 80	Public lectures in various cities, 1922
CW 81	Renewal-Impulses for Culture and Science–Berlin College Course
CW 82	So that the Human Being Can Become a Complete Human Being
CW 83	Western and Eastern World-Contrast. Paths to Understanding It through Anthroposophy
CW 84	What Did the Goetheanum Intend and What Should Anthroposophy Do?

Lectures to the Members of the Anthroposophical Society

CW 88	Concerning the Astral World and Devachan
CW 89	Consciousness – Life – Form. Fundamental Principles of a Spiritual-Scientific Cosmology
CW 90	Participant Notes from the Lectures during the Years 1903-1905
CW 91	Participant Notes from the Lectures during the Years 1903-1905
CW 92	The Occult Truths of Ancient Myths and Sagas
CW 93	The Temple Legend and the Golden Legend
CW 93a	Fundamentals of Esotericism
CW 94	Cosmogony. Popular Occultism. The Gospel of John. The Theosophy in the Gospel of John
CW 95	At the Gates of Theosophy
CW 96	Origin-Impulses of Spiritual Science. Christian Esotericism in the Light of New Spirit-Knowledge
CW 97	The Christian Mystery
CW 98	Nature Beings and Spirit Beings – Their Effects in Our Visible World
CW 99	The Theosophy of the Rosicrucians
CW 100	Human Development and Christ-Knowledge
CW 101	Myths and Legends. Occult Signs and Symbols
CW 102	The Working into Human Beings by Spiritual Beings
CW 103	The Gospel of John
CW 104	The Apocalypse of John
CW 104a	From the Picture-Script of the Apocalypse of John
CW 105	Universe, Earth, the Human Being: Their Being and Development, as well as Their Reflection in the Connection between Egyptian Mythology and Modern Culture
CW 106	Egyptian Myths and Mysteries in Relation to the Active Spiritual Forces of the Present
CW 107	Spiritual-Scientific Knowledge of the Human Being
CW 108	Answering the Questions of Life and the World through Anthroposophy
CW 109	The Principle of Spiritual Economy in Connection with the Question of Reincarnation. An Aspect of the Spiritual Guidance of Humanity
CW 110	The Spiritual Hierarchies and Their Reflection in the Physical World. Zodiac, Planets and Cosmos
CW 111	Contained in CW 109
CW 112	The Gospel of John in Relation to the Three Other Gospels, Especially the Gospel of Luke
CW 113	The Orient in the Light of the Occident. The Children of Lucifer and the Brothers of Christ
CW 114	The Gospel of Luke

CW 115 Anthroposophy – Psychosophy – Pneumatosophy
CW 116 The Christ-Impulse and the Development of I-Consciousness
CW 117 The Deeper Secrets of the Development of Humanity in Light of the Gospels
CW 118 The Event of the Christ-Appearance in the Etheric World
CW 119 Macrocosm and Microcosm. The Large World and the Small World. Soul-Questions, Life-Questions, Spirit-Questions
CW 120 The Revelation of Karma
CW 121 The Mission of Individual Folk-Souls in Connection with Germanic-Nordic Mythology
CW 122 The Secrets of the Biblical Creation-Story. The Six-Day Work in the First Book of Moses
CW 123 The Gospel of Matthew
CW 124 Excursus in the Area of the Gospel of Mark
CW 125 Paths and Goals of the Spiritual Human Being. Life Questions in the Light of Spiritual Science
CW 126 Occult History. Esoteric Observations of the Karmic Relationships of Personalities and Events of World History
CW 127 The Mission of the New Spiritual Revelation. The Christ-Event as the Middle-Point of Earth Evolution
CW 128 An Occult Physiology
CW 129 Wonders of the World, Trials of the Soul, and Revelations of the Spirit
CW 130 Esoteric Christianity and the Spiritual Guidance of Humanity
CW 131 From Jesus to Christ
CW 132 Evolution from the View Point of the Truth
CW 133 The Earthly and the Cosmic Human Being
CW 134 The World of the Senses and the World of the Spirit
CW 135 Reincarnation and Karma and their Meaning for the Culture of the Present
CW 136 The Spiritual Beings in Celestial Bodies and the Realms of Nature
CW 137 The Human Being in the Light of Occultism, Theosophy and Philosophy
CW 138 On Initiation. On Eternity and the Passing Moment. On the Light of the Spirit and the Darkness of Life
CW 139 The Gospel of Mark
CW 140 Occult Investigation into the Life between Death and New Birth. The Living Interaction between Life and Death
CW 141 Life between Death and New Birth in Relationship to Cosmic Facts
CW 142 The Bhagavad Gita and the Letters of Paul
CW 143 Experiences of the Supersensible. Three Paths of the Soul to Christ
CW 144 The Mysteries of the East and of Christianity

CW 145	What Significance Does Occult Development of the Human Being Have for the Sheaths – Physical Body, Etheric Body, Astral Body, and Self?
CW 146	The Occult Foundations of the Bhagavad Gita
CW 147	The Secrets of the Threshold
CW 148	Out of Research in the Akasha: The Fifth Gospel
CW 149	Christ and the Spiritual World. Concerning the Search for the Holy Grail
CW 150	The World of the Spirit and Its Extension into Physical Existence; The Influence of the Dead in the World of the Living
CW 151	Human Thought and Cosmic Thought
CW 152	Preliminary Stages to the Mystery of Golgotha
CW 153	The Inner Being of the Human Being and Life Between Death and New Birth
CW 154	How does One Gain an Understanding of the Spiritual World? The Flowing in of Spiritual Impulses from out of the World of the Deceased
CW 155	Christ and the Human Soul. Concerning the Meaning of Life. Theosophical Morality. Anthroposophy and Christianity
CW 156	Occult Reading and Occult Hearing
CW 157	Human Destinies and the Destiny of Peoples
CW 157a	The Formation of Destiny and the Life after Death
CW 158	The Connection Between the Human Being and the Elemental World. Kalevala – Olaf Asteson – The Russian People – The World as the Result of the Influences of Equilibrium
CW 159	The Mystery of Death. The Nature and Significance of Middle Europe and the European Folk Spirits
CW 160	In CW 159
CW 161	Paths of Spiritual Knowledge and the Renewal of the Artistic Worldview
CW 162	Questions of Art and Life in Light of Spiritual Science
CW 163	Coincidence, Necessity and Providence. Imaginative Knowledge and the Processes after Death
CW 164	The Value of Thinking for a Knowledge That Satisfies the Human Being. The Relationship of Spiritual Science to Natural Science
CW 165	The Spiritual Unification of Humanity through the Christ-Impulse
CW 166	Necessity and Freedom in the Events of the World and in Human Action
CW 167	The Present and the Past in the Human Spirit
CW 168	The Connection between the Living and the Dead
CW 169	World-being and Selfhood
CW 170	The Riddle of the Human Being. The Spiritual Background of Human History. Cosmic and Human History, Vol. 1
CW 171	Inner Development-Impulses of Humanity. Goethe and the Crisis of the 19th Century. Cosmic and Human History, Vol. 2

CW 172	The Karma of the Vocation of the Human Being in Connection with Goethe's Life. Cosmic and Human History, Vol. 3
CW 173	Contemporary-Historical Considerations: The Karma of Untruthfulness, Part One. Cosmic and Human History, Vol. 4
CW 174	Contemporary-Historical Considerations: The Karma of Untruthfulness, Part Two. Cosmic and Human History, Vol. 5
CW 174a	Middle Europe between East and West. Cosmic and Human History, Vol. 6
CW 174b	The Spiritual Background of the First World War. Cosmic and Human History, Vol. 7
CW 175	Building Stones for an Understanding of the Mystery of Golgotha. Cosmic and Human Metamorphoses
CW 176	Truths of Evolution of the Individual and Humanity. The Karma of Materialism
CW 177	The Spiritual Background of the Outer World. The Fall of the Spirits of Darkness. Spiritual Beings and Their Effects, Vol. 1
CW 178	Individual Spiritual Beings and their Influence in the Soul of the Human Being. Spiritual Beings and their Effects, Vol. 2
CW 179	Spiritual Beings and Their Effects. Historical Necessity and Freedom. The Influences on Destiny from out of the World of the Dead. Spiritual Beings and Their Effects, Vol. 3
CW 180	Mystery Truths and Christmas Impulses. Ancient Myths and their Meaning. Spiritual Beings and Their Effects, Vol. 4
CW 181	Earthly Death and Cosmic Life. Anthroposophical Gifts for Life. Necessities of Consciousness for the Present and the Future.
CW 182	Death as Transformation of Life
CW 183	The Science of the Development of the Human Being
CW 184	The Polarity of Duration and Development in Human Life. The Cosmic Pre-History of Humanity
CW 185	Historical Symptomology
CW 185a	Historical-Developmental Foundations for Forming a Social Judgment
CW 186	The Fundamental Social Demands of Our Time–In Changed Situations
CW 187	How Can Humanity Find the Christ Again? The Threefold Shadow-Existence of our Time and the New Christ-Light
CW 188	Goetheanism, a Transformation-Impulse and Resurrection-Thought. Science of the Human Being and Science of Sociology
CW 189	The Social Question as a Question of Consciousness. The Spiritual Background of the Social Question, Vol. 1
CW 190	Impulses of the Past and the Future in Social Occurrences. The Spiritual Background of the Social Question, Vol. 2
CW 191	Social Understanding from Spiritual-Scientific Cognition. The Spiritual Background of the Social Question, Vol. 3

CW 192 Spiritual-Scientific Treatment of Social and Pedagogical Questions
CW 193 The Inner Aspect of the Social Riddle. Luciferic Past and Ahrimanic Future
CW 194 The Mission of Michael. The Revelation of the Actual Mysteries of the Human Being
CW 195 Cosmic New Year and the New Year Idea
CW 196 Spiritual and Social Transformations in the Development of Humanity
CW 197 Polarities in the Development of Humanity: West and East Materialism and Mysticism Knowledge and Belief
CW 198 Healing Factors for the Social Organism
CW 199 Spiritual Science as Knowledge of the Foundational Impulses of Social Formation
CW 200 The New Spirituality and the Christ-Experience of the 20th Century
CW 201 The Correspondences Between Microcosm and Macrocosm. The Human Being – A Hieroglyph of the Universe. The Human Being in Relationship with the Cosmos: 1
CW 202 The Bridge between the World-Spirituality and the Physical Aspect of the Human Being. The Search for the New Isis, the Divine Sophia. The Human Being in Relationship with the Cosmos: 2
CW 203 The Responsibility of Human Beings for the Development of the World through their Spiritual Connection with the Planet Earth and the World of the Stars. The Human Being in Relationship with the Cosmos: 3
CW 204 Perspectives of the Development of Humanity. The Materialistic Knowledge-Impulse and the Task of Anthroposophy. The Human Being in Relationship with the Cosmos: 4
CW 205 Human Development, World-Soul, and World-Spirit. Part One: The Human Being as a Being of Body and Soul in Relationship to the World. The Human Being in Relationship with the Cosmos: 5
CW 206 Human Development, World-Soul, and World-Spirit. Part Two: The Human Being as a Spiritual Being in the Process of Historical Development. The Human Being in Relationship with the Cosmos: 6
CW 207 Anthroposophy as Cosmosophy. Part One: Characteristic Features of the Human Being in the Earthly and the Cosmic Realms. The Human Being in Relationship with the Cosmos: 7
CW 208 Anthroposophy as Cosmosophy. Part Two: The Forming of the Human Being as the Result of Cosmic Influence. The Human Being in Relationship with the Cosmos: 8
CW 209 Nordic and Central European Spiritual Impulses. The Festival of the Appearance of Christ. The Human Being in Relationship with the Cosmos: 9

CW 210	Old and New Methods of Initiation. Drama and Poetry in the Change of Consciousness in the Modern Age
CW 211	The Sun Mystery and the Mystery of Death and Resurrection. Exoteric and Esoteric Christianity
CW 212	Human Soul Life and Spiritual Striving in Connection with World and Earth Development
CW 213	Human Questions and World Answers
CW 214	The Mystery of the Trinity: The Human Being in Relationship with the Spiritual World in the Course of Time
CW 215	Philosophy, Cosmology, and Religion in Anthroposophy
CW 216	The Fundamental Impulses of the World-Historical Development of Humanity
CW 217	Spiritually Active Forces in the Coexistence of the Older and Younger Generations. Pedagogical Course for Youth
CW 217a	Youth's Cognitive Task
CW 218	Spiritual Connections in the Forming of the Human Organism
CW 219	The Relationship of the World of the Stars to the Human Being, and of the Human Being to the World of the Stars. The Spiritual Communion of Humanity
CW 220	Living Knowledge of Nature. Intellectual Fall and Spiritual Redemption
CW 221	Earth-Knowing and Heaven-Insight
CW 222	The Imparting of Impulses to World-Historical Events through Spiritual Powers
CW 223	The Cycle of the Year as Breathing Process of the Earth and the Four Great Festival-Seasons. Anthroposophy and the Human Heart (Gemüt)
CW 224	The Human Soul and its Connection with Divine-Spiritual Individualities. The Internalization of the Festivals of the Year
CW 225	Three Perspectives of Anthroposophy. Cultural Phenomena observed from a Spiritual-Scientific Perspective
CW 226	Human Being, Human Destiny, and World Development
CW 227	Initiation-Knowledge
CW 228	Science of Initiation and Knowledge of the Stars. The Human Being in the Past, the Present, and the Future from the Viewpoint of the Development of Consciousness
CW 229	The Experiencing of the Course of the Year in Four Cosmic Imaginations
CW 230	The Human Being as Harmony of the Creative, Building, and Formative World-Word
CW 231	The Supersensible Human Being, Understood Anthroposophically
CW 232	The Forming of the Mysteries
CW 233	World History Illuminated by Anthroposophy and as the Foundation for Knowledge of the Human Spirit

CW 233a Mystery Sites of the Middle Ages: Rosicrucianism and the Modern Initiation-Principle. The Festival of Easter as Part of the History of the Mysteries of Humanity
CW 234 Anthroposophy. A Summary after 21 Years
CW 235 Esoteric Observations of Karmic Relationships in 6 Volumes, Vol. 1
CW 236 Esoteric Observations of Karmic Relationships in 6 Volumes, Vol. 2
CW 237 Esoteric Observations of Karmic Relationships in 6 Volumes, Vol. 3: The Karmic Relationships of the Anthroposophical Movement
CW 238 Esoteric Observations of Karmic Relationships in 6 Volumes, Vol. 4: The Spiritual Life of the Present in Relationship to the Anthroposophical Movement
CW 239 Esoteric Observations of Karmic Relationships in 6 Volumes, Vol. 5
CW 240 Esoteric Observations of Karmic Relationships in 6 Volumes, Vol. 6
CW 243 The Consciousness of the Initiate
CW 245 Instructions for an Esoteric Schooling
CW 250 The Building-Up of the Anthroposophical Society. From the Beginning to the Outbreak of the First World War
CW 251 The History of the Goetheanum Building-Association
CW 252 Life in the Anthroposophical Society from the First World War to the Burning of the First Goetheanum
CW 253 The Problems of Living Together in the Anthroposophical Society. On the Dornach Crisis of 1915. With Highlights on Swedenborg's Clairvoyance, the Views of Freudian Psychoanalysts, and the Concept of Love in Relation to Mysticism
CW 254 The Occult Movement in the 19th Century and Its Relationship to World Culture. Significant Points from the Exoteric Cultural Life around the Middle of the 19th Century
CW 255 Rudolf Steiner during the First World War
CW 255a Anthroposophy and the Reformation of Society. On the History of the Threefold Movement
CW 255b Anthroposophy and Its Opponents, 1919-1921
CW 256 How Can the Anthroposophical Movement Be Financed?
CW 256a Futurum, Inc. / International Laboratories, Inc.
CW 256b The Coming Day, Inc.
CW 257 Anthroposophical Community-Building
CW 258 The History of and Conditions for the Anthroposophical Movement in Relationship to the Anthroposophical Society. A Stimulus to Self-Contemplation
CW 259 The Year of Destiny 1923 in the History of the Anthroposophical Society. From the Burning of the Goetheanum to the Christmas Conference
CW 260 The Christmas Conference for the Founding of the General Anthroposophical Society

CW 260a The Constitution of the General Anthroposophical Society and the School for Spiritual Science. The Rebuilding of the Goetheanum
CW 261 Our Dead. Addresses, Words of Remembrance, and Meditative Verses, 1906-1924
CW 262 Rudolf Steiner and Marie Steiner-von Sivers: Correspondence and Documents, 1901-1925
CW 263/1 Rudolf Steiner and Edith Maryon: Correspondence: Letters, Verses, Sketches, 1912-1924
CW 264 On the History and the Contents of the First Section of the Esoteric School from 1904 to 1914. Letters, Newsletters, Documents, Lectures
CW 265 On the History and from the Contents of the Ritual-Knowledge Section of the Esoteric School from 1904 to 1914. Documents, and Lectures from the Years 1906 to 1914, as Well as on New Approaches to Ritual-Knowledge Work in the Years 1921-1924
CW 266/1 From the Contents of the Esoteric Lessons. Volume 1: 1904-1909. Notes from Memory of Participants. Meditation texts from the notes of Rudolf Steiner
CW 266/2 From the Contents of the Esoteric Lessons. Volume 2: 1910-1912. Notes from Memory of Participants
CW 266/3 From the Contents of the Esoteric Lessons. Volume 3: 1913, 1914 and 1920-1923. Notes from Memory of Participants. Meditation texts from the notes of Rudolf Steiner
CW 267 Soul-Exercises: Vol. 1: Exercises with Word and Image Meditations for the Methodological Development of Higher Powers of Knowledge, 1904-1924
CW 268 Soul-Exercises: Vol. 2: Mantric Verses, 1903-1925
CW 269 Ritual Texts for the Celebration of the Free Christian Religious Instruction. The Collected Verses for Teachers and Students of the Waldorf School
CW 270 Esoteric Instructions for the First Class of the School for Spiritual Science at the Goetheanum 1924, 4 Volumes
CW 271 Art and Knowledge of Art. Foundations of a New Aesthetic
CW 272 Spiritual-Scientific Commentary on Goethe's "Faust" in Two Volumes. Vol. 1: Faust, the Striving Human Being
CW 273 Spiritual-Scientific Commentary on Goethe's "Faust" in Two Volumes. Vol. 2: The Faust-Problem
CW 274 Addresses for the Christmas Plays from the Old Folk Traditions
CW 275 Art in the Light of Mystery-Wisdom
CW 276 The Artistic in Its Mission in the World. The Genius of Language. The World of Self-Revealing Radiant Appearances – Anthroposophy and Art. Anthroposophy and Poetry
CW 277 Eurythmy. The Revelation of the Speaking Soul

CW 277a The Origin and Development of Eurythmy
CW 278 Eurythmy as Visible Song
CW 279 Eurythmy as Visible Speech
CW 280 The Method and Nature of Speech Formation
CW 281 The Art of Recitation and Declamation
CW 282 Speech Formation and Dramatic Art
CW 283 The Nature of Things Musical and the Experience of Tone in the Human Being
CW 284/285 Images of Occult Seals and Pillars. The Munich Congress of Whitsun 1907 and Its Consequences
CW 286 Paths to a New Style of Architecture. "And the Building Becomes Human"
CW 287 The Building at Dornach as a Symbol of Historical Becoming and an Artistic Transformation Impulse
CW 288 Style-Forms in the Living Organic
CW 289 The Building-Idea of the Goetheanum: Lectures with Slides from the Years 1920-1921
CW 290 The Building-Idea of the Goetheanum: Lectures with Slides from the Years 1920-1921
CW 291 The Nature of Colors
CW 291a Knowledge of Colors. Supplementary Volume to CW 291
CW 292 Art History as Image of Inner Spiritual Impulses
CW 293 General Knowledge of the Human Being as the Foundation of Pedagogy
CW 294 The Art of Education, Methodology and Didactics
CW 295 The Art of Education: Seminar Discussions and Lectures on Lesson Planning
CW 296 The Question of Education as a Social Question
CW 297 The Idea and Practice of the Waldorf School
CW 297a Education for Life: Self-Education and the Practice of Pedagogy
CW 298 Rudolf Steiner in the Waldorf School
CW 299 Spiritual-Scientific Observations on Speech
CW 300a Conferences with the Teachers of the Free Waldorf School in Stuttgart, 1919 to 1924, in 3 Volumes, Vol. 1
CW 300b Conferences with the Teachers of the Free Waldorf School in Stuttgart, 1919 to 1924, in 3 Volumes, Vol. 2
CW 300c Conferences with the Teachers of the Free Waldorf School in Stuttgart, 1919 to 1924, in 3 Volumes, Vol. 3
CW 301 The Renewal of Pedagogical-Didactical Art through Spiritual Science
CW 302 Knowledge of the Human Being and the Forming of Class Lessons
CW 302a Education and Teaching from a Knowledge of the Human Being
CW 303 The Healthy Development of the Human Being

CW 304 Methods of Education and Teaching Based on Anthroposophy
CW 304a Anthroposophical Knowledge of the Human Being and Pedagogy
CW 305 The Soul-Spiritual Foundational Forces of the Art of Education. Spiritual Values in Education and Social Life
CW 306 Pedagogical Praxis from the Viewpoint of a Spiritual-Scientific Knowledge of the Human Being. The Education of the Child and Young Human Beings
CW 307 The Spiritual Life of the Present and Education
CW 308 The Method of Teaching and the Life-Requirements for Teaching
CW 309 Anthroposophical Pedagogy and Its Prerequisites
CW 310 The Pedagogical Value of a Knowledge of the Human Being and the Cultural Value of Pedagogy
CW 311 The Art of Education from an Understanding of the Being of Humanity
CW 312 Spiritual Science and Medicine
CW 313 Spiritual-Scientific Viewpoints on Therapy
CW 314 Physiology and Therapy Based on Spiritual Science
CW 315 Curative Eurythmy
CW 316 Meditative Observations and Instructions for a Deepening of the Art of Healing
CW 317 The Curative Education Course
CW 318 The Working Together of Doctors and Pastors
CW 319 Anthroposophical Knowledge of the Human Being and Medicine
CW 320 Spiritual-Scientific Impulses for the Development of Physics 1: The First Natural-Scientific Course: Light, Color, Tone, Mass, Electricity, Magnetism
CW 321 Spiritual-Scientific Impulses for the Development of Physics 2: The Second Natural-Scientific Course: Warmth at the Border of Positive and Negative Materiality
CW 322 The Borders of the Knowledge of Nature
CW 323 The Relationship of the various Natural-Scientific Fields to Astronomy
CW 324 Nature Observation, Mathematics, and Scientific Experimentation and Results from the Viewpoint of Anthroposophy
CW 324a The Fourth Dimension in Mathematics and Reality
CW 325 Natural Science and the World-Historical Development of Humanity since Ancient Times
CW 326 The Moment of the Coming Into Being of Natural Science in World History and Its Development Since Then
CW 327 Spiritual-Scientific Foundations for Success in Farming. The Agricultural Course
CW 328 The Social Question
CW 329 The Liberation of the Human Being as the Foundation for a New Social Form
CW 330 The Renewal of the Social Organism

CW 331	Work-Council and Socialization
CW 332	The Alliance for Threefolding and the Total Reform of Society. The Council on Culture and the Liberation of the Spiritual Life
CW 332a	The Social Future
CW 333	Freedom of Thought and Social Forces
CW 334	From the Unified State to the Threefold Social Organism
CW 335	The Crisis of the Present and the Path to Healthy Thinking
CW 336	The Great Questions of the Times and Anthroposophical Spiritual Knowledge
CW 337a	Social Ideas, Social Reality, Social Practice, Vol. 1: Question-and-Answer Evenings and Study Evenings of the Alliance for the Threefold Social Organism in Stuttgart, 1919-1920
CW 337b	Social Ideas, Social Realities, Social Practice, Vol. 2: Discussion Evenings of the Swiss Alliance for the Threefold Social Organism
CW 338	How Does One Work on Behalf of the Impulse for the Threefold Social Organism?
CW 339	Anthroposophy, Threefold Social Organism, and the Art of Public Speaking
CW 340	The National-Economics Course. The Tasks of a New Science of Economics, Volume 1
CW 341	The National-Economics Seminar. The Tasks of a New Science of Economics, Volume 2
CW 342	Lectures and Courses on Christian Religious Work, Vol. 1: Anthroposophical Foundations for a Renewed Christian Religious Working
CW 343	Lectures and Courses on Christian Religious Work, Vol. 2: Spiritual Knowledge – Religious Feeling – Cultic Doing
CW 344	Lectures and Courses on Christian Religious Work, Vol. 3: Lectures at the Founding of the Christian Community
CW 345	Lectures and Courses on Christian Religious Work, Vol. 4: Concerning the Nature of the Working Word
CW 346	Lectures and Courses on Christian Religious Work, Vol. 5: The Apocalypse and the Work of the Priest
CW 347	The Knowledge of the Nature of the Human Being According to Body, Soul and Spirit. On Earlier Conditions of the Earth
CW 348	On Health and Illness. Foundations of a Spiritual-Scientific Doctrine of the Senses
CW 349	On the Life of the Human Being and of the Earth. On the Nature of Christianity
CW 350	Rhythms in the Cosmos and in the Human Being. How Does One Come To See the Spiritual World?
CW 351	The Human Being and the World. The Influence of the Spirit in Nature. On the Nature of Bees
CW 352	Nature and the Human Being Observed Spiritual-Scientifically
CW 353	The History of Humanity and the World-Views of the Folk Cultures
CW 354	The Creation of the World and the Human Being. Life on Earth and the Influence of the Stars

SIGNIFICANT EVENTS IN THE LIFE OF RUDOLF STEINER

1829: June 23: birth of Johann Steiner (1829-1910)—Rudolf Steiner's father—in Geras, Lower Austria.

1834: May 8: birth of Franciska Blie (1834-1918)—Rudolf Steiner's mother—in Horn, Lower Austria. "My father and mother were both children of the glorious Lower Austrian forest district north of the Danube."

1860: May 16: marriage of Johann Steiner and Franciska Blie.

1861: February 25: birth of *Rudolf Joseph Lorenz Steiner* in Kraljevec, Croatia, near the border with Hungary, where Johann Steiner works as a telegrapher for the South Austria Railroad. Rudolf Steiner is baptized two days later, February 27, the date usually given as his birthday.

1862: Summer: the family moves to Mödling, Lower Austria.

1863: The family moves to Pottschach, Lower Austria, near the Styrian border, where Johann Steiner becomes stationmaster. "The view stretched to the mountains...majestic peaks in the distance and the sweet charm of nature in the immediate surroundings."

1864: November 15: birth of Rudolf Steiner's sister, Leopoldine (d. November 1, 1927). She will become a seamstress and live with her parents for the rest of her life.

1866: July 28: birth of Rudolf Steiner's deaf-mute brother, Gustav (d. May 1, 1941).

1867: Rudolf Steiner enters the village school. Following a disagreement between his father and the schoolmaster, whose wife falsely accused the boy of causing a commotion, Rudolf Steiner is taken out of school and taught at home.

1868: A critical experience. Unknown to the family, an aunt dies in a distant town. Sitting in the station waiting room, Rudolf Steiner sees her "form," which speaks to him, asking for help. "Beginning with this experience, a new soul life began in the boy, one in which not only the outer trees and mountains spoke to him, but also the worlds that lay behind them. From this moment on, the boy began to live with the spirits of nature...."

1869: The family moves to the peaceful, rural village of Neudorfl, near Wiener-Neustadt in present-day Austria. Rudolf Steiner attends the village school. Because of the "unorthodoxy" of his writing and spelling, he has to do "extra lessons."

1870: Through a book lent to him by his tutor, he discovers geometry: "To grasp something purely in the spirit brought me inner happiness. I know that I first learned happiness through geometry." The same tutor allows him to draw, while other students still struggle with their reading and writing. "An artistic element" thus enters his education.

1871: Though his parents are not religious, Rudolf Steiner becomes a "church child," a favorite of the priest, who was "an exceptional character." "Up to the age of ten or eleven, among those I came to know, he was far and away the most significant." Among other things, he introduces Steiner to Copernican, heliocentric cosmology. As an altar boy, Rudolf Steiner serves at Masses, funerals, and Corpus Christi processions. At year's end, after an incident in which he escapes a thrashing, his father forbids him to go to church.

1872: Rudolf Steiner transfers to grammar school in Wiener-Neustadt, a five-mile walk from home, which must be done in all weathers.

1873-75: Through his teachers and on his own, Rudolf Steiner has many wonderful experiences with science and mathematics. Outside school, he teaches himself analytic geometry, trigonometry, differential equations, and calculus.

1876: Rudolf Steiner begins tutoring other students. He learns bookbinding from his father. He also teaches himself stenography.

1877: Rudolf Steiner discovers Kant's *Critique of Pure Reason*, which he reads and rereads. He also discovers and reads von Rotteck's *World History*.

1878: He studies extensively in contemporary psychology and philosophy.

1879: Rudolf Steiner graduates from high school with honors. His father is transferred to Inzersdorf, near Vienna. He uses his first visit to Vienna "to purchase a great number of philosophy books"—Kant, Fichte, Schelling, and Hegel, as well as numerous histories of philosophy. His aim: to find a path from the "I" to nature.

October 1879-1883: Rudolf Steiner attends the Technical College in Vienna—to study mathematics, chemistry, physics, mineralogy, botany, zoology, biology, geology, and mechanics—with a scholarship. He also attends lectures in history and literature, while avidly reading philosophy on his own. His two favorite professors are Karl Julius Schröer (German language and literature) and Edmund Reitlinger (physics). He also audits lectures by Robert Zimmerman on aesthetics and Franz Brentano on philosophy. During this year he begins his friendship with Moritz Zitter (1861-1921), who will help support him financially when he is in Berlin.

1880: Rudolf Steiner attends lectures on Schiller and Goethe by Karl Julius Schröer, who becomes his mentor. Also "through a remarkable combination of circumstances," he meets Felix Koguzki, a "herb gatherer" and healer, who could "see deeply into the secrets of nature." Rudolf Steiner will meet and study with this "emissary of the Master" throughout his time in Vienna.

1881: January: "... I didn't sleep a wink. I was busy with philosophical problems until about 12:30 a.m. Then, finally, I threw myself down on my couch. All my striving during the previous year had been to research whether the following statement by Schelling was true or not: *Within everyone dwells a secret, marvelous capacity to draw back from the stream of time—out of the self clothed in all that comes to us from outside—into our innermost being and there, in the immutable form of the Eternal, to look into ourselves*. I believe, and I am still quite certain of it, that I discovered this capacity in myself; I had long had an inkling of it. Now the whole of idealist philosophy stood before me in modified form. What's a sleepless night compared to that!"

Rudolf Steiner begins communicating with leading thinkers of the day, who send him books in return, which he reads eagerly.

July: "I am not one of those who dives into the day like an animal in human form. I pursue a quite specific goal, an idealistic aim—knowledge of the truth! This cannot be done offhandedly. It requires the greatest striving in the world, free of all egotism, and equally of all resignation."

August: Steiner puts down on paper for the first time thoughts for a "Philosophy of Freedom." "The striving for the absolute: this human yearning is freedom." He also seeks to outline a "peasant philosophy," describing what the worldview of a "peasant"—one who lives close to the earth and the old ways—really is.

1881-1882: Felix Koguzki, the herb gatherer, reveals himself to be the envoy of another, higher initiatory personality, who instructs Rudolf Steiner to penetrate Fichte's philosophy and to master modern scientific thinking as a preparation for right entry into the spirit. This "Master" also teaches him the double (evolutionary and involutionary) nature of time.

1882: Through the offices of Karl Julius Schröer, Rudolf Steiner is asked by Joseph Kurschner to edit Goethe's scientific works for the *Deutschen National-Literatur* edition. He writes "A Possible Critique of Atomistic Concepts" and sends it to Friedrich Theodore Vischer.

1883: Rudolf Steiner completes his college studies and begins work on the Goethe project.

1884: First volume of Goethe's *Scientific Writings* (CW 1) appears (March). He lectures on Goethe and Lessing, and Goethe's approach to science. In July, he enters the household of Ladislaus and Pauline Specht as tutor to the four Specht boys. He will live there until 1890. At this time, he meets Josef Breuer (1842-1925), the coauthor with Sigmund Freud of *Studies in Hysteria*, who is the Specht family doctor.

1885: While continuing to edit Goethe's writings, Rudolf Steiner reads deeply in contemporary philosophy (Edouard von Hartmann, Johannes Volkelt, and Richard Wahle, among others).

1886: May: Rudolf Steiner sends Kurschner the manuscript of *Outlines of Goethe's Theory of Knowledge* (CW 2), which appears in October, and which he sends out widely. He also meets the poet Marie Eugenie Delle Grazie and writes "Nature and Our Ideals" for her. He attends her salon, where he meets many priests, theologians, and philosophers, who will become his friends. Meanwhile, the director of the Goethe Archive in Weimar requests his collaboration with the *Sophien* edition of Goethe's works, particularly the writings on color.

1887: At the beginning of the year, Rudolf Steiner is very sick. As the year progresses and his health improves, he becomes increasingly "a man of letters," lecturing, writing essays, and taking part in Austrian cultural life. In August-September, the second volume of Goethe's *Scientific Writings* appears.

1888: January-July: Rudolf Steiner assumes editorship of the "German Weekly" (*Deutsche Wochenschrift*). He begins lecturing more intensively, giving, for example, a lecture titled "Goethe as Father of a New Aesthetics." He meets and becomes soul friends with Friedrich Eckstein (1861-1939), a vegetarian, philosopher of symbolism, alchemist, and musician, who will introduce him to various spiritual currents (including Theosophy) and with whom he will meditate and interpret esoteric and alchemical texts.

1889: Rudolf Steiner first reads Nietzsche (*Beyond Good and Evil*). He encounters Theosophy again and learns of Madame Blavatsky in the Theosophical circle around Marie Lang (1858-1934). Here he also meets well-known figures of Austrian life, as well as esoteric figures like the occultist Franz Hartman and Karl Leinigen-Billigen (translator of C.G. Harrison's *The Transcendental Universe*.) During this period, Steiner first reads A.P. Sinnett's *Esoteric Buddhism* and Mabel Collins's *Light on the Path*. He also begins traveling, visiting Budapest, Weimar, and Berlin (where he meets philosopher Edouard von Hartmann).

1890: Rudolf Steiner finishes volume 3 of Goethe's scientific writings. He begins his doctoral dissertation, which will become *Truth and Science* (CW 3). He also meets the poet and feminist Rosa Mayreder (1858-1938), with whom he can exchange his most intimate thoughts. In September, Rudolf Steiner moves to Weimar to work in the Goethe-Schiller Archive.

1891: Volume 3 of the Kurschner edition of Goethe appears. Meanwhile, Rudolf Steiner edits Goethe's studies in mineralogy and scientific writings for the *Sophien* edition. He meets Ludwig Laistner of the Cotta Publishing Company, who asks for a book on the basic question of metaphysics. From this will result, ultimately, *The Philosophy of Freedom* (CW 4), which will be published not by Cotta but by Emil Felber. In October, Rudolf Steiner takes the oral exam for a doctorate in philosophy, mathematics, and mechanics at Rostock University, receiving his doctorate on the twenty-sixth. In November, he gives his first lecture on Goethe's "Fairy Tale" in Vienna.

1892: Rudolf Steiner continues work at the Goethe-Schiller Archive and on his *Philosophy of Freedom*. *Truth and Science*, his doctoral dissertation, is published. Steiner undertakes to write introductions to books on Schopenhauer and Jean Paul for Cotta. At year's end, he finds lodging with Anna Eunike, née Schulz (1853-1911), a widow with four daughters and a son. He also develops a friendship with Otto Erich Hartleben (1864-1905) with whom he shares literary interests.

1893: Rudolf Steiner begins his habit of producing many reviews and articles. In March, he gives a lecture titled "Hypnotism, with Reference to Spiritism." In September, volume 4 of the Kurschner edition is completed. In November, *The Philosophy of Freedom* appears. This year, too, he meets John Henry Mackay (1864-1933), the anarchist, scholar, and biographer of Max Stirner.

1894: Rudolf Steiner meets Elisabeth Förster Nietzsche, the philosopher's sister, and begins to read Nietzsche in earnest, beginning with the as yet unpublished *Antichrist*. He also meets Ernst Haeckel (1834-1919). In the fall, he begins to write *Nietzsche, A Fighter against His Time* (CW 5).

1895: May, *Nietzsche, A Fighter against His Time* appears.

1896: January 22: Rudolf Steiner sees Friedrich Nietzsche for the first and only time. Moves between the Nietzsche and the Goethe-Schiller Archives, where he completes his work before year's end. He falls out with Elisabeth Förster Nietzsche, thus ending his association with the Nietzsche Archive.

1897: Rudolf Steiner finishes the manuscript of *Goethe's Worldview* (CW 6). He moves to Berlin with Anna Eunike and begins editorship of the *Magazin fur Literatur*. From now on, Steiner will write countless reviews, literary and philosophical articles, and so on. He begins lecturing at the "Free Literary Society." In September, he attends the Zionist Congress in Basel. He sides with Dreyfus in the Dreyfus affair.

1898: Rudolf Steiner is very active as an editor in the political, artistic, and theatrical life of Berlin. He becomes friendly with John Henry Mackay and poet Ludwig Jacobowski (1868-1900). He joins Jacobowski's circle of writers, artists, and scientists—"The Coming Ones" (*Die Kommenden*)—and contributes lectures to the group until 1903. He also lectures at the "League for College Pedagogy." He writes an article for Goethe's sesquicentennial, "Goethe's Secret Revelation," on the "Fairy Tale of the Green Snake and the Beautiful Lily."

1898-99: "This was a trying time for my soul as I looked at Christianity.... I was able to progress only by contemplating, by means of spiritual perception, the evolution of Christianity .... Conscious knowledge of real Christianity began to dawn in me around the turn of the century. This seed continued to develop. My soul trial occurred shortly before the beginning of the twentieth century. It was decisive for my soul's development that I stood spiritually before the Mystery of Golgotha in a deep and solemn celebration of knowledge."

1899: Rudolf Steiner begins teaching and giving lectures and lecture cycles at the Workers' College, founded by Wilhelm Liebknecht (1826-1900). He will continue to do so until 1904. Writes: *Literature and Spiritual Life in the Nineteenth Century; Individualism in Philosophy*; *Haeckel and His Opponents; Poetry in the Present;* and begins what will become (fifteen years later) *The Riddles of Philosophy* (CW 18). He also meets many artists and writers, including Käthe Kollwitz, Stefan Zweig, and Rainer Maria Rilke. On October 31, he marries Anna Eunike.

1900: "I thought that the turn of the century must bring humanity a new light. It seemed to me that the separation of human thinking and willing from the spirit had peaked. A turn or reversal of direction in human evolution seemed to me a necessity." Rudolf Steiner finishes *World and Life Views in the Nineteenth Century* (the second part of what will become *The Riddles of Philosophy*) and dedicates it to Ernst Haeckel. It is published in March. He continues lecturing at *Die Kommenden*, whose leadership he assumes after the death of Jacobowski. Also, he gives the Gutenberg Jubilee lecture before 7,000 typesetters and printers. In September, Rudolf Steiner is invited by Count and Countess Brockdorff to lecture in the Theosophical Library. His first lecture is on Nietzsche. His second lecture is titled "Goethe's Secret Revelation." October 6, he begins a lecture cycle on the mystics that will become *Mystics after Modernism* (CW 7). November-December: "Marie von Sivers appears in the audience...." Also in November, Steiner gives his first lecture at the Giordano Bruno Bund (where he will continue to lecture until May, 1905). He speaks on Bruno and modern Rome, focusing on the importance of the philosophy of Thomas Aquinas as monism.

1901: In continual financial straits, Rudolf Steiner's early friends Moritz Zitter and Rosa Mayreder help support him. In October, he begins the lecture cycle *Christianity as Mystical Fact* (CW 8) at the Theosophical Library. In November, he gives his first "Theosophical lecture" on Goethe's "Fairy Tale" in Hamburg at the invitation of Wilhelm Hubbe-Schleiden. He also attends a gathering to celebrate the founding of the Theosophical Society at Count and Countess Brockdorff's. He gives a lecture cycle, "From Buddha to Christ," for the circle of the *Kommenden*. November 17, Marie von Sivers asks Rudolf Steiner if Theosophy needs a Western-Christian spiritual movement (to complement Theosophy's Eastern emphasis). "The question was posed. Now, following spiritual laws, I could begin to give an answer...." In December, Rudolf Steiner writes his first article for a Theosophical publication. At year's end, the Brockdorffs and possibly Wilhelm Hubbe-Schleiden ask Rudolf Steiner to join the Theosophical Society and undertake the leadership of the German section. Rudolf Steiner agrees, on the condition that Marie von Sivers (then in Italy) work with him.

1902: Beginning in January, Rudolf Steiner attends the opening of the Workers' School in Spandau with Rosa Luxemberg (1870-1919). January 17, Rudolf Steiner joins the Theosophical Society. In April, he is asked to become general secretary of the German Section of the Theosophical Society, and works on preparations for its founding. In July, he visits London for a Theosophical congress. He meets Bertram Keightly, G.R.S. Mead, A.P. Sinnett, and Annie Besant, among others. In September, *Christianity as Mystical Fact* appears. In October, Rudolf

Steiner gives his first public lecture on Theosophy ("Monism and Theosophy") to about three hundred people at the Giordano Bruno Bund. On October 19-21, the German Section of the Theosophical Society has its first meeting; Rudolf Steiner is the general secretary, and Annie Besant attends. Steiner lectures on practical karma studies. On October 23, Annie Besant inducts Rudolf Steiner into the Esoteric School of the Theosophical Society. On October 25, Steiner begins a weekly series of lectures: "The Field of Theosophy." During this year, Rudolf Steiner also meets Ita Wegman (1876-1943), who will become his close collaborator in his final years.

1903: Rudolf Steiner holds about 300 lectures and seminars. In May, the first issue of the periodical *Luzifer* appears. In June, Rudolf Steiner visits London for the first meeting of the Federation of the European Sections of the Theosophical Society, where he meets Colonel Olcott. He begins to write *Theosophy* (CW 9).

1904: Rudolf Steiner continues lecturing at the Workers' College and elsewhere (about 90 lectures), while lecturing intensively all over Germany among Theosophists (about 140 lectures). In February, he meets Carl Unger (1878-1929), who will become a member of the board of the Anthroposophical Society (1913). In March, he meets Michael Bauer (1871-1929), a Christian mystic, who will also be on the board. In May, *Theosophy* appears, with the dedication: "To the spirit of Giordano Bruno." Rudolf Steiner and Marie von Sivers visit London for meetings with Annie Besant. June: Rudolf Steiner and Marie von Sivers attend the meeting of the Federation of European Sections of the Theosophical Society in Amsterdam. In July, Steiner begins the articles in *Luzifer-Gnosis* that will become *How to Know Higher Worlds* (CW 10) and *Cosmic Memory* (CW 11). In September, Annie Besant visits Germany. In December, Steiner lectures on Freemasonry. He mentions the High Grade Masonry derived from John Yarker and represented by Theodore Reuss and Karl Kellner as a blank slate "into which a good image could be placed."

1905: This year, Steiner ends his non-Theosophical lecturing activity. Supported by Marie von Sivers, his Theosophical lecturing—both in public and in the Theosophical Society—increases significantly: "The German Theosophical Movement is of exceptional importance." Steiner recommends reading, among others, Fichte, Jacob Boehme, and Angelus Silesius. He begins to introduce Christian themes into Theosophy. He also begins to work with doctors (Felix Peipers and Ludwig Noll). In July, he is in London for the Federation of European Sections, where he attends a lecture by Annie Besant: "I have seldom seen Mrs. Besant speak in so inward and heartfelt a manner…." "Through Mrs. Besant I have found the way to H.P. Blavatsky." September to October, he gives a course of thirty-one lectures for a small group of esoteric students. In October, the annual meeting of the German Section of the Theosophical Society, which still remains very small, takes place. Rudolf Steiner reports membership has risen from 121 to 377 members. In November, seeking to establish esoteric "continuity," Rudolf Steiner and Marie von Sivers participate in a "Memphis-Misraim" Masonic ceremony. They pay forty-five marks for membership. "Yesterday, you saw how little remains of former esoteric institutions." "We are dealing only with a 'framework'... for the present, nothing lies behind it. The occult powers have completely withdrawn."

1906: Expansion of Theosophical work. Rudolf Steiner gives about 245 lectures, only 44 of which take place in Berlin. Cycles are given in Paris, Leipzig, Stuttgart, and Munich. Esoteric work also intensifies. Rudolf Steiner begins writing *An Outline of Esoteric Science* (CW 13). In January, Rudolf Steiner receives permission (a patent) from the Great Orient of the Scottish A & A Thirty-Three Degree Rite of the Order of the Ancient Freemasons of the Memphis-Misraim Rite to direct a chapter under the name "Mystica Aeterna." This will become the "Cognitive-Ritual Section" (also called "Misraim Service") of the Esoteric School. (See: *Freemasonry and Ritual Work: The Misraim Service* (CW 265). During this time, Steiner also meets Albert Schweitzer. In May, he is in Paris, where he visits Edouard Schuré. Many Russians attend his lectures (including Konstantin Balmont, Dimitri Mereszkovski, Zinaida Hippius, and Maximilian Woloshin). He attends the General Meeting of the European Federation of the Theosophical Society, at which Col. Olcott is present for the last time. He spends the year's end in Venice and Rome, where he writes and works on his translation of H.P. Blavatsky's *Key to Theosophy*.

1907: Further expansion of the German Theosophical Movement according to the Rosicrucian directive to "introduce spirit into the world"—in education, in social questions, in art, and in science. In February, Col. Olcott dies in Adyar. Before he dies, Olcott indicates that "the Masters" wish Annie Besant to succeed him: much politicking ensues. Rudolf Steiner supports Besant's candidacy. April-May: preparations for the Congress of the Federation of European Sections of the Theosophical Society—the great, watershed Whitsun "Munich Congress," attended by Annie Besant and others. Steiner decides to separate Eastern and Western (Christian-Rosicrucian) esoteric schools. He takes his esoteric school out of the Theosophical Society (Besant and Rudolf Steiner are "in harmony" on this). Steiner makes his first lecture tours to Austria and Hungary. That summer, he is in Italy. In September, he visits Edouard Schuré, who will write the introduction to the French edition of *Christianity as Mystical Fact* in Barr, Alsace. Rudolf Steiner writes the autobiographical statement known as the "Barr Document." In *Luzifer–Gnosis*, "The Education of the Child" appears.

1908: The movement grows (membership: 1,150). Lecturing expands. Steiner makes his first extended lecture tour to Holland and Scandinavia, as well as visits to Naples and Sicily. Themes: St. John's Gospel, the Apocalypse, Egypt, science, philosophy, and logic. *Luzifer-Gnosis* ceases publication. In Berlin, Marie von Sivers (with Johanna Mücke (1864-1949) forms the *Philosophisch-Theosophisch* (after 1915 *Philosophisch-Anthroposophisch*) *Verlag* to publish Steiner's work. Steiner gives lecture cycles titled *The Gospel of St. John* (CW 103) and *The Apocalypse* (104).

1909: *An Outline of Esoteric Science* appears. Lecturing and travel continues. Rudolf Steiner's spiritual research expands to include the polarity of Lucifer and Ahriman; the work of great individualities in history; the Maitreya Buddha and the Bodhisattvas; spiritual economy (CW 109); the work of the spiritual hierarchies in heaven and on earth (CW 110). He also deepens and intensifies his research into the Gospels, giving lectures on the Gospel of St. Luke (CW 114) with the first mention of two Jesus children. Meets and becomes friends with Christian Morgenstern (1871-1914). In April, he lays the foundation stone for the Malsch model—the building that will lead to the first Goetheanum. In May, the International Congress of the Federation of European Sections of the Theosophical Society takes place in Budapest. Rudolf Steiner receives the Subba Row medal for *How to Know Higher Worlds.* During this time, Charles W. Leadbeater discovers Jiddu Krishnamurti (1895-1986) and proclaims him the future "world teacher," the bearer of the Maitreya Buddha and the "reappearing Christ." In October, Steiner delivers seminal lectures on "anthroposophy," which he will try, unsuccessfully, to rework over the next years into the unfinished work, *Anthroposophy (A Fragment)* (CW 45).

1910: New themes: *The Reappearance of Christ in the Etheric* (CW 118); *The Fifth Gospel; The Mission of Folk Souls* (CW 121); *Occult History* (CW 126); the evolving development of etheric cognitive capacities. Rudolf Steiner continues his Gospel research with *The Gospel of St. Matthew* (CW 123). In January, his father dies. In April, he takes a month-long trip to Italy, including Rome, Monte Cassino, and Sicily. He also visits Scandinavia again. July-August, he writes the first mystery drama, *The Portal of Initiation* (CW 14). In November, he gives "psychosophy" lectures. In December, he submits "On the Psychological Foundations and Epistemological Framework of Theosophy" to the International Philosophical Congress in Bologna.

1911: The crisis in the Theosophical Society deepens. In January, "The Order of the Rising Sun," which will soon become "The Order of the Star in the East," is founded for the coming world teacher, Krishnamurti. At the same time, Marie von Sivers, Rudolf Steiner's coworker, falls ill. Fewer lectures are given, but important new ground is broken. In Prague, in March, Steiner meets Franz Kafka (1883-1924) and Hugo Bergmann (1883-1975). In April, he delivers his paper to the Philosophical Congress. He writes the second mystery drama, *The Soul's Probation* (CW 14). Also, while Marie von Sivers is convalescing,

Rudolf Steiner begins work on *Calendar 1912/1913*, which will contain the "Calendar of the Soul" meditations. On March 19, Anna (Eunike) Steiner dies. In September, Rudolf Steiner visits Einsiedeln, birthplace of Paracelsus. In December, Friedrich Rittelmeyer, future founder of the Christian Community, meets Rudolf Steiner. The *Johannes-Bauverein*, the "building committee," which would lead to the first Goetheanum (first planned for Munich), is also founded, and a preliminary committee for the founding of an independent association is created that, in the following year, will become the Anthroposophical Society. Important lecture cycles include *Occult Physiology* (CW 128); *Wonders of the World* (CW 129); *From Jesus to Christ* (CW 131). Other themes: esoteric Christianity; Christian Rosenkreutz; the spiritual guidance of humanity; the sense world and the world of the spirit.

1912: Despite the ongoing, now increasing crisis in the Theosophical Society, much is accomplished: *Calendar 1912/1913* is published; eurythmy is created; both the third mystery drama, *The Guardian of the Threshold* (CW 14) and *A Way of Self-Knowledge* (CW 16) are written. New (or renewed) themes included life between death and rebirth and karma and reincarnation. Other lecture cycles: *Spiritual Beings in the Heavenly Bodies and in the Kingdoms of Nature* (CW 136); *The Human Being in the Light of Occultism, Theosophy, and Philosophy* (CW 137); *The Gospel of St. Mark* (CW 139); and *The Bhagavad Gita and the Epistles of Paul* (CW 142). On May 8, Rudolf Steiner celebrates White Lotus Day, H.P. Blavatsky's death day, which he had faithfully observed for the past decade, for the last time. In August, Rudolf Steiner suggests the "independent association" be called the "Anthroposophical Society." In September, the first eurythmy course takes place. In October, Rudolf Steiner declines recognition of a Theosophical Society lodge dedicated to the Star of the East and decides to expel all Theosophical Society members belonging to the order. Also, with Marie von Sivers, he first visits Dornach, near Basel, Switzerland, and they stand on the hill where the Goetheanum will be built. In November, a Theosophical Society lodge is opened by direct mandate from Adyar (Annie Besant). In December, a meeting of the German section occurs at which it is decided that belonging to the Order of the Star of the East is incompatible with membership in the Theosophical Society. December 28: informal founding of the Anthroposophical Society in Berlin.

1913: Expulsion of the German section from the Theosophical Society. February 2-3: Foundation meeting of the Anthroposophical Society. Board members include: Marie von Sivers, Michael Bauer, and Carl Unger. September 20: Laying of the foundation stone for the *Johannes Bau* (Goetheanum) in Dornach. Building begins immediately. The third mystery drama, *The Soul's Awakening* (CW 14), is completed. Also: *The Threshold of the Spiritual World* (CW 147). Lecture cycles include: *The Bhagavad Gita and the Epistles of Paul* and *The Esoteric*

Meaning of the Bhagavad Gita (CW 146), which the Russian philosopher Nikolai Berdyaev attends; *The Mysteries of the East and of Christianity* (CW 144); *The Effects of Esoteric Development* (CW 145); and *The Fifth Gospel* (CW 148). In May, Rudolf Steiner is in London and Paris, where anthroposophical work continues.

1914: Building continues on the *Johannes Bau* (Goetheanum) in Dornach, with artists and coworkers from seventeen nations. The general assembly of the Anthroposophical Society takes place. In May, Rudolf Steiner visits Paris, as well as Chartres Cathedral. June 28: assassination in Sarajevo ("Now the catastrophe has happened!"). August 1: War is declared. Rudolf Steiner returns to Germany from Dornach—he will travel back and forth. He writes the last chapter of *The Riddles of Philosophy*. Lecture cycles include: *Human and Cosmic Thought* (CW 151); *Inner Being of Humanity between Death and a New Birth* (CW 153); *Occult Reading and Occult Hearing* (CW 156). December 24: marriage of Rudolf Steiner and Marie von Sivers.

1915: Building continues. Life after death becomes a major theme, also art. Writes: *Thoughts during a Time of War* (CW 24). Lectures include: *The Secret of Death* (CW 159); *The Uniting of Humanity through the Christ Impulse* (CW 165).

1916: Rudolf Steiner begins work with Edith Maryon (1872-1924) on the sculpture "The Representative of Humanity" ("The Group"—Christ, Lucifer, and Ahriman). He also works with the alchemist Alexander von Bernus on the quarterly *Das Reich*. He writes *The Riddle of Humanity* (CW 20). Lectures include: *Necessity and Freedom in World History and Human Action* (CW 166); *Past and Present in the Human Spirit* (CW 167); *The Karma of Vocation* (CW 172); *The Karma of Untruthfulness* (CW 173).

1917: Russian Revolution. The U.S. enters the war. Building continues. Rudolf Steiner delineates the idea of the "threefold nature of the human being" (in a public lecture March 15) and the "threefold nature of the social organism" (hammered out in May-June with the help of Otto von Lerchenfeld and Ludwig Polzer-Hoditz in the form of two documents titled *Memoranda*, which were distributed in high places). August-September: Rudolf Steiner writes *The Riddles of the Soul* (CW 20). Also: commentary on "The Chemical Wedding of Christian Rosenkreutz" for Alexander Bernus (*Das Reich*). Lectures include: *The Karma of Materialism* (CW 176); *The Spiritual Background of the Outer World: The Fall of the Spirits of Darkness* (CW 177).

1918: March 18: peace treaty of Brest-Litovsk—"Now everything will truly enter chaos! What is needed is cultural renewal." June: Rudolf Steiner visits Karlstein (Grail) Castle outside Prague. Lecture cycle: *From Symptom to Reality in Modern History* (CW 185). In mid-November, Emil Molt, of the Waldorf-Astoria Cigarette Company, has the idea of founding a school for his workers' children.

1919: Focus on the threefold social organism: tireless travel, countless lectures, meetings, and publications. At the same time, a new public stage of Anthroposophy emerges as cultural renewal begins. The coming years will see initiatives in pedagogy, medicine, pharmacology, and agriculture. January 27: threefold meeting: " We must first of all, with the money we have, found free schools that can bring people what they need." February: first public eurythmy performance in Zurich. Also: "Appeal to the German People" (CW 24), circulated March 6 as a newspaper insert. In April, *Towards Social Renewal* (CW 23) appears—"perhaps the most widely read of all books on politics appearing since the war." Rudolf Steiner is asked to undertake the "direction and leadership" of the school founded by the Waldorf-Astoria Company. Rudolf Steiner begins to talk about the "renewal" of education. May 30: a building is selected and purchased for the future Waldorf School. August-September, Rudolf Steiner gives a lecture course for Waldorf teachers, *The Foundations of Human Experience (Study of Man)* (CW 293). September 7: Opening of the first Waldorf School. December (into January): first science course, the *Light Course* (CW 320).

1920: The Waldorf School flourishes. New threefold initiatives. Founding of limited companies *Der Kommende Tag* and *Futurum A.G.* to infuse spiritual values into the economic realm. Rudolf Steiner also focuses on the sciences. Lectures: *Introducing Anthroposophical Medicine* (CW 312); *The Warmth Course* (CW 321); *The Boundaries of Natural Science* (CW 322); *The Redemption of Thinking* (CW 74). February: Johannes Werner Klein—later a cofounder of the Christian Community—asks Rudolf Steiner about the possibility of a "religious renewal," a "Johannine church." In March, Rudolf Steiner gives the first course for doctors and medical students. In April, a divinity student asks Rudolf Steiner a second time about the possibility of religious renewal. September 27-October 16: anthroposophical "university course." December: lectures titled *The Search for the New Isis* (CW 202).

1921: Rudolf Steiner continues his intensive work on cultural renewal, including the uphill battle for the threefold social order. "University" arts, scientific, theological, and medical courses include: *The Astronomy Course* (CW 323); *Observation, Mathematics, and Scientific Experiment* (CW 324); the *Second Medical Course* (CW 313); *Color*. In June and September-October, Rudolf Steiner also gives the first two "priests' courses" (CW 342 and 343). The "youth movement" gains momentum. Magazines are founded: *Die Drei* (January), and—under the editorship of Albert Steffen (1884-1963)—the weekly, *Das Goetheanum* (August). In February-March, Rudolf Steiner takes his first trip outside Germany since the war (Holland). On April 7, Steiner receives a letter regarding "religious renewal," and May 22-23, he agrees to address the question in a practical way. In June, the Klinical-Therapeutic Institute opens in Arlesheim under the direction of Dr. Ita Wegman. In August, the Chemical-Pharmaceutical Laboratory opens in Arlesheim (Oskar Schmiedel and Ita Wegman are directors). The Clinical Therapeutic Institute is inaugurated in Stuttgart (Dr. Ludwig Noll is director); also the Research Laboratory in Dornach (Ehrenfried Pfeiffer and Gunther Wachsmuth are directors). In November-December, Rudolf Steiner visits Norway.

1922: The first half of the year involves very active public lecturing (thousands attend); in the second half, Rudolf Steiner begins to withdraw and turn toward the Society—"The Society is asleep." It is "too weak" to do what is asked of it. The businesses—*Der Kommende Tag* and *Futura A.G.*—fail. In January, with the help of an agent, Steiner undertakes a twelve-city German lecture tour, accompanied by eurythmy performances. In two weeks he speaks to more than 2,000 people. In April, he gives a "university course" in The Hague. He also visits England. In June, he is in Vienna for the East-West Congress. In August-September, he is back in England for the Oxford Conference on Education. Returning to Dornach, he gives the lectures *Philosophy, Cosmology, and Religion* (CW 215), and gives the third priests' course (CW 344). On September 16, The Christian Community is founded. In October-November, Steiner is in Holland and England. He also speaks to the youth: *The Youth Course* (CW 217). In December, Steiner gives lectures titled *The Origins of Natural Science* (CW 326), and *Humanity and the World of Stars: The Spiritual Communion of Humanity* (CW 219). December 31: Fire at the Goetheanum, which is destroyed.

1923: Despite the fire, Rudolf Steiner continues his work unabated. A very hard year. Internal dispersion, dissension, and apathy abound. There is conflict—between old and new visions—within the society. A wake-up call is needed, and Rudolf Steiner responds with renewed lecturing vitality. His focus: the spiritual context of human life; initiation science; the course of the year; and community building. As a foundation for an artistic school, he creates a series of pastel sketches. Lecture cycles: *The Anthroposophical Movement; Initiation Science* (CW 227) (in England at the Penmaenmawr Summer School); *The Four Seasons and the Archangels* (CW 229); *Harmony of the Creative Word* (CW 230); *The Supersensible Human* (CW 231), given in Holland for the founding of the Dutch society. On November 10, in response to the failed Hitler-Ludendorf putsch in Munich, Steiner closes his Berlin residence and moves the *Philosophisch-Anthroposophisch Verlag* (Press) to Dornach. On December 9, Steiner begins the serialization of his *Autobiography: The Course of My Life* (CW 28) in *Das Goetheanum*. It will continue to appear weekly, without a break, until his death. Late December-early January: Rudolf Steiner refounds the Anthroposophical Society (about 12,000 members internationally) and takes over its leadership. The new board members are: Marie Steiner, Ita Wegman, Albert Steffen, Elizabeth Vreede, and Guenther Wachsmuth. (See *The Christmas*

Meeting for the Founding of the General Anthroposophical Society (CW 260). Accompanying lectures: *Mystery Knowledge and Mystery Centers* (CW 232); *World History in the Light of Anthroposophy* (CW 233). December 25: the Foundation Stone is laid (in the hearts of members) in the form of the "Foundation Stone Meditation."

1924: January 1: having founded the Anthroposophical Society and taken over its leadership, Rudolf Steiner has the task of "reforming" it. The process begins with a weekly newssheet ("What's Happening in the Anthroposophical Society") in which Rudolf Steiner's "Letters to Members" and "Anthroposophical Leading Thoughts" appear (CW 26). The next step is the creation of a new esoteric class, the "first class" of the "University of Spiritual Science" (which was to have been followed, had Rudolf Steiner lived longer, by two more advanced classes). Then comes a new language for Anthroposophy—practical, phenomenological, and direct; and Rudolf Steiner creates the model for the second Goetheanum. He begins the series of extensive "karma" lectures (CW 235-40); and finally, responding to needs, he creates two new initiatives: biodynamic agriculture and curative education. After the middle of the year, rumors begin to circulate regarding Steiner's health. Lectures: January-February, *Anthroposophy* (CW 234); February: *Tone Eurythmy* (CW 278); June: *The Agriculture Course* (CW 327); June-July: Speech [?] Eurythmy (CW 279); *Curative Education* (CW 317); August: (England, "Second International Summer School"), *Initiation Consciousness: True and False Paths in Spiritual Investigation* (CW 243); September: *Pastoral Medicine* (CW 318). On September 26, for the first time, Rudolf Steiner cancels a lecture. On September 28, he gives his last lecture. On September 29, he withdraws to his studio in the carpenter's shop; now he is definitively ill. Cared for by Ita Wegman, he continues working, however, and writing the weekly installments of his *Autobiography* and *Letters to the Members/Leading Thoughts* (CW 26).

1925: Rudolf Steiner, while continuing to work, continues to weaken. He finishes *Extending Practical Medicine* (CW 27) with Ita Wegman.

On March 30, around ten in the morning, Rudolf Steiner dies.

INDEX